THE FUGITIVE

RECAPTURED

17.95

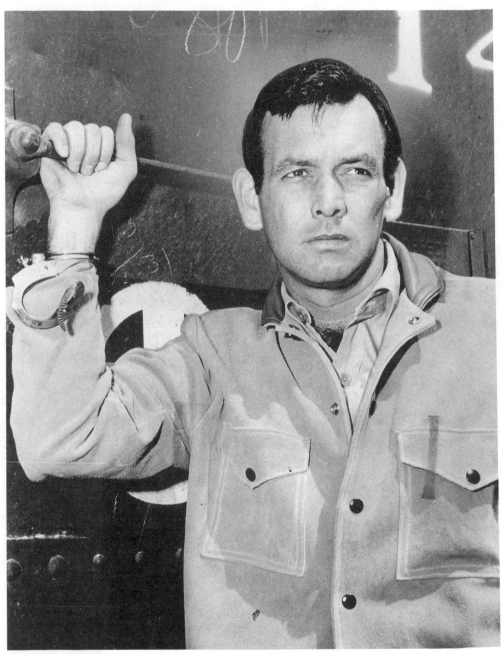

David Janssen, The Fugitive.

THE FUGITIVE
RECAPTURED

**THE 30TH ANNIVERSARY
COMPANION
TO A TELEVISION CLASSIC**

ED ROBERTSON

**Foreword by
BARRY MORSE**

**Introduction by
STEPHEN KING**

POMEGRANATE PRESS, LTD.

LOS ANGELES   LONDON

This is a Pomegranate Press, Ltd. book.

Library of Congress Catalog Card Number: 93-084409

Tradepaper Edition ISBN: 0938817-34-5

First Printing: September 1993

For Pomegranate Press, Ltd.:

Editor: Kathryn Leigh Scott
Book Design: Benjamin R. Martin
Book Cover Design: Heidi Frieder
Book Cover Photograph: Gene Trindl
Typography Consultant: Leroy Chen

Printed and bound in The United States of America
by
McNaughton & Gunn, Inc.
Saline, Michigan

POMEGRANATE PRESS, LTD.
Post Office Box 8261
Universal City, California 91608

DEDICATION

A character might appear one way on paper, as the writer originally defined him. But the minute you bring in an actor to play the role, the character changes. What emerges, finally, is an amalgam in which the actor absorbs the written character and the written character absorbs the actor.

With David Janssen and Richard Kimble, it became one of those rare, nearly perfect meldings. To a remarkable degree, actor and character became one. David Janssen *was* the Fugitive.

ALAN ARMER
Series Producer, 1963-1966

On behalf of the many fans around the globe who love him, and miss him, this book is dedicated to David Janssen (1931-1980)

ED ROBERTSON
April 1993

David Janssen.

TABLE OF CONTENTS

ACKNOWLEDGMENTS

Richard Kimble would never have reached his goal without the help of a whole lot of people. Likewise, the story of his life on the run could not have been written without the help of many, many, many people.

For their time, patience, and professionalism in granting interviews and answering dozens and dozens of questions, I thank Barry Morse, Roy Huggins, Alan Armer, Stanford Whitmore, George Eckstein, Suzanne Pleshette, Jacqueline Scott, Don Brinkley, Philip Saltzman, Hank Searls, Bob Rubin, Steve Lodge, Ken Gilbert, Jack Wilson, John Conwell, Leonard Goldenson, Sutton Roley, John Meredyth Lucas, James Sheldon, Christian Nyby I, Peter Rugolo, Walter Schenck, Larry Gianakos, Dorothy Hopper, Richard Chaffee, Arthur Fellows, Carol Rossen, Richard Anderson, William Conrad, Lois Nettleton, Berniece Janssen, Wilton Schiller, David Thorburn, and Stephen King.

I am also indebted to Dave Brown, Jason Allen, Ann Mathis, Gene Trindl, Alan and David Grossman of NuVentures Video, Ann Gaines of *MAD Magazine*, Nancy Hildebrandt of *The Chicago Sun-Times,* John Yodice and Dave Charmatz of Arts & Entertainment, David Chin, Bob Charger, Frank Free, Rod Bushnell, Alan Caplan, Dave Fielding, Ron Baxter, Buck Delventhal, Mariam Morley, Scott Emblidge, Carol Beran, Clinton Bond, Ginny Draper, and Ricky Weisbroth.

Special thanks to:

Kay McAfee, my "Arkansas pen pal" with whom I have shared countless hours swapping ideas over the phone, for providing many of the wonderful photos that appear in this book;

Barry Morse, Steve Lodge, Carol Rossen, Richard Anderson, and Berniece Janssen, for contributing pictures from their personal collections;

Roy Huggins, for the use of his original screenplay concept of *The Fugitive*;

Phyllis Fellows, for her help in reviewing her husband's comments (Arthur passed away in 1992);

Rusty Pollard, the head of the *On the Run* fan club, whose breathless enthusiasm has helped me in ways I cannot begin to describe;

Bob Rubin, whose numerous "little suggestions" truly enabled me to capture the feel of really being behind the scenes;

Bonnie Dash, my partner on many of the interviews for this book;

My parents, my family (particularly my sister JoAnn Collins and my brother-in-law Thom Anderson), and Tony Maddox, Michael Wright, Chris Sweeney, Bob Gorsch, and Corinne Cottle, for their love, support and encouragement;

and Cathy McCarthy—I owe you big time.

Finally....my father called me one night shortly after Pomegranate Press agreed to publish this book. He had just finished reading the book proposal that led to the sale of *The Fugitive Recaptured.*

"So, what do you think, Dad?" I asked.

"Well, I don't know," he said. "I mean, it's very good, what you wrote. I enjoyed reading it very much. It's just that—well, I don't know if it's good because it's 'good,' or whether it's good because my son wrote it."

I started to laugh. "Oh, that's okay, Dad—you can say it's good because I wrote it!"

My father passed away one month before this book went to press. This is probably the first time I've ever told him just how much that phone conversation meant to me. Thanks, Dad. I love you.

FOREWORD

I've been lucky enough to have been consistently engaged in some branch or other of the entertainment industry for nearly 60 years, and I've found that it isn't always the case that if you're involved in something which is hugely popular, it's necessarily also highly enjoyable.

But *The Fugitive* was, for me, *immensely* enjoyable. Not only because of its great and lasting popularity, but even more because of the splendid group of people whom it brought together: Quinn Martin, who formulated the structure of the whole thing; the writers, who contributed so many marvelously diverse scripts; our brilliantly skillful and tireless crew; and of course our hero, dear David Janssen.

Thirty years on, the series has become a classic of its kind. All too many of our colleagues are no longer with us; but I meet every day enthusiastic young people who are thrilled and moved today by a drama that we made long before they were born.

By the scrupulous research and tasteful presentation of his book, Ed Robertson has created a brilliant record of one of the outstanding achievements of television history, of which I for one am proud to have been a part. It will fascinate viewers of all generations.

BARRY MORSE
February 1993

Kimble and Gerard: Janssen and Morse.

INTRODUCTION

The Fugitive was a groundbreaking television series because it featured a hero who was totally powerless. Everybody who watched The Fugitive could identify with Richard Kimble. David Janssen spoke for a whole generation of people—kids like me, who grew up feeling slightly alienated from all the values of our parents. We felt like fugitives in a sense. The Greek chorus that was heard from one end of this country to another was "Turn that goddam thing down!" Our music changed, our mores changed, and I looked at that guy and I said, "Yes, I feel like him. I know what it's like to be falsely accused." And I loved the way Kimble lived, to be able to move from town to town like that. He was the sort of character that people at the time wanted to sublimate themselves in.

Lt. Gerard, on the other hand, really scared me as kid. Barry Morse was so good—he brought an element of reality to Gerard that a lot of TV characters didn't have. Whereas most series characters remain emotionally static, Gerard actually seemed to grow less and less tightly wrapped as the show continued. Gerard was completely nuts—at least I thought so. Kimble had made him crazy, and as The Fugitive went on you could see him heading further and further into freako land.

The Fugitive broke all the stereotypes. It was at the time (and still is, when you see the reruns) absolutely the best series done on American television. There was nothing better than The Fugitive—it just turned everything on its head.

STEPHEN KING

William Conrad, who narrated all 120 episodes of *The Fugitive*, with David Janssen.

PROLOG

One of the most popular television programs of the 1960s endeared audiences worldwide to one man and his struggle to clear himself of a crime he did not commit. *The Fugitive.*

On Tuesday, September 17, 1963, at 10:00 p.m., William Conrad's stern but soothing voice introduced television viewers to Dr. Richard Kimble (David Janssen), a respected pediatrician from Stafford, Indiana, who had been convicted of murdering his wife Helen two years earlier. For months the Kimbles had argued over Helen's unwillingness to adopt a child after learning that she could not bear her own. One night, after storming out of the house following another quarrel, Dr. Kimble was just returning home when he witnessed Fred Johnson (Bill Raisch), a fiendish-looking one-armed man, running from the vicinity of his house. After nearly running over Johnson with his car, Dr. Kimble raced into his home and found Helen murdered.

Although Kimble believed it was Johnson who killed his wife, no one else witnessed the murder, no neighbors heard or saw Johnson, and the police—despite the thorough investigation of Lieutenant Philip Gerard (Barry Morse)—found no trace of the man. Based on circumstantial evidence, the jury found Dr. Kimble guilty and sentenced him to die in the electric chair. After several failed appeals, Kimble, accompanied by Lt. Gerard, boarded a train headed for the death house.

Kimble glanced into the train window but saw only the darkness of the night. The end was only moments away. "But," intoned William Conrad, "in that darkness, fate moves its huge hand." The train derailed, and in the ensuing confusion Kimble escaped. On that September night, he began a lonely, paranoid flight from the law, and a desperate search for the one-armed man—the only person who can clear his name and save him from execution. An exile, Kimble drifted from place to place, from rural town to big city, in search of any clue that could lead him to the man with one arm. Like Jean Valjean, his counterpart in Victor Hugo's *Les Miserables*, Kimble faced a particular nemesis—the implacable Lt. Gerard, whose relentless search for the Fugitive soon became an all-consuming obsession.

Each week, tens of millions of television viewers watched *The Fugitive* and hoped that Kimble could elude the authorities long enough to find the one-armed man and clear his own name. The quest for exoneration reached a dramatic climax on August 29, 1967, when Kimble confronted the one-armed man in the series' final prime-time episode. Seventy-two percent of the total TV audience in the United States alone watched *The Fugitive* that night, a figure which remains one of the highest-rated broadcasts in American television history.

But would you believe that *The Fugitive* nearly did not make it to the television screen? Although he never once doubted that audiences would accept his idea, series creator Roy Huggins abandoned *The Fugitive* for nearly two years because *everyone* he consulted—friends, colleagues, his lawyer, even his dentist—found the idea absolutely repulsive. Huggins finally found a lone supporter in ABC president Leonard Goldenson, who declared *The Fugitive* "the best idea for a television series I've ever heard" after Huggins presented the concept at a meeting with ABC executives in 1962.

But the series still faced nothing but opposition before it premiered in September 1963. Even ABC was split. One programming vice-president denounced *The Fugitive* as "a slap in the face of the American judicial system" moments after Goldenson had approved the program.

But television audiences embraced *The Fugitive* because of two factors everyone who opposed the series had overlooked. First, "Richard Kimble is innocent," as William Conrad reminds us at the beginning of every episode. And second, "This was a TV series about a hero who was totally powerless, and people identified with him," as novelist Stephen King observed about his favorite TV show. "It turned everything on its head."

Indeed, in a TV world populated by winners like Perry Mason, Dr. Kimble was a loser, a man condemned by society with no recourse to prove his innocence. *Anyone* who watched *The Fugitive* could identify with him, because *everyone* has felt the sting of a false accusation or an unjust punishment.

"The thing that gets me the angriest is being blamed for something I didn't do," said series writer/producer George Eckstein. "I'm sure this is true for a great many people. *The Fugitive* is the ultimate version of that syndrome: Kimble's life is on the line for something he didn't do. This series tapped a nerve. A lot of us go around with that sting in our psyche. We feel that somehow people think we're one thing, when we're really another."

In January 1990, the Arts and Entertainment cable television network (A&E) revitalized *The Fugitive* by introducing the Emmy Award-winning drama to a new generation of viewers. Since its revival, *The Fugitive* has spawned at least two fan clubs in this country (*On the Run* and *The Fugitives*) and a third in France (*The David Janssen Appreciation Society*); NuVentures Video has made the series available on home video; and Warner Brothers has produced a feature film version (starring Harrison Ford as the Fugitive) for release in late 1993. Thirty years after its network premiere, *The Fugitive* remains as magnetic as ever. According to an A&E spokesman, the tremendously positive audience response to *The Fugitive* convinced A&E in 1992 to renew the program for another three years. And in April 1993, *TV GUIDE*, as part of its 40th anniversary salute to the All-Time Best TV, named *The Fugitive* the best Dramatic Series of the 1960s.

For 13 years, the final episode of *The Fugitive* held the record for the highest-rated broadcast in television history. Although that record has twice been eclipsed—first by *Dallas* in 1980, then by *M*A*S*H* in 1983—*The Fugitive* continues to leave its imprint on television. Kimble's exoneration in the final episode marked the first instance of a TV series resolving its premise. Since *The Fugitive* left the air in 1967, many other successful television programs have followed its lead by ending their network runs with a definitive concluding episode—programs such as *The Mary Tyler Moore Show*, *M*A*S*H*, *Dallas*, *Cheers*, even *The Tonight Show Starring Johnny Carson*.

In addition, *The Fugitive* has proliferated dozens of similar programs featuring a wandering, disadvantaged protagonist who helps people—*Run For Your Life*, *The Invaders*, *The Immortal*, *Kung Fu*, *The Incredible Hulk*, *Hot Pursuit*, and *The Golden Years*, to name a few. Some shows have parodied it (*Get Smart*, *Run, Buddy, Run*, *It's Garry Shandling's Show*), while others have made playful allusions to it (an announcement paging "Dr. Richard Kimble" on *St. Elsewhere*, a one-armed character named "Philip Gerard" on *Twin Peaks*).

The Fugitive's influence extends further. It enhanced the already solid reputations of series creator Roy Huggins and executive producer Quinn Martin, two of the most influential figures in the history of television drama. It provided a springboard for many talented writers, producers and directors, including Richard Levinson and William Link, Glen A. Larson, Hampton Fancher, Burt Brinckerhoff, Lou Antonio, Burt Metcalfe, Walter Brough, Bob Rubin, Ken Gilbert, Steve Lodge, Richard Donner, Mark Rydell, and Sydney Pollack. It boasted a litany of prominent and talented guest stars, such as Suzanne Pleshette, Angie Dickinson, Ron Howard, Carroll O'Connor, Brian Keith, Bruce Dern, Telly Savalas, Leslie Nielsen, Carol Rossen, Jack Klugman, Robert Duvall, Ossie Davis, Lee Grant, Kurt Russell, Greg Morris, Sheree North, Richard Anderson, Diane Baker, William Shatner, Dabney Coleman, James Farentino, Carol Lawrence, Donald Pleasence, Edward Asner, Mickey Rooney, Beau Bridges, Charles Bronson, and Jack Lord.

And it made David Janssen a star.

The Fugitive wasn't just a highly-watched, hugely profitable television series. It was an international phenomenon. Every Tuesday night for four years, people of all ages in over 70 countries dropped what they were doing at 10:00 p.m. and took up the cause of Dr. Richard Kimble. Not since Lucy Ricardo gave birth to Little Ricky in 1953 had one television character so seized the collective human spirit. Whenever Kimble felt fear, we held our breath, and when he escaped unharmed, we sighed in relief. Whenever Kimble looked over his shoulder, every single viewer the world over felt the Fugitive's sense of urgency. David Janssen held us all together—as Richard Kimble, he became a symbol that inspired us to continue hoping and persisting, even at our lowest ebb.

What follows is a long-overdue history devoted to this timeless classic. We'll meet many of the key people who put together the show we have continued to love for thirty years—including Roy Huggins, who created *The Fugitive*; Stanford Whitmore, whose script for the pilot episode set the entire series in motion; and producers Alan Armer and George Eckstein, the two people who understood *The Fugitive* better than anyone else. We'll go behind the scenes and gain insight into Richard Kimble and Philip Gerard from Barry Morse and from writers Don Brinkley, Philip Saltzman, and Hank Searls. And we'll take in memories of *The Fugitive*'s beloved star, David Janssen, from the people who knew him the best—the guest stars, the production staff, and the crew members.

So let's get started... and together, we'll re-capture *The Fugitive*.

ED ROBERTSON

Morse and Janssen in *Corner of Hell.*

Roy Huggins.

ACT I

"The Most Repulsive Concept in History"

"Dan, I Have Something That Everybody Hates"

Bret Maverick, the silver-tongued gambler who dressed in black and ran at the first sign of trouble. Gerald Lloyd "Kookie" Kookson, the hair-combing, ultra-cool parking attendant with a lingo all his own. Jim Rockford, the classic TV private eye once described as a curve ball in a world of fast balls. Richard Kimble, the Fugitive. Each of these characters are permanently etched in the minds of TV lovers the world over. Each was the center of enormously successful programs that changed the face of television drama. Each was formed out of the mind of one innovative man: Roy Huggins.

Huggins, born in 1914, began his career as a novelist. His first book *The Double Take* (1946) introduced Stu Bailey, "the private eye with an Ivy-League look and a dock-walloper's punch" whose adventures were adapted to the screen (*I Love Trouble*, which Huggins scripted) and later to television (as *77 Sunset Strip*, which Huggins created and produced). After several successful years as a motion picture writer (*The Fuller Brush Man, The Lady Gambles, Three Hours to Kill*) and director (*Hangman's Knot*, which he also wrote), Huggins moved into television in 1955. He immediately established a solid reputation for himself by producing a string of hit series for Warner Brothers—*Cheyenne* (ABC, 1955-63), *Maverick* (ABC, 1957-62, for which he won an Emmy in 1959), *77 Sunset Strip* (ABC, 1958-64). After leaving Warners in 1960, Huggins received a lucrative offer from Columbia Pictures to produce feature films. But Huggins wanted to stay in television.

"It was true then, as it is today, that creative people in Hollywood have the single-minded goal of getting out of television and into theatrical films," he explained. "But there are exceptions and I was one of them. I knew that in theatrical films I would never get the kind of freedom I wanted, unless I was in charge of the studio. And at that time the movies were in decline—weekly attendance had fallen from 80 million in 1946 to about 20 million in 1960. Television had taken away the traditional mass audience from the major studios. I had decided that the movies were going to continue to decline, and that the real money was in television."

Huggins turned down the offer from Columbia. "I made a mistake about the movies," he chuckled. "But I wanted to stay in television. I decided that I wanted to develop a series, sell it, and finish my Ph.D. work at UCLA, where I had studied as an undergraduate.

"I then sat down at home and I started thinking. I wanted to create a contemporary series that would contain the elements that make westerns so appealing. The shows I had been working on from the time I came into television were westerns, starting with *Cheyenne* and moving onto *Maverick*. Although I was tired of producing westerns, I loved the freedom of the western hero. I wanted to transfer that total freedom of the western protagonist who could wander from place to place, and do anything he wanted, and have a relationship with a woman, and move on—onto a character in a contemporary setting.

"At first I thought it couldn't be done. If you put a man like that in a contemporary environment, he'll look like a bum. The audience wouldn't accept him: they'd hate him. "But then the answer hit me: he has to be a fugitive from injustice. He must have been accused of a crime, and it must be a capital crime, and he must have exhausted all of his appeals so that he is truly a fugitive. And if they catch him, he dies! That is the only way I could have put the classic western hero in a modern setting—the man cannot stay in one place because he is a fugitive, and so he must move on, and so forth."

It is widely assumed Huggins based *The Fugitive* on *Les Miserables* (1862), Victor Hugo's epic novel about a thief who tries to escape his criminal past and the determined police officer who refuses to let him. But that isn't the case. "I did mention *Les Miserables* in my presentation to ABC, but that wasn't what really triggered the idea," said Huggins. "The only source I drew from was the western.... I then wrote the concept of *The Fugitive* in two hours, including the signature (opening scene) that introduces Richard Kimble and states his predicament. I then put those pages, three in number, away and went to bed, but I was so wound up over this idea I couldn't sleep.

"The following morning I reread those pages very carefully, the way I always approach ideas I write in a half-dream at three o'clock in the morning. By the time I was finished, I was convinced that I had written a concept that was worth a fortune and was a work of genius—but it turned out to be the most repulsive concept in the history of man!

"Shortly after writing the treatment of *The Fugitive*, I signed a contract which put me in charge of television at 20th Century-Fox, and I thought my contract was so good that I would give them *The Fugitive*. In effect, I would be making it a 'gift' to 20th Century-Fox, but also it would make me a very successful head of production, and I would be getting a percentage of the profits, and all the rest of it.

"After signing the Fox deal, I got on an airplane to come home. Seated next to me was my boss Peter Levathes, president of Fox Television. We got to talking about what we were going to do, and I said, 'Well, I have the first show: it's called *The Fugitive*,' and I told him precisely what *The Fugitive* was.

"Peter Levathes looked at me, and I could read his mind (and it turned out that this is exactly what he was thinking): 'My God, what kind of horrendous mistake have we made?' He didn't even comment. He instantly dropped it, and said, 'Let me tell you about an idea I have called *Jules Verne*.' And he proceeded to talk about doing a series about Jules Verne stories.

"When we got [to Los Angeles], Levathes had a private meeting with Fox executive Bill Self, and he told Self the conclusion he had drawn about me. I was put into a strange little office, and I called my lawyer, and I said, 'I think I've made a huge mistake. I told Mr. Levathes a series idea that I have, and I think he wants to get me out of here. So why don't you get me out first? Let's strike first.'

"My lawyer talked me out of it. He said, 'Roy, this'll pass. It's only one show. You have this great reputation which you will hurt if you quit at this early stage,' and he gave me quite a pitch. So I said, 'Well, look. I will reserve my decision about dropping this job for a little longer.'

"By the way, I told my lawyer about *The Fugitive*, and he also fell silent!"

Despite Levathes' reaction, Huggins continued to believe in the potential appeal of his idea. "If you go back into the '40s, and late '30s, you will find film after film after film in which the story is about the protagonist who has been falsely accused, and he must prove that he is innocent," he said. "That was so common that I felt it was appropriate to call that 'the American theme.'"

What Huggins calls the "American theme" is an offshoot of the era of *film noir*, movies with a gritty, urban setting that often depicted such themes as guilt and salvation. The heroes of such pictures—including *I Am a Fugitive from a Chain Gang*, *The Big Clock*, *Stranger on the Third Floor*, and *The Wrong Man*—were often insecure loners who were tied to the past and unsure about the future. These films also had a permeating effect on television in the 1950s and 60s, particularly as urban detective series such as *M Squad*, *Naked City* and Quinn Martin's *The Untouchables* became increasingly popular. "It had been proved, time and time again, that American audiences respond to that theme," said Huggins. "After I had thought of the idea, I said to myself, 'This is the American theme; this can't possibly fail.'"

Huggins sought out everyone in television whose opinion he respected—writers, directors, producers and friends—and told them about *The Fugitive*. Everyone he consulted found the idea absolutely repulsive. "Some of them reacted in an embarrassed way," he recalled. "My agent actually looked ill, as if he might be thinking, 'I've got to drop this guy!' I told it to Howard Browne *(Scotch on the Rocks)*, one of my closest writer friends, and Howard looked at me and said, 'Roy, you have a great reputation in television—if you want to keep that, don't tell this idea to any of the networks.'" (Browne apparently changed his mind about *The Fugitive*; he wrote the fourth season episode "A Clean and Quiet Town.")

By this time, even Huggins was convinced that *The Fugitive* was a terrible idea. "If enough people tell you you're blind, you better get yourself a dog," he said. "I put *The Fugitive* on a shelf and decided that Levathes was right, and that I would have to try to win my way back into his confidence, which I had lost totally by telling him *The Fugitive*."

Although he continued to help Levathes develop shows for 20th Century-Fox, Huggins never regained the studio's confidence. The two men had disparate ideas on what would make a good series. "I fought every one of their ideas, and all of them failed," Huggins said. Fox eventually relieved Huggins of his duties in early 1962. (Levathes was fired a short while later; in fact, the entire television department at Fox soon shut down.) A little sour on the business, Huggins decided to drop out of television and pursue something he had put off for too many years.

"I had a brother who was a professor at the University of Arizona, and he lived a very happy life," explained Huggins. "That was the life I wanted, and that was the life I had planned. I had done two years of graduate work [in political philosophy] when I got shuttled off doing government work during World War II, and I had always planned to go back and finish. But I was doing so well in television that I kept putting off what I had always planned to do. But when Fox simply went belly up, as a result of both its motion picture and television policies, I asked to be accepted into the graduate school at UCLA, which was not an easy thing to accomplish. In order to take me, someone else had to be bumped."

Shortly after he was accepted at UCLA, Huggins was contacted by Dan Melnick, ABC's vice president of program development. Leonard Goldenson, the president of the network, wanted a meeting with Huggins. "ABC was in serious trouble. They were in ratings trouble, and Goldenson was trying to save the network," Huggins recalled. "So he called Dan Melnick and said, 'Here is a list of people, and I want to see each one of them.' Melnick called me and told me that Leonard wanted to meet me. I told Dan that there was no point in that because I had left television and that I was trying to get my Ph.D., that I probably would then go into academic work, and that I had no interest in television.

"As much as I liked Leonard Goldenson (which I did; he's a very decent man), I discovered that Melnick was absolutely petrified! He put it this way to me: 'Roy, I can't go to Leonard Goldenson and tell him you won't meet with him!' And since he put it that way, and since I had liked him (we had worked together earlier in television), I said, 'Dan, look. I have something in a drawer that everybody hates! And I mean they hate it, they find it distasteful. They don't just not like it, they are offended by it! But it is an idea called *The Fugitive*, and if you want me to meet with Leonard Goldenson, I will do so, and I will tell him about *The Fugitive*."

Huggins met with Goldenson and several other prominent ABC executives, including Thomas Moore, the network's head of programming. "I started to tell the concept of *The Fugitive*. In the middle of it, Tom Moore got up and left the room," Huggins recalled. "Other people were drumming on the arms of their chairs, or swinging their feet, or looking at their watches. It was not easy for me to continue. Two minutes later, Tom Moore came out of the other room, carrying a suitcase; he went to the door and said, 'Roy, sorry, I gotta catch a plane!' He made it very clear that he had heard enough of this piece of you-know-what.

"I finished the presentation, and there was this dreadful silence. Leonard was waiting for people to speak up. No one was going to speak up until Leonard spoke,"

Huggins continued. "Leonard then looked at me and said, 'Roy, that is the best idea for a television series that I have ever heard.'

"And I thought, 'My God, I wasn't wrong after all!' Leonard was the first man that heard my idea and actually liked it. Leonard understood it—before he came to ABC, he ran Paramount Pictures, one of the studios that had made all those films about the man falsely accused."

Goldenson liked the idea because it was different from anything on television at that time. "I felt that it was distinctive, and that the novelty of it would catch on," Goldenson recalled. "Fortunately, it did."

But Goldenson was surprised to learn that Huggins was not available to produce *The Fugitive*. Apparently no one told him that Huggins had already enrolled at UCLA, probably because nobody expected the series to be approved.

"Leonard was absolutely astonished," said Huggins. "No one had ever said to him 'I'll set it up for you but I won't be producing it.' That was unheard of. So Leonard looked around at the other people and said 'Who would we like to have Roy set this up with?' They didn't have any idea."

Huggins suggested Quinn Martin. "I knew that Quinn was a very efficient producer, and he had done some successful shows (*The Untouchables*), and I wanted the show to be a success," he said. "I mentioned several names, and they accepted two or three of them. But the first one I met was Quinn Martin."

After selling ABC the television rights to *The Fugitive*, Huggins and Martin worked out a deal: QM Productions would produce the series, while Huggins would receive credit for creating it. (Huggins maintained ownership of all other rights to *The Fugitive*.) If Martin wasn't aware of all the problems he inherited, Huggins quickly filled in the details, such as the programming executive who had the temerity to denounce *The Fugitive* moments after Goldenson had okayed the series.

"Julius Barnathan stood up [after Goldenson voiced his approval] and said, 'I hate it,'" Huggins recalled. "He made a speech about how un-American it was, how it was a slap in the face of American justice, week after week, and he thought it was awful. Now, he's a very brave man, because his boss has just declared that it's the best idea he ever heard!"

But Huggins knew that Martin faced a more formidable opponent in Thomas Moore, whose dissent was voiced in a manner far more telling than Barnathan's diatribe. "Tom Moore hated it so much he walked out," Huggins reiterated. "I said to myself, 'He is going to give whoever does this show nothing but trouble.'"

Martin had already worked his way into the good graces of both Moore and ABC by virtue of producing *The Untouchables* (1959-63). But Huggins knew that enough infighting over *The Fugitive* existed to warrant concern, so he remained on board long enough to help Martin get the new series off the ground.

Martin, born Martin Cohen in 1922, grew up in the motion picture industry (his father Leonard was a film editor). After graduating as an English major from the University of California/Berkeley, Martin himself started off as an editor at Universal Pictures, then gradually worked his way into television as a script writer for many series. "I had known Quinn when we were both at ZIV Studios," said Sutton Roley, who directed many of Martin's programs. "I came out from New York, and Quinn was at ZIV in the sound department. He was married to Madelyn Pugh at the time, who (along with Bob Carroll) was one of the major writers on *I Love Lucy*. Then Quinn left ZIV and became a writer/producer on such anthology shows as *The Jane Wyman Theater* (NBC, 1955-58). Then Madelyn Pugh had something to do with him being brought into Desilu Productions, where he worked as a writer/producer on *Desilu Playhouse* (CBS, 1958-60). One of the shows he did for Desilu was a special called *The Untouchables*, and it pulled such great numbers and a voluminous number of letters from the public. Because of the great response, another network [ABC] decided to make it into a series, and Quinn was made the producer. *The Untouchables* was the real start of Quinn Martin—that really put him in the foreground of television producers, as far as the networks were concerned. He did a great job on it."

Based on the memoirs of government agent Eliot Ness, *The Untouchables* was an excitingly-written and well-produced excursion into the Chicago crime wars of the Prohibition era. Although criticized on two fronts—(1) the censors thought it was too violent; and (2) many Italian-American groups were upset over its portrayal of Italians as gangsters—*The Untouchables* became one of ABC's first successful series. The rat-a-tat-tat narration of newspaper columnist Walter Winchell gave the series a newsreel/documentary-like style that Martin would finally hone in many of his subsequent programs. After its second season (1960-61), with *The Untouchables* ranked as the eighth-most popular program on television, Martin left to start his own company, QM Productions. His first series as an independent producer was *The New Breed* (ABC, 1961-62).

"People compare me to the old moguls of the movies," Martin told Robert Alley and Horace Newcombe in *The Producer's Medium: Conversations with Creators of American TV* (Oxford University Press, 1983). "I really am a controller. I believe in control. When I say I am a benevolent dictator, I really mean that. I was always brought up that the guy at the top had the responsibility of control. Now that is an offshoot of my environment.... I grew up in [Hollywood] and grew up seeing strong father-figure images: [Louis B.] Mayer, [Harry] Cohn, [Jack] Warner, [Adolph] Zukor. So I patterned my style without even thinking about it ....

"I don't mean to sound like a braggart when I say control. I was given total control by a network [ABC] which was looking desperately to get on the boards and I really pulled it off. I was the only one who did in those days. I had [three] shows in the top ten for ABC [*The Untouchables*, *The Fugitive*, *The F.B.I.*] at a time when it was really tough, because we used to start off with fifty stations short the first of every year and have to prove ourselves—be tougher than anybody. I earned my stripes in a very tough market."

A strong believer in organization, Martin delegated the various responsibilities of TV production and hired the best people available to carry them out. "We all worked together to a point where the company is the producer," Martin told *The Producer's Medium*. "I'm the executive producer and the [line] producer is really a story editor. There's nothing wrong with [delegating responsibility]. I think it's the only way you can have mass-produced quality [in a short amount of time]." (The production staff, technical crew, and cast of *The Fugitive* had seven working days to produce one episode, then immediately began work on the next segment, and so forth.)

Martin was one of the first producers who really exploited the visual possibilities of television, according to scholar David Thorburn. "He was very conscious of the extent to which black-and-white photography, that sort of shadowed effect that was created by these dark streets [in both *The Untouchables* and *The Fugitive*], was an explicit echo of *film noir*," said Thorburn, who interviewed Martin in 1978 for his forthcoming book on television. "He saw *The Fugitive* as a show that tried to recapture some of the ambience of *film noir*. He was conscious of the extent to which television was a modified, 'smalled' form of the movies. He tried to have *The Untouchables* edited in a movie-like way, with more cuts than were usual on television, and with fewer fade-outs. He was also conscious of the camera angle as a strategy that could compensate for the fact that vast panoramas don't work well on television. There are a number of almost artsy shots in *The Untouchables* that consciously aim for effects that are appropriate to the small screen—shots through windows or shots in which the camera will gaze through the legs of a chair which then frames a face in the background. Martin knew he had introduced a movie-like quality to television film production with *The Untouchables*." (We will expand these thoughts when we discuss episode 48, "Nicest Fella You'd Ever Want to Meet.")

The motion-picture quality was not the only distinguishing feature of Martin's programs. For nearly twenty years, TV viewers could recognize a Martin series by the superimposed "Act I," "Act II," "Act III," "Act IV," and "Epilog" that began each segment of every episode. While these affectations certainly catered to Martin's eccentricities, they also underscored his keen understanding of the medium. According to Thorburn, Martin believed it was important to differentiate between the television program and the commercials that sponsored it. The format that would become his signature was Martin's way of acknowledging the commercial interruptions without sacrificing any of the dramatic integrity of his programs.

"Martin wanted a clear signal to the audience that we're coming to a break now," said Thorburn. "One of the most important contributions Martin made to television was his sense that television was a segmented form. The commercial environment of television required that you create mini-dramas that come to a kind of mini-climax just before the commercial, and have sharp demarcations identifying themselves as separate segments. In other words, it was his way of trying to keep the commercial interruptions from contaminating his programs."

Martin divided dramatic television into three components: "melodrama," or plot and action; "theme," or social relevance; and "emotion," the human element. Martin believed that the emotional component was the most important of the three because it was the one element that best reflected his dramatic ideals—his intention of presenting things as they should be—and that emotional content governed the ratio between melodrama and theme. For Martin, emotion was what made a program "honest:" it cut across all socio-economic lines and affected people on a fundamentally human level. In his view, a program with a proper emotional balance was a program that would appeal to the mass general audience across the country. "If things are emotionally correct, you then hit everybody," Martin told *The Producer's Medium.* "I always try to make sure that the characters are motivated properly, that people get a feeling of what's going on. I've always been rather proud that my shows have really hit a very broad section. I get the college kids and I get the truck drivers."

"You Can't Hate Anybody Named Lincoln"

Martin completely understood Huggins' concept and knew how he could exploit it. But he first needed a story for the pilot (the test film designed to "launch" the series). Huggins' three-page screenplay provided him with the basic premise—Richard Kimble was innocent; he had seen a gaunt, red-haired man fleeing from his home; he was convicted of his wife's murder on circumstantial evidence; and he escaped the death house as a result of a train wreck. The pilot had to (1) convince the network's remaining skeptics that *The Fugitive* was a worthy investment; (2) resolve any ethical conflict surrounding Kimble's fugitive status; and (3) elicit sympathy from the viewing public and potential sponsors. To write the pilot, Martin summoned Stanford Whitmore, the talented screenwriter who was the script editor on *The New Breed*, which ABC had just canceled.

"I went in to see Quinn, and he handed me three pages and said 'Sit down on the couch and read these and tell me what you think,'" recalled Whitmore, a onetime novelist who had already made the successful transition to film and television writing. His resume included *War Hunt* (1962), the film that introduced Robert Redford to movie audiences, and several episodes of *Staccato* (NBC, 1959-60), the critically acclaimed but little-watched clone of *Peter Gunn* (NBC/ABC, 1958-61) that starred future director John Cassavetes (*Faces, Husbands, A Woman Under the Influence*) as a jazz musician/private eye.

"If I remember right, the first sequence was written in screenplay form, and that was of the train wreck," Whitmore continued. "And then Roy wrote, 'And thus begins an exciting new series called *The Fugitive,*' and then he went into a couple pages of philosophizing about the appeal of such a show. He brought up as an illustration *Shane*, the mysterious drifter who came into town and set everything right, and then moved on. So I said to Quinn, 'Okay, sure, I think I could have fun with this thing!'"

In order to "hit the mass general audience," the pilot needed two key ingredients. The first was a matter of approach. "Martin felt the essence of *The Fugitive* was that this upper middle-class figure (and a doctor) was forced to go underground and become part of the working-class," according to David Thorburn. "The interest of the series would reside in the fact that this professional figure was forced to take on a series of menial jobs—bartender, ditch digger, [apprentice] carpenter, etc. Martin believed the audience would identify with those experiences."

"In most television programs, even if a guy has a job, you don't remember it after the series went off the air," added Stephen King. "But I remember a lot of different jobs that Richard Kimble had. I could believe him chopping the cabbages down there in Texas, or Louisiana, and I could believe him parking cars in Michigan. It was the only show on television where it even sort of hinted that there was a job somewhere besides being a cop or a cowboy, at that time. This guy did everything. They were real jobs and real backgrounds. In most TV shows, even if the main character had a job and you know what it is, they never have to do it. You know, Ben Cartwright and his boys (*Bonanza*) had a ranch, but they never had to run it—it apparently ran itself! All they did was sit around the table, and Hop Sing would bring them coffee and they'd drink it. Or a truer example was *Doctor Kildare*, who had time to solve everybody's problems."

The second, and most important, key ingredient of the pilot was creating a decent protagonist. After Martin told him of the network's apprehension about *The Fugitive*, Whitmore knew how he wanted to proceed. "Some people back there felt that the sponsors would not want to be identified with someone who was running from the law," he said. "Quinn and I pointed out to them that the guy was *innocent*—but with their wonderful logic, they said that didn't make any difference. ABC was nervous that the sponsors might shy away from even being associated with a fugitive, because a 'fugitive' had a bad connotation.

"So I said to Quinn, 'I'll fix this guy up good, and no sponsor will want to run from him!' and in the pilot episode, I gave him the alias 'Jim Lincoln.' I said to Quinn, 'Okay, now, you can't hate anybody named Lincoln.'"

With his aim at the collective heartstrings of the American television audience, Whitmore employed several other devices calculated to garner sympathy for the fugitive Kimble. "I thought what Kimble should do for the overall story is rescue someone, and preferably a woman for the romantic aspect, and for the bittersweet quality of having to move on," he continued. "I think Vera Miles played it—she was a cocktail pianist in a bar in Tucson, Kimble was a bartender, and she had a husband [played by Brian Keith] who was powerful and somewhat demented; he was sort of sadistically harassing his wife.

"And then the second shamelessly calculated piece of business was that she had a son, and Kimble ('Lincoln') was going to save her, and he was also going to befriend the son, he was going to do something nice. We were going to have a scene with the kid."

Martin liked where the story was headed, so he left Whitmore alone to finish the first draft. "I discovered at the end that I still had another trick up my sleeve for shameless calculation," Whitmore continued. "The pilot ends really in nice black-and-white stuff. There's this railroad yard, and Kimble is leaving town after having fixed everything. Lo and behold, there is a stray kitten that he encounters, and he picks up the kitten. He would, of course, like to take the kitten with him, but he cannot, because he is a fugitive, and he must go on.

"Well, if you didn't like Kimble after that..."

Whitmore completed the first draft. Martin then forwarded the script to Kellam DeForest, a researcher for ABC's Errors and Omissions Division who reviewed scripts for any potentially liable material. DeForest noticed a remarkable similarity between Dr. Kimble's red-haired stranger and a prominent character in a well-publicized news story. "Kellam called Quinn," Whitmore recalled, "and he said, 'My God, this red-haired man—Huggins stole it from the Sam Sheppard case!'"

Samuel Sheppard, an osteopath from Cleveland, Ohio, was convicted of bludgeoning his wife to death in 1954. Sheppard claimed that the real perpetrator was a bushy-haired stranger whom he saw running around in the neighborhood. The story made headlines all over the nation and eventually provided the basis for a made-for-television movie, *Guilty or Innocent: The Sam Sheppard Murder Case* (NBC, 1975), featuring George Peppard as Dr. Sheppard. The case was in its eighth year of appeal by the time *The Fugitive* premiered in 1963. Interestingly enough, the Supreme Court dismissed Sheppard's conviction during the program's third season (1965-66). In so ruling, the court stated that the "virulent publicity" surrounding *The Fugitive* (at that time the fifth-highest rated show on television) had sufficiently obscured the facts of the Sheppard case.

"Shortly after the show began, I received a letter from a woman in Boston who asked me where I got the idea for *The Fugitive*," Huggins recalled. "I was a little suspicious, because I knew that Sheppard's lawyer (F. Lee Bailey) had his offices in Boston. After I wrote the woman back, I found out that she was indeed Bailey's secretary. She needn't have bothered writing, though, because I was not at all influenced by the Sam Sheppard case."

Nevertheless, the parallel was too coincidental, so Martin and Whitmore went back to the drawing board. "We sat around Quinn's office and we said, 'What are we going to do about this—who is going to be the villain of the piece? What distinctive quality is this guy going to have?'" Whitmore said. "And I remembered when I was a kid that what always scared me about horror movies was that they always had someone with a club foot dragging the leg. It was really kind of old-fashioned, melodramatic horror, but it always worked on me. But I said, scratch that, because he's got to be some kind of a worthy adversary for Kimble at some point, and if the guy is handicapped, and simply can't move about .... And then we talked, and I said, 'What about one arm, the guy's missing an arm?' And Quinn said, 'That's terrific.'

"Then we spent about twenty minutes trying to decide whether it was the right arm or the left arm. I know I suggested that it be the right arm, because most people are right-handed, and consequently their right hand would get them into trouble. And so was born the 'one-armed man.'"

But then another small glitch was discovered. "Our original pilot script was supposed to be set in the state of Wisconsin," noted Barry Morse. "After the series was launched, some citizen—whether within our organization or outside it, I don't know— pointed out that the whole premise of *The Fugitive* would fall to the ground, punctured, if the location were set in Wisconsin, because at that time, there was no capital punishment in the state of Wisconsin! And so, arbitrarily, the locale of the series was shifted to Indiana."

Whitmore corroborates this story. "I distinctly remember writing in the pilot that Kimble said he was from Wisconsin," he said. "Why they changed it to Indiana, I have no idea. But if it was changed for that reason, undoubtedly Kellam (who never missed anything) would come up with it and discover something like that, and then say, 'Wait a minute, we've got to change it to a state that has capital punishment.'" (Two years after *The Fugitive* premiered, Indiana also repealed the death penalty.)

With these details straightened out, Martin then sent a copy of the script to Huggins, who had remained in the background up to this point. After reviewing Whitmore's revised script, Huggins addressed two elements that needed changing. He first objected to the idea of having Dr. Kimble maintain the same alias for the entire series. "I found that out by accident," Huggins recalled. "I was reading the pilot script, and his name in that script was Jim Lincoln. At some point, I asked Quinn, 'Of course, his name isn't gonna be Jim Lincoln next week, is it?' 'Oh, sure, that's his name!,' he said. 'That's the name he's going to use. We can't have him have a different name every week—it'll confuse the audience.' And I said, 'Hey, wait a minute. The guy is a fugitive. When he moves on, he moves on for a reason, and he's not going to take the name with him.'"

It's clear that Martin took heed, as evidenced by an observation Gerard makes to Monica in Whitmore's revised shooting script. After Monica (the Vera Miles character) declares her allegiance to Kimble, Gerard observes: "'Lincoln!' He'll have to change that now." This footage, however, was cut from the final print.

One other element of the pilot was excised at Huggins' suggestion. "I discovered that Quinn was going to have the man keeping a diary, on the old theory in this town that all protagonists have to have someone to talk to," he explained. "I mean, when I took over *Cheyenne*, [the character] had a 'comic' partner. I said, 'We get rid of the comic partner,' and their response was 'But whom will he have to talk to?' I said, 'You find they always have someone to talk to in 'B' pictures. In 'A' pictures, they don't have anybody to talk to! The scenes are dramatized—they aren't talked about.' And so, I won that point.

"Well, again, now here it was, God knows how much later, and I was getting the same answer. 'Well, you gotta keep a diary, because he hasn't got anybody to talk to.' And I said, 'Wait a minute. He is carrying a diary in his pocket that says I am a fugitive from a murder conviction. In your pilot, he is arrested. They will find the diary! He doesn't need any diary. He doesn't need someone to talk to, and he doesn't need a diary.' So the diary was thrown out."

Martin quickly recognized the rationale behind Huggins' suggestions. "It was not difficult for me to persuade Quinn that a mistake was being made," Huggins said. "Otherwise, I was quite pleased with the pilot. I thought that the script was well conceived. With those two things out of the way, I felt certain that the project was off to a good start."

Martin and Whitmore then met with the ABC brass to discuss the next step: casting. According to Hollywood legend, over 50 actors interviewed for the lead role, including such prominent names as James Franciscus (*Naked City, Mr. Novak*), Anthony Franciosa (*The Name of the Game*), and Robert Lansing (*87th Precinct, Twelve O'Clock High*). But according to Whitmore, this is one instance where legend has it wrong. "I have met an awful lot of actors in this town who claim they turned down *The Fugitive*, and I just smile at all that," he said, "because Quinn had no one else in mind but David Janssen. I mean, he wanted him from the beginning, and that was that."

Martin had kept his eye on Janssen ever since their days at Universal Pictures in the 1950s (Martin was a film editor, Janssen a contract player). "I saw a lot of him [back then]," Martin told *Newsweek* in 1965. "He struck me as a person that would never fade into the woodwork." Certainly Janssen had already established himself as a familiar (if not famous) screen performer by the time Martin offered him *The Fugitive*. He made his film debut as a teenager in 1945 (*It's a Pleasure*, with Sonja Henie), and had worked extensively in television, including a successful run as the glib *Richard Diamond, Private Detective* (CBS/NBC, 1957-60).

A fine athlete during his years at Fairfax High School in Hollywood, Janssen (born David Harold Meyer in 1931) twisted his knee during a pole vaulting exhibition—an injury that would dog him the rest of his life. His mother Berniece, a former Ziegfeld showgirl and onetime Miss Universe runner-up, encouraged him to take up acting. At age 18 he landed a contract with 20th Century-Fox Studios where well-meaning producers, aghast at the size of his large ears, used rubber cement to pin them back. That didn't work (the ears lay too flat). The producers then wanted his ears fixed surgically, but Janssen objected to that. Fox also wanted to alter Janssen's hairline, but when the producers couldn't do anything about that, they let him go.

Janssen then moved on to Universal-International and appeared in 32 pictures where he played, as he put it, an "agreer." "The star would approach me and ask, 'Don't you think so, Harry?' and I'd agree, and disappear," Janssen told *TV Guide* in 1965. But he soon caught the eye of TV producer (and onetime movie star) Dick Powell, who saw in Janssen a younger version of himself. Powell, who played Richard Diamond on radio, cast Janssen as the private eye for the TV version. "He was brash then," recalled Philip Saltzman. "I was working at Four Star Productions, where David filmed *Richard Diamond*. I was a story editor on *The Alcoa/Goodyear Theater* (NBC, 1958-60), which was also produced by Four Star, and David's office was right across the hall from my producer's. David used to come into my office, and we'd sit around and talk, and he was always doing Cary Grant imitations—you know, turning his head and saying, 'Judy, Judy.'"

But Janssen struggled (at least, in his own mind) after *Richard Diamond* was canceled. Despite a steady diet of work (*Route 66, Naked City, Cain's Hundred, Death Valley Days*), he wanted to succeed in the movies—a goal that would never materialize. "The thing that I remember about David was that I don't think he knew how good he was," said Whitmore. "When *The Fugitive* was riding high, television was still the 'stepchild'—the really important stuff was to be in features. And although David was in features (*Twenty Plus Two, King of the Roaring Twenties, Dondi*), he never became the 'great movie star,' the Robert Redford sort of thing. I think it always nagged him a little. And that was too bad, because he was a terrific personality. He was a hard-working, reliable person. He was a real professional. But I think he undervalued himself."

Huggins thought Janssen was an excellent choice. "I had used him on other shows and had thought very highly of him," he said. "David was a good friend of mine; we used to play poker together. I don't remember at what point his name came up—it may have been brought up by Quinn. But, yes, he became the only one that I could even see as the Fugitive."

In lieu of a salary, Janssen negotiated a deal in which he would receive ten percent of the series' profits. "David was not only a wonderful person, but he was a very smart guy," said Whitmore. "I think he understood better than I did the possibilities of this." By the time *The Fugitive* left the air in 1967, Janssen had earned over $4.5 million.

However, as line producer Alan Armer points out, Martin had to deal with one small detail before Janssen could shoot the pilot. "David had a commitment with somebody," recalled Armer, who produced the first three seasons of the series. "Somebody had optioned him for a series, and in order for David to be able to do the pilot, Quinn put up some of his own money to buy him out of whatever the other contract was. And, obviously, that was a good investment!" (Martin credited Armer with producing the pilot although he did not actually hire Armer until after the pilot was completed. Armer was busy producing *The Untouchables* at the time the pilot was filmed.)

After meeting and discussing the script with Janssen, Whitmore began working on the second draft, while Martin sought his only choice to play Lieutenant Philip Gerard, the character he once described as the *sine qua non* of the series.

Barry Morse once estimated that he has played over 2000 parts on stage, screen, radio and television over the course of his 60-year career. "I've never performed on the high wire, on ice, or under water, but I'm ready if need be," he once joked. Born in London, England in 1918, he won at age 15 the principal scholarship at the Royal Academy of Dramatic Art—the youngest person admitted to the Academy at the time. In his final term, he won the BBC Award and the title role in *Henry V*; he then played in a number of repertory companies in theaters throughout England, as well as in London's West End. He also worked as a director, then began acting on BBC radio in 1936; appeared in many BBC television shows beginning in 1937; and then later branched into films (his first was *The Goose Steps Out*, in 1940). He married actress Sydney Sturgess in 1939; their daughter Melanie was born in 1945, their son Hayward in 1947. The Morse family moved to Canada in 1951, where he appeared in countless films, and TV and radio productions for the CBC. He has worked as an actor, director and writer all over the world, from Austria to New Zealand.

"By the time we began *The Fugitive*, I had worked intermittently in the U.S., over a period of five or six years," said Morse. "We had not ever set up residence there, but from around 1957 or '58, I had been commuting both to New York and L.A. to do individual shows—things like *The U.S. Steel Hour*, *Studio One*, *Twilight Zone*, dozens of the popular shows of that time."

Among other shows, Morse had appeared in several episodes of *The Untouchables*. "Quinn Martin was a man of quite uncommon good sense, good taste, and general decency, which was by no means universally the case among Hollywood producers," said Morse. "I came to know him and to like him. And one fine day, when I was in Hollywood, Quinn rang me up and said, 'Look, I'm planning a new series, and there's a character in it that I'd like you to play—not exactly a running character, but a recurring character, in that the character won't be in every episode of the series.' He said, 'I don't want to tell you anything more about it, but I'll send you 'round the script, and let's have lunch.'

"And so this script arrived which had to do with a man falsely accused of the murder of his wife, and his pursuit by a dedicated officer of the law. The character of the 'man on the run' was a decent, admirable character (unmistakably 'middle American'), and the law officer was even more archetypically 'middle America,' conceived and written in the then quite conventional way of the 'raincoat and fedora' kind of detective.

"Now, to that point I had played all kinds of different American characters, even for Quinn Martin on *The Untouchables* (I can remember playing some kind of East Side thug in one episode). I didn't realize it was implicitly something of a compliment that producers and directors never hesitated to hire me to play all sorts of different types of American characters. And I'd have to admit that I'm a little vain about my skill with accents. While I was a student at the Royal Academy, I had developed a sort of 'flexible inner ear' that enabled me to reproduce, more or less, any accent after I was exposed to it for a little while. I think *The Fugitive* was the only instance up to that time where a British actor played an American character in a TV series.

"At any rate, I thought that both these characters in this proposed pilot for *The Fugitive* were so 'down the middle' in terms of American characterization, that he couldn't possibly want me to play the man on the run or the law officer, and I thought the only solution must be that somebody had sent me the wrong script! So when I met Quinn for lunch a day or so later, I was all set to explain this to him when he launched into an enthusiastic description of the outline of this proposed series, and made it quite clear that he wanted me to play the detective!"

Morse initially resisted the idea. "I said, 'Quinn, look, the character as I see it in this pilot script is a thoroughly conventional rendering of an American detective (as seen in the movies).' 'Well, that's the trouble, you see,' Quinn said. 'I know that. The character, as presently expressed, is too much 'on the nose.' And he said, 'I know you're always interested in developing slightly offbeat characters, so why don't you think about it and see if you can't develop something that's a bit more unusual?'

"Although I had made several television pilots before, I had not worked in quite this circumstance [of developing a character] before. It was interesting, but somewhat alarming, to be faced with that much responsibility. But I recognized immediately that this script that we had, the skeletal elements of *The Fugitive*, was a modern remake of *Les Miserables*. I mentioned this to Quinn, and he said, 'Well, yes, that is true, although we're naturally not advertising that, but it is a sort of modern rendition of the outline of *Les Miserables*.'

"Now, I've always thought that we in the arts (whichever art we're in) are all 'shoplifters.' Everybody, from Shakespeare onwards and downwards, who enters any of our activities must acknowledge that we are shoplifters. But once you've acknowledged that, make sure that when you set out on a shoplifting expedition, you go always to Cartier's, and never to Woolworth's!

"Well, on that basis, and with that idea in mind, I thought that Victor Hugo wasn't a bad 'role model,' if we were going to have a role model for our author. And so, I went back to *Les Miserables*, and especially to the character of Javert, the police officer who becomes engrossed with the pursuit of the hero, Jean Valjean," Morse continued. "Now, this may seem to be a very highfalutin' way of setting about what was, after all, thought to be a fairly commonplace exercise in Hollywood—the making of a television series pilot. But, it seemed to me, that we might as well go to the best places for our 'shoplifting,' and that certainly more 'flesh' could be put on this character, something a little less like the conventional 'Hollywood dick,' so much beloved and so much overplayed in so many movies. I wanted to develop over a period of time a more complex and less usual sort of character for this detective who was to be the 'nemesis' of our hero.

"It's interesting, by the way, that faintly French ring to the name 'Gerard,'" Morse observed. "There may have been some even subconscious echoes of *Les Miserables* in the choice of that name."

It was more than a subconscious echo; it was a deliberate take. "I gave Lieutenant Gerard the name 'Gerard' because I was having a little fun," said Whitmore. "I wanted to see if anybody might recognize that 'Gerard' was close to 'Javert.'"

With Morse set to play Gerard, Martin then hired prominent director Walter Grauman (*Lady in a Cage*), and Vera Miles (*The Searchers*, *The Man Who Shot Liberty Valance*) and Brian Keith (*Family Affair*, *Hardcastle and McCormick*) as the marqueé guest stars. In February 1963, the cast and crew traveled to Tucson, Arizona to film "Fear in a Desert City," the pilot episode. "They could always spend a little more for the pilot," said Whitmore. "I knew Tucson, and I kind of wanted to get away from the look of Hollywood, and Quinn wanted to establish a different location. He wanted to get away from L.A., where you always had the same palm trees in the background."

Shooting the pilot was easy. Convincing the skeptics at ABC that *The Fugitive* was a winner was an entirely different matter.

Brian Keith, Vera Miles and David Janssen in the pilot, *Fear in a Desert City*.

ACT II

The Pilot:

FEAR IN A DESERT CITY

"Fate Moves Its Huge Hand..."

At the heart of [*The Fugitive*] is the preoccupation with guilt and salvation which has been called the American Theme," wrote Roy Huggins in his 1960 network presentation of *The Fugitive*. "Kimble is pursued, and in the eyes of the law he is guilty. But no American of any persuasion will find him so. The idea of natural law is too deeply embedded in the American spirit for anyone to question Kimble's right, after all recourse to law has been exhausted, to preserve his own life. Even Hobbes, the great philosopher of authoritarianism, acknowledged one circumstance in which a man has a right to resist Leviathan: when an attempt is made to take his life on mistaken grounds." (Huggins' complete presentation is reprinted as Appendix 1. See page 182.)

Some six months stood between the completion of the pilot episode in early March 1963 and *The Fugitive*'s scheduled premiere in September. In addition to the usual headaches associated with producing a television series, Quinn Martin had to contend with the dissension at ABC over *The Fugitive*. Despite network president Leonard Goldenson's support, the likes of programming head Thomas Moore continued to grumble about the new series. Martin was also beginning to experience some of the same problems Huggins went through—his closest friends had their doubts about *The Fugitive*.

"I had known Quinn Martin from the days when he was a sound editor at the old ZIV studios," said writer/producer Don Brinkley (*Medical Center, Trapper John, M.D.*). "We were old friends. I had done a number of his other shows—*The Untouchables, The New Breed, The Jane Wyman Theater*. When he was telling me about *The Fugitive*, and showed me the pilot, I said, 'Well, it's a great idea, but what do you do for your 14th show? You're going to run out of ideas in about 13 shows.' Quinn said, 'Well, I'll take the chance.' And that's how much I know!" (Brinkley would contribute five scripts to *The Fugitive*.)

Brinkley certainly had a point. Many series before and since *The Fugitive* have failed because they could not sustain the premise, no matter how innovative, for the entire length of a television season. (In 1963, a full season ranged from 30 to 39 episodes.) Television producers invest millions of dollars in new programs every year in the hope that the shows last long enough—usually three or four seasons, or about 100 episodes—to go into syndication, or the "rerun" circuit. When that happens, the producer licenses the series to an independent program distributor who then markets the entire package of episodes to local stations across the country. Depending on how popular the program was during its original network run, a producer can, at the very least, recoup the initial investment. In some cases, syndication sales can result in major profits. In 1987, for example, producers Marcy Carsey and Tom Werner sold the rebroadcast rights to *The Cosby Show* (NBC, 1984-1992), the highest-rated television program at the time, to 175 independent television stations for over $500 million.

"ABC wondered what direction *The Fugitive* would take after the pilot—what kind of stories we would be telling," said Stanford Whitmore. "So Quinn and I sat down and, in the space of about twenty minutes, came up with ten stories, very quickly and very easily. That was a lot of fun, because we didn't have to resolve them—they were really just kind of premises. I remember at the time that Quinn liked fights—boxing, and so did I, and I said 'Look, this guy's a doctor—suppose he gets a job as a cut man for a prize fighter?' Quinn said, 'Great! That's a story [the episode "Decision in the Ring"]!' We really thought them up rapidly. Then Quinn sent off that list of proposed stories to ABC, and that apparently comforted them where they could see where we'd be going after the pilot show, what kind of situations he would be getting involved with."

Martin then recognized something else about Huggins' concept that the network had overlooked—*The Fugitive* was based on a premise that was completely elastic. The pilot episode demonstrated that the actual search for Kimble was a secondary, albeit important, element of the overall story. The true drama, and ultimately what made *The Fugitive* so appealing, was the moral dilemma Kimble confronted each week (i.e., he had to resolve the conflict facing the people he became involved with that week without endangering his own life). Since he had to leave town at the end of each episode, Kimble could land anywhere, in any job, and the story would still make sense.

"*The Fugitive* was an anthology show with a running character. That was the big advantage of it," said director Sutton Roley. "Most series have running characters, like cops or lawyers or doctors or whatever, and those characters do the same job each and every week; whereas David Janssen in *The Fugitive* could be thrown into an entirely different type of situation each week. It was always moving, it had people in it, but it was primarily a character show. It dealt with people."

In the tradition of the many dramatic programs (*Playhouse 90*, *Studio One*, *The U.S. Steel Hour*) that populated television throughout the 1950s and '60s, many episodes of *The Fugitive* consisted of small character studies of the various people and towns Kimble encountered during his search for the one-armed man. Kimble and the basic fugitive concept served as the skeleton around which the scripts were wrapped.

ABC president Leonard Goldenson thought it was a great approach. "I felt that it was certainly an exciting way to be telling a story about an innocent person trying to prove that he was innocent," he said.

The elasticity of the premise gave *The Fugitive* the sort of "forward motion" characteristic of another narrative genre—the novel. "I got the sense that the writers on *The Fugitive* were telling one whole story," observed Stephen King. "The concept itself was a novelistic concept—you had a main character who had a potentially life-threatening or life-ending problem, as opposed to Ward Bond in *Wagon Train*, who simply had to keep 'wagon training,' and then people came on and he solved their problems. If you imagine a group therapy session of popular TV characters, with people sitting in chairs around in a circle, most of the characters—guys like the Wagonmaster, or Gil Favor in *Rawhide* or possibly George Maharis and Marty Milner in *Route 66*—would never raise their hands. But if you raised your hand, they would be able to solve your problems.

"Then you have this other, very small group of characters, like Paul Bryan from *Run for Your Life*, or Harlan from *The Golden Years* (King's 1991 series which borrowed elements of *The Fugitive*), or Richard Kimble—these characters are constantly raising their hands. Harlan's saying, 'I'm having a problem because I was involved with an accident—I'm an old man who's growing younger and everybody's hunting for me.' And then Kimble raises his hand and says, 'They want to kill me in the death house. They think I killed my wife, and I have to find the man. Have you seen this man? I have a problem and I need to find this man.' So there's a novelistic situation.

"The only thing about *The Fugitive* that doesn't happen in a novel (because the series ran for four years) is that the problem remains static: I'm looking for the one-armed man, and this guy pops up in different places," King continued. "But the concept is still more realistic than the standard situation on something like *Murder, She Wrote* or *Perry Mason*, where week after week these things happen to other people. With a character like Richard Kimble, it's natural that things should happen to him, because he has to keep outrunning the police."

The Fugitive also owes some of its success to the "cliffhanger" element of the oldtime Saturday afternoon matinee adventures. "When this pilot was produced, all the experts pronounced that it couldn't possibly succeed, or even get on the air, because it had no successful ending," recalled Barry Morse. "Well, of course, they had completely ignored the impact of the cinema serials of the 1930s and '40s, and to go a little further back, that of the literary serials of the 19th century. [In both of these cases], the very absence of an ending in the ordinary sense of the word, so far from being a disadvantage, served as a powerful immense hook."

The Fugitive also relies on the assumption that, although narrow escapes and lucky coincidences abound, the viewers will suspend their disbelief so long as the writing holds up and the characters remain appealing. "If the audience is really involved, you can [make that assumption]," Martin told TV Guide in 1964. "Look at Westerns—they do the same thing. Nobody really thinks the hero will be gunned down in the duel at high noon. But everyone watches as if he might." Thus it is that "Nightmare at Northoak" and "The End Game" (two episodes in which Gerard comes tantalizingly close to capturing Kimble) remain exciting to watch 30 years later. Even though we know that Kimble will escape, it's still fun to see just how he does it. The writing continues to convey the inherent tension of the series' premise. "You get that little frisson every time Kimble walks through a bus station past his own poster on the wall," added King.

Although Martin was certain that television audiences would take to his new series, he still needed to convince ABC that The Fugitive would appeal to potential sponsors as well. While the network arranged for several advance showings of the pilot before its September premiere, Martin recruited Janssen and Morse to help promote the series. "Among all the other opinions collected on the basis of this pilot, there was a huge split of reaction to the two characters, Kimble and Gerard," said Morse. "On the one hand, there was immense sympathy, an immense warmth, that was felt from people who recorded their impressions of the pilot episode—support and sympathy towards the character of Richard Kimble, of course. Well, the natural counterpart was the response to Gerard!

"Quinn Martin was very amused by this. I remember him saying to me, just before the show went on the air, 'Boy, all the people in the commercial world are very worried about you!'

"And I said, 'What do you mean, me?'

"And he said, 'Well, this performance of yours. Because they keep coming to me and saying, 'We've done all this audience testing, and they love David. But, boy oh boy, do they ever hate that guy Morse—you gotta get him out of there!'

"And Quinn said, 'No, no, no! That's the whole point!' Because in the climate of those days," continued Morse, "it was totally unheard of to have in a series a character whom you were deliberately meant to dislike!" Indeed, this was some fifteen years before the era wherein American television audiences willingly embraced such prominent villains as J.R. Ewing (Dallas) and Alexis Carrington (Dynasty).

"It was very rare for an actor to want to play such a character," Morse continued. "But, of course, as Quinn patiently pointed out to anyone who would listen, the more animosity, the more resistance there was to Gerard, by simple mathematical process, the more sympathy there would be created for Richard Kimble—for David. So that intensity of response was, implicitly, a great testimony to the strength of what we were delivering."

The response to the two characters is also a testimony to Whitmore's strength as a writer, for his script elicited just the sort of response he and Martin had counted on. Morse, for one, is quick to point this out. "Actors don't half-often enough acknowledge the importance of the quality of the writing," he said. "But it is, after all, in any dramatic offering, the writing where the battle is won and lost."

Roy Huggins was also pleased with the pilot script. "Whitmore did a very, very good job," he said. "He and Quinn did exactly what they should have done to present Richard Kimble with great sympathy."

With network president Leonard Goldenson's faith in the program sustained, ABC ordered a full season (30 episodes) and scheduled The Fugitive for Tuesday nights at 10:00 p.m. "Fear in a Desert City" aired September 17, 1963. Nearly three years to the day when the idea first took root in Huggins' mind, and having withstood every conceivable argument against its existence, Richard Kimble's quest for the one-armed man had finally begun.

The early reviews were encouraging. "The measure of *The Fugitive* is that a viewer has a hankering to stick around for another week and see how and under what circumstances David Janssen successfully eludes the law," noted *The New York Times Review on Television* (September 25, 1963). "Quinn Martin's professional touch and its cast of eminently qualified stars gives this series promise."

"If you're looking for something different . . . , you could do far worse than to try this ABC show," wrote Cleveland Amory (*TV Guide*, January 11, 1964). "It is not, as its title suggests, merely another gun run where the good guys get the bad guys in the end. Rather, it is an adult drama excitingly and often excellently written, in which one good guy, who cannot turn to any authority to help him, has to get the bad guys before the end—because, for him, literally, there is no end."

Years later, Huggins recalls meeting with Goldenson long after *The Fugitive* became a huge success. "Leonard said, 'Did you ever have any trouble when you told that idea to people?' And I laughed, and I said, 'Why, Leonard?' And he said, 'Because I had nothing but trouble! I got letters from the American Legion, from the Bar Association, from my own people—*my own people* opposed me every inch of the way, and I almost canceled the show! And you know, the funny thing is, Roy, that once it went on the air, we didn't hear from any of these people!'"

Huggins knows the reason why. "The American people never saw a thing wrong with it," he said. "That is the American theme [rooting for the underdog], and they recognized it."

"Here's an innocent man who's fighting for his life, against all odds, and the public was pulling for him to find that person," added Goldenson. "People like pulling for an innocent person."

Plot Synopsis

[We see a train heading into the night. An omniscient narrator introduces us to two of its passengers....]

Name: Richard Kimble. Profession: Doctor of Medicine. Destination: Death Row, State Prison.

Richard Kimble has been tried and convicted for the murder of his wife. But laws are made by men, carried out by men. And men are imperfect.

Richard Kimble is innocent.

Proved guilty, what Richard Kimble could not prove was that moments before discovering his wife's body he encountered a man running from the vicinity of his home. A man with one arm. A man he had never seen before. A man who has not yet been found.

Richard Kimble ponders his fate as he looks at the world for the last time... and sees only darkness. But in that darkness, fate moves its huge hand.

[The train derails, and in the confusion Dr. Kimble makes his escape. In each subsequent episode of *The Fugitive*, an abbreviated version of the foregoing introduction restates the premise and re-establishes the mood of the series.]

THE FUGITIVE

a QM Production

Starring

DAVID JANSSEN

as The Fugitive

Also Starring

BARRY MORSE

as Lieutenant Philip Gerard

Tonight's episode

FEAR IN A DESERT CITY

Written by Stanford Whitmore. Directed by Walter Grauman.

Guest Cast: Vera Miles (Monica Welles), Brian Keith (Edward Welles), Harry Townes (Sgt. Burden), Dabbs Greer (Sgt. Fairfield), Barney Phillips (Cleve Brown), Abigail Shelton (Evelyn), Donald Losby (Mark Welles), Bryan O'Byrne (Ticket Agent), Paul Birch (Police Captain Carpenter).

Prolog. *Now six months a fugitive, this is Richard Kimble with a new identity, and for as long as it is safe, a new name. . . James Lincoln. He thinks of the day when he might find the man with one arm, but now is now. And this is how it is with him.*

Another journey, another place. Walk neither too fast, nor too slow. Beware the eyes of strangers. Keep moving.

[Kimble chooses a hotel.]

The right one? Or will it be a mistake? Is this the trap where it will end?

Safe. For now.

Another room. Windows look out—and look in. Get busy.

[Kimble stares at his reflection in the mirror and applies black dye to his hair.]

Look closely. Be sure of this: they'll never stop looking. He'll never stop. Not Lieutenant Gerard.

Synopsis. In Tucson, Arizona, Dr. Kimble finds a job as a bartender at the Branding Iron Saloon, where he falls for the pianist, Monica Welles. Monica has been trying to shield herself and her son Mark from her husband Edward Welles, a wealthy businessman who is insanely jealous. Welles quickly discovers Kimble's involvement with his family and influences two police detectives to run Kimble out of town. With no other choice,

Kimble arranges to leave, but not before he sees Monica and tells her his secret. Extremely moved by the Fugitive's plight, Monica decides that she and Mark will leave with Kimble and protect him from Gerard. However, an enraged Welles quickly determines Monica's plan and tries to head them off at the bus depot. Welles confronts Kimble just as he, Monica and Mark are about to board a bus for San Diego.

Epilog. *Now six months, two weeks, and another thousand miles a fugitive, this is Richard Kimble. And this is how it is with him.*

One of *The Fugitive*'s most recognized characteristics, the distinctive voice of William Conrad as the Narrator provided a sense of direction not only for Dr. Kimble, but for millions of television viewers across the globe. "That was one of Quinn's little quirks: he liked the narrator," noted Stanford Whitmore of the device Martin had previously used on *The Untouchables* (the breathless delivery of syndicated newspaper columnist Walter Winchell). "A lot of people say that a narrator is a crutch—and it can be a crutch. But it also can be terrifically effective. It can bridge scenes, time, and almost subliminally make an audience feel the way you want them to feel. And it gives you an opportunity [as a writer] to write some good stuff that you can't put into the mouths of characters who are in a dramatic situation. The narrator can stand back and make these comments."

William Conrad was an inspired choice. He had already narrated *The Bullwinkle Show* (ABC/NBC, 1959-63) and had starred as Matt Dillon in the radio version of *Gunsmoke.* Conrad with his booming delivery still has one of the most recognized voices in the entertainment industry, rivaled only by that of James Earl Jones. When Whitmore discovered that Conrad would narrate *The Fugitive*, he deliberately scripted the Narrator's speeches to cater to the actor's commanding voice. "I wanted to give Bill the kind of words that he could really make sound important and ominous, such as the way he says in the beginning, 'Fate moves its huge hand,'" Whitmore said.

Conrad spent several years as a successful TV producer and director (*Klondike, 77 Sunset Strip*) before Martin coaxed him back into acting to play *Cannon* (CBS, 1971-76); he has since starred in *Nero Wolfe* (NBC, 1981) and *Jake and the Fatman* (CBS, 1987-92).

Usually limited to a few brief, sometimes terse remarks to open and close each episode, the role of the Narrator is extended in this first episode. Here the Narrator is the guiding force for not only the story, but for the Fugitive as well. As Kimble checks into the hotel, for example, the Narrator becomes an extension of the Fugitive's consciousness that allows us to hear exactly what Kimble is thinking: "The right one? Or will it be a mistake? Is this the trap where it will end?" This is particularly important in that Kimble has no dialogue in his first scenes: his thoughts and emotions are communicated entirely through the Narrator. (The Narrator is used similarly in "Glass Tightrope," "The End Game," and "End of the Line.")

These first scenes with Kimble are tremendously well done. Moving perfectly in sync with Conrad's narrative, David Janssen pantomimes the Fugitive's fear and paranoia. There's also a nice quality in the way Janssen delivers his first lines ("My name is Jim Lincoln"). He conveys the sense that, even though Kimble has been using disposable aliases for six months, he still has to remind himself of who he's supposed to be. Only once, in the third season's "Landscape with Running Figures," does Kimble make the mistake of forgetting his adopted name (he signs in for work as "Richard Kimble").

"Fear" provides several other instances of Kimble's learning how to act like a fugitive. In the patrol car sequence (Act III), Kimble displays remarkable composure throughout the entire time Burden and Fairfield drive him home. Despite being "pushed around," Kimble demonstrates the ability to think on his feet. "Put yourself in my place: a stranger, no one to vouch for me, no friend who's a lawyer," he tells Burden. "I can't demand a thing. I have to sit here and take it." In this instance he shows some of the savvy he needs to survive pressure situations. Compare this to the sequence in Act I where Ed Welles makes Kimble flinch ("What makes you think I was talking about you?").

However, his triumph is quickly undermined. Kimble doesn't anticipate the detectives' following him to the hotel. This is a mistake he will rarely make again. Naturally, he cannot stop them from searching his room without calling attention to himself. In fact the hotel search reveals the one vulnerable chink that Kimble can never quite mask: he usually acts very nervous, and very guilty, in front of the police. Again, Janssen is excellent in this sequence—he looks completely shaken by the time the detectives leave Kimble's apartment.

Stanford Whitmore was particularly pleased with Walter Grauman's direction of the sequence where Kimble confides in Monica (Act III). "If you'll look at that scene, Wally went away from the closeup of the agony of Richard Kimble having to say 'I'm innocent,'" he said. "I think part of it is played on Vera Miles' reaction, and Kimble has one final little line in there ['I was a doctor'], which is very, very close to self pity. But David almost threw it away. It was so underplayed, yet I thought it was tremendously effective. When I saw it, I was really impressed, because I said, 'This is something where the audience supplies all the sympathy,' instead of having him crammed down their throat, like 'Feel sorry for me, I'm innocent, I'm being hunted, I must always run.'

"That one scene is, I think, the kind of thing you get from people who work together on a show and understand what you're trying to get at," Whitmore continued. "Walter deserves a lot just for that one scene alone." Certainly, the tight shots of Janssen's face capture Kimble's anguish and vulnerability. The eyes tell all. With the possible exception of the nightmare sequence from "Nightmare at Northoak" (which would air later that season), this is the only time Kimble shows us just how much Gerard frightens him.

As brilliant as Janssen is in "Fear," the pilot contains one sequence that did not require a whole lot of acting. Keep an eye on his reaction when Brian Keith throws him against the bus during their brawl in Act IV. Keith hit him so hard that Janssen broke three ribs—an early indication of the tremendous physical toll the series would take on the 32-year-old soon-to-be star.

Despite his inner conflict—his inherent instinct to do good versus the instinct to survive—the humanitarian Kimble is fairly easy to define. Figuring out Lieutenant Philip Gerard is an entirely different matter. Because he appears in less than one-third of the series' 120 episodes (and rarely for more than a few minutes at a time), Gerard is an enigma—yet he is clearly the most fascinating character of the series, due in large part to the intelligent, intricate manner in which he is portrayed by Barry Morse.

Understanding what makes Gerard tick requires an understanding of the law as Gerard sees it. "The police officer as 'an instrument of the law' is a concept which is fundamental to the whole operation of any legal system, but it doesn't seem to be quite so readily accepted and understood among the public at large," explained Morse. "As I see it, any society which has a legal, judicial system has three functions, really, within it. It has *the police investigative process*, which deals with the uncovering of crime and the apprehension of criminals; *the judicial system* (judges and juries), which disposes the punishment or acquittal of those charged with criminal offenses; and *the prison system*, which enforces whatever punishment has been decreed for this or that criminal act. The police officer within that legal structure cannot permit himself to have question or doubt because he must be, above and beyond everything else, *impartial*. Many police officers in many societies have gotten into deep, deep trouble by allowing their partiality to influence their actions.

"Gerard would say that it is no part of his business to question the decision of a jury as to the guilt or otherwise of a person who has been charged with a crime—his function is to make sure that the process laid down by the judge and jury is carried out. He is a 'functionary,' or an 'instrument,' of the law: he is involved in the carrying out of the law, not in the making of it. If aspects of the law need to be changed, if the decision of that judge and that jury needs to be challenged, there are processes of appeal, there are processes of review in the law—if you happen not to agree with capital punishment! Those are perfectly legitimate questions, *but they do not concern me in my function as a police officer*. As he himself said in the pilot, 'Let others debate and conclude—I was an instrument of the law, and [still] am.'"

Gerard's steadfast, rigid interpretation of his role as "instrument" of the law enables us to understand (at least partially) why he is so insistent upon capturing Kimble himself. Despite the freak nature of the train accident, Gerard holds himself personally responsible for Kimble's escape. The accident which prevented the law from carrying out its proper conclusion (the convicted violator meeting his end) was beyond Gerard's control—yet he somehow blames himself. Therefore, finding Kimble and bringing him to execution becomes Gerard's personal mission—his obsession.

In his first scene (with Paul Birch as Captain Carpenter), Morse plays Gerard as a man with a quiet determination—a far cry from how that sequence originally went. "I first wrote Gerard as a little like Captain Ahab (*Moby Dick*), but I didn't know Barry Morse was going to play it," recalled Whitmore. "I remember watching the first cut of the pilot with Quinn and with Wally Grauman, and there's this one scene where Gerard is on the other side of this glass map, and the captain asks him to take a vacation, and Gerard nearly bites his head off! I mean, Barry played it like a raving lunatic, and Quinn said, 'This guy should be hospitalized!'

"Quinn then said to me, 'Stan, for God's sake, Barry Morse is used to acting on the stage: you give him something a little extreme [the pilot script describes Gerard as 'a man whose dedication borders on fanaticism'], and he'll really get into it!' So I had to rewrite that scene, just to kind of calm the character down a little bit, because Barry was playing it as it was written, and as Wally directed it. Then we re-shot that scene."

Morse also recalled his initial performance. "It was considerably 'over the top,'" he said. "I think there were two things at issue. One was the superficial, purely theatrical, presentation of the character, which was served up in my view in a Hollywood stereotype manner, complete with the hat and the raincoat. The other was *Les Misérables*, where you have Javert presented as being somebody who by modern psychiatric standards probably should be hospitalized!

"As we continued to work on the pilot, it began to appear to a fair number of people, quite independently, that there was something other and better and less stereotypical that could be made out of this character Gerard. There didn't have to be a snarling, snappy, obsessive antagonist, because there would be more life in the whole thing if he were rather more complex. And so, gradually, other colors were added to the character."

Morse then discussed some of the ways in which he added color to Gerard over the course of the series. "I used to get mail from viewers who noticed that over a period of time, I used both hands to write or to operate things with," he said. "I am instinctively left-handed, but I developed a certain degree of ambidexterity, and I thought that might be interesting and intriguing to viewers as being an outward sign of this somewhat divided nature which poor Philip Gerard had. And so, perhaps months apart, if I was involved in writing something, I would in one instance use my left hand, and in another use my right. I also began to use glasses as time went by—my own, because more often than not I had them with me in my pocket. It seemed to me that it would be a hint of the march of time, if one started to see Gerard wearing glasses.

"But then, of course, the interpretation of the character began to emerge in more subtle, less tangible ways. I hope I found ways of illustrating Gerard's sense of dichotomy—his own instinctive responses to situations set against the 'code' which he had drilled himself to observe rigidly—as the series progressed."

Aside from David Janssen's performances, the most captivating aspect of *The Fugitive* is the stirring theme music composed by jazz artist Pete Rugolo. Since the Arts and Entertainment cable television network began rebroadcasting the series in 1990, at least three *Fugitive* fan clubs have been formed; the topic that fans want to know the most about is the series' music.

"John Elizalde, who was Quinn Martin's music supervisor, called me and came to my house and told me that he wanted me to look at the pilot," said Rugolo, who was scoring music for Universal Television at the time. Prior to moving into television, Rugolo was a musical director at Mercury Records, where he arranged for and directed such jazz greats as Billy Eckstine, Sarah Vaughan, Patti Page and Stan Kenton.

"I looked at the *Fugitive* pilot and I liked it and I decided to do it," he said. "They had me write about two or three hours of music, and they told me what they wanted. They showed me the main title, how Kimble would be running a lot during the series. So I came up with the idea of the 'Fugitive' theme music at the beginning."

Because Rugolo was under contract at Universal, he wasn't able to come into the Goldwyn Studios where *The Fugitive* was filmed to score each episode individually. "At Universal, I scored every picture; I looked at it and talked it over with the producer and the director and so forth," he explained. "But for *The Fugitive*, no. All I actually saw was the pilot. They gave me a few scripts and they gave me an idea of what the show would be about, so I wrote several cues based on the 'Fugitive' theme—sad versions, neutral music, chases, a love theme, 'story' music (music you hear while the radio's playing), every possible kind of theme and variations. I also wrote a theme for Lt. Gerard—it was like a police theme ('bah-bah-bah-bumm!'), so that anytime you saw Gerard, they'd start it off."

On the basis of watching the pilot episode, Rugolo composed a library of music that music director Elizalde and music editor Ken Wilhoit drew from as they scored the episodes. Rugolo did not, however, write all the music used on the series. "In those days you were able to buy other libraries of music, since there were so many shows and so many hours of music available," he said. "They could deal with the publisher, and they would get little arrangements on those kind of things as the show went on. They used all the thematic material that I wrote for *The Fugitive*, but there are other things they needed that I didn't write." (The series used music that had been featured on such shows as *Gunsmoke*, *The Twilight Zone* and *The Outer Limits*.)

Because the musicians' union at that time permitted American television studios to record music for their shows in different countries, Elizalde arranged to have the *Fugitive* music recorded in London, England. However, Rugolo was unable to record the music himself. "In those days, they also had a law that the composer from the United States could not conduct the music over there," he said. "So John supervised it and had someone else conduct the music. They used a big symphony orchestra with wonderful musicians, and they did a beautiful job. Then [music editor] Ken Wilhoit would put the music where he needed it. He did a wonderful job—he made me sound good!"

Rugolo never released an album of his own based on his compositions for *The Fugitive*. "That's kind of a sad story," he recalled. "I was asked by Warner Brothers to make an album of *The Fugitive*, because in those days they were recording a lot of those albums with TV themes (Rugolo did one for *Richard Diamond, Private Detective*). The producer called me, and I wrote all the different arrangements, and I had set up a recording date with him. But the producer got fired at the last minute, and for some reason Warners didn't want to go through with it! I probably should have called some companies to see if they were interested, but I never followed through. I still have a whole album of music for *The Fugitive* sitting in my basement. It's a shame it was never recorded, because I think that it would have been a pretty good album." It's safe to say that many would agree.

Rugolo was pleased to hear that, 30 years later, his compositions for *The Fugitive* continue to have an impact on the fans. "Oh, that's wonderful," he said. "I think it really does help to create the mood of the show."

FUGE FACTS

Television scholar David Thorburn watched "Fear in a Desert City" with Quinn Martin as part of an interview with the producer in 1978. "Martin was very proud of his ability to choose actors who were appropriate to the medium of television," he said. "At a certain point during the interview, he said 'Well, how about if we go and look at a segment of *The Fugitive*?,' and we went into a projection room and we watched the first episode. At various points, he stopped the film and we talked about what we had seen, what sorts of effects he had aimed for, and so forth."

Martin stopped the film at the end of the patrol car sequence with Janssen, Harry Townes and Dabbs Greer. "After we looked at this scene, Martin said 'Look, this is an example of how I think performers on television operate,'" said Thorburn. "He pointed to Dabbs Greer and Harry Townes as examples of actors who projected a kind of 'internal danger'—they were able to project an air of menace, something from within. Martin also emphasized the extent to which they were not 'conventionally handsome' performers— he thought that added to the air of menace and danger they projected. You can feel a sadistic quality in the way the cops question Kimble in that scene, and the quietness with which they speak reinforces that element." (Townes and Greer both made multiple appearances on *The Fugitive*, as well as in many other Martin programs.)

Martin felt that this sequence was one of the most important scenes of the entire series, according to Thorburn. "He felt that this scene explained the heart of *The Fugitive*'s appeal: that all human beings feel guilty in a vague way without knowing what they're guilty of," explained Thorburn. "Although Martin never invoked Kafka, it was clear to me that he understood that *The Fugitive* dramatized the fear that ordinary people have of authority in general, and the sense that authority is potentially dangerous to them even if they're innocent. Martin was proud of the scene because he felt that it dramatized that subject very clearly: it established an assumption on which the rest of the series would be based."

Paul Birch appears as Captain Carpenter, the only character on *The Fugitive* besides Richard Kimble who has any sort of control over Lieutenant Gerard. Although his scenes are brief, and his lines accordingly scant, Birch manages to carry some weight to his role (perhaps due to the actor's imposing build). In Carpenter's only scene, he questions Gerard's motivation behind pursuing Kimble: he suspects that Gerard thinks the one-armed man really exists. Although Carpenter never gets Gerard to admit his reasons for keeping the Kimble matter alive, the captain will continue to ask this question in subsequent episodes. Because Carpenter respects Gerard's abilities as a police officer, he continues to grant the lieutenant leave to follow Kimble-related leads. But the captain is no jelly fish—he always requires Gerard to be back in Stafford within a couple days to return to the other cases at hand, and even pulls rank on Gerard in one episode ("The End is But the Beginning").

Carpenter appeared in several episodes during the first two seasons, then was never seen again. (Birch died in 1969; the character was never replaced.) Although no explanation was ever given, the captain's disappearance had a dramatic effect on Gerard: it made the character even more of a threat. Without Carpenter (or any subsequent captain) to report to, Gerard becomes in effect a free agent who can come and go as he pleases. Indeed, in the final two seasons, we rarely, if ever, see Gerard in his office—he's always out and about, apparently devoted to tracking down Kimble 24 hours a day.

It would seem logical that a man on the run would resort to a steady array of facial disguises—lengthening his hair, growing a full mustache or beard—in order to hide his identity. But Dr. Kimble, over the course of the series, never did much more than brush his hair with black dye. While preparing for *The Fugitive*, David Janssen and Quinn Martin spent a lot of time in various small towns and police stations, and among the things they looked into was the best manner of disguise to use on the series. "The police told us that nearly 99 percent of all men on the run rarely do more to delude their pursuers [than change their hair color]," Janssen told *Newsweek* in 1965. "They don't have the money for plastic surgery."

Although Morse and Janssen became good friends off the set, ABC tried to discourage them from being seen together in public because that was considered "bad" for the series. "Our paths didn't cross all that often within the series," said Morse. "But the network was very much concerned about the possibility of our being seen in each other's company socially. They really took this sort of thing seriously—it would be as if King Lear was seen taking his daughters out to dinner on his night off!"

In 1964 Pocket Books published *Fear in a Desert Town*, an unauthorized adaptation of the pilot that took many liberties with Stanford Whitmore's screenplay to create a much different (but less satisfying) story. Among the noticeable changes:

Ed Welles is renamed Mark Welles.

Monica Welles is reduced to a spineless, pathetic whimperer. While she certainly deserves pity, she also suffers from such lack of self esteem (she resignedly accepts her husband's abuse) that you almost wish Kimble wouldn't bother with her.

The waitress Evelyn and bar owner Cleve, who are little more than walk-ons in the pilot, become major characters. Evelyn is Kimble's love interest (including a one-night stand), while Cleve assists Kimble in his escape at the conclusion of the story.

Carpenter, Burden and Fairfield are all given first names—Ed, Elroy and Wilson, respectively. Burden and Fairfield are considerably more sleazy—they accept a bribe not only from Welles, but from anyone else with a little money.

After escaping from the train wreck, Kimble stumbles onto a satchel full of money.

Gerard absolutely hates Kimble. In a pointed bit of dialogue, he tells Kimble how much he resents doctors. The novel also suggests that Kimble hated Helen.

Roy Huggins didn't like the Pocket Books adaptation for another reason: copyright infringement. Although he had relinquished the TV rights to *The Fugitive*, Huggins kept all other property rights, including merchandise rights. To this day, no product based on *The Fugitive* can be manufactured without his consent. (Ideal issued a board game based on *The Fugitive*, but Huggins did not become aware of this until long after the product left the market.) Huggins won a lawsuit against Pocket Books; no other adaptation based on the series ever appeared.

Get Smart paid homage to "Fear in a Desert City" in its 1968 parody of *The Fugitive*, "Don't Look Back." Maxwell Smart is framed for murder and armed robbery, and his only hope of clearing himself is to find a one-handed man—the KAOS agent who pulled off the crime along with his partner (who was disguised as Max). Written by Chris Hayward and Phil Mazzella and directed by Don Adams, "Don't Look Back" totally lampoons the style of *The Fugitive*, complete with an omniscient narrator. In Act II, Max's identity is discovered by the owner of a roadside diner, but Max convinces the owner of his innocence. As Max runs off to the next town, the narrator intones "Beware the eyes of strangers, and even friends: keep moving"—an allusion to the prolog narration of "Fear in a Desert City." (*It's Garry Shandling's Show* also parodied *The Fugitive* in a 1983 episode.)

David Janssen, as Dr. Richard Kimble with his wife, Helen Kimble, played by Diane Brewster.

ACT III

THE EPISODES

FIRST SEASON, 1963-1964

PRODUCTION CREDITS

Starring David Janssen as The Fugitive
Also Starring Barry Morse as Lt. Philip Gerard
and William Conrad as The Narrator

Executive Producer: Quinn Martin
Created by: Roy Huggins
Producer: Alan A. Armer
Associate Producer: Arthur Weiss
Assistant to the Executive Producer: Arthur Fellows

Production Manager: Fred Ahern
Directors of Photography: Lloyd Ahern, Carl Guthrie, Fred Mendl, Meredith Nicholson
Music: Peter Rugolo
Production Design: Claudio Guzman (pilot only)
Assistant to the Producer: John Conwell
Film Editors: Larry Heath, Walter Hannemann, Jerry Young, Mars Fay
Art Director: Serge Krizman
Assistant Directors: Maxwell Henry (pilot only), Paul Wurtzel, Lloyd Allen, James E. Newcomb, William Shanks, Read Kilgore
Property Masters: Irving Sindler, Don Smith
Chief Electricians: Lester Miller, Robert Farmer, James Potevin, Vaughn Ashen
2nd Camera Operators: Roger C. Sherman, Joe August Jr., Richard A. Kelley
Special Photographic Effects: Howard Anderson
Music Supervisors: John Elizalde, Ken Wilhoit
Music Editor: Ted Roberts (pilot only)
Set Decorator: Charles Thompson (pilot only), Sandy Grace
Makeup Artist: Walter Schenck
Costume Supervisors: Bob Wolfe, Elmer Ellsworth
Hairdresser: Lavaughn Speer (pilot only), Lynn Burke
Assistant Film Editors: Tom Neff, Jr., John Shouse, John Post, Carl Mahakian
Script Supervisors: Billy Vernon (pilot only), Duane Toler, Frances McDowell
Sound: The Goldwyn Studio
Casting: Kerwin Coughlin (pilot only)
Production Mixer: John Kean
Sound Editor: Chuck Overhulser
Re-Recording: Clem Portman

PROLOG: FIRST SEASON

In the beginning, it was very tough," recalled producer Alan Armer. "You're struggling to find out what your series is, what kind of stories you can tell, what kind of stories work, what kind of stories don't work. You're making some mistakes, and you're having some victories. So the first year was kind of uneven."

From the production end, that would seem to be the case. The series underwent several changes in personnel during its first weeks on the air. But the episodes themselves, with just a few exceptions, were excellent and after several weeks the series began to build a solid and loyal audience. By the end of the season, *The Fugitive* established itself as one of the most popular programs on the ABC television network, with an average of 21 million viewers a week.

"The audience was terribly involved with the series," said Armer. "The rooting interest for Kimble was stunning—we would get letters and phone calls, pleading with us to let the poor devil have another trial!" In response, Martin commissioned Stanford Whitmore to write "The Girl from Little Egypt," a "prequel" to the pilot episode in which Kimble flashes back to the trial and the night of the murder.

The opening sequence (Kimble and Gerard seated on the train) underwent several changes over the course of the season. After a few episodes the narration was pared down, although it still recapped the premise of the series for the benefit of those watching *The Fugitive* for the first time. However, for a couple of episodes toward the end of the season ("Never Stop Running," "Storm Center"), the narration was eliminated altogether from the opening. These episodes begin with the close-up of the frog sitting on the rock, followed by the cut to Kimble stumbling through the meadow. "I guess somebody must've had a thing for frogs," joked Stanford Whitmore. "I don't know about the frog. I remember seeing it, and I kind of wondered what's the frog doing there?"

Whitmore does recall coming up with the idea behind the most visually striking element of the opening sequence. "In the sessions with Quinn where we would just sort of sit around Quinn's office and put our feet up," he said, "I remember saying 'Hey, Quinn, what if he comes out of the train wreck and magically the handcuffs just sever, but part of them are still on his wrist, and the light flashed off his handcuffs, and it jumps out and becomes the title.'

'And Quinn said, 'Hey, that's a great idea, let's do it!'

'And I said, 'Can you do it?'

'He said, 'Sure, they can do anything in the lab.'

'It was just kind of an idle remark, an easy suggestion. And I said, 'Well, why not?' Because I usually don't concern myself with stuff like that.

'But Quinn liked it, and he said, 'Let's do it that way.'"

Episode 2

THE WITCH

Original Airdate: September 24, 1963

Written by William D. Gordon.

Directed by Andrew McCollough.

Guest Cast: Patricia Crowley (Emily Norton), Madeleine Sherwood (Mrs. Ammory), Arch Johnson (Ty Tyson), Gina Gillespie (Jenny Ammory), Crahan Denton (H.R. Ammory), Elisha Cook (Sailor), George Mitchell (William Sturgis), Ray Teal (McNay), Claudia Bryar (Mrs. Sturgis).

Prolog. *Now ten months after his escape, take Richard Kimble, unjustly convicted of murder, put him down in the Missouri hills, a handyman, driving a truck for a local fuel and feed company. Once again, he has changed his identity: he has become Jim Fowler, a stranger in town.*

Synopsis. Young Jenny Ammory is a pathological liar who uses an encounter with Kimble as an excuse for failing to turn in her homework. When Kimble makes a delivery at the school, Jenny identifies him as the man who attacked her. As Jenny's teacher Emily speaks to Kimble, the girl runs home and tells her mother that she saw Emily and Kimble "in the barn." Emily and Kimble are both advised to leave town. Kimble tries to clear Emily by catching Jenny in a lie, but his strategy backfires: the townsfolk believe Jenny and decide to lynch Kimble.

Epilog. *This is Jim Fowler, about to die. He will last long enough to take the bus out of Hainesville, Missouri, and then a new identity must emerge, a new identity to hide the path of his flight, and the path of his search for the man whose crime has made Richard Kimble the Fugitive.*

Kimble's training in pediatrics enables him to recognize why Jenny lies so much: the girl is lonely (her only friend is a rag doll she calls Nyet) and has been neglected by her parents. The Fugitive manages to communicate with her even after he exposes her as a liar. After finding Kimble in the woods (Act IV), Jenny realizes that the new man is clearly frightened by the town's sudden turn against him. Kimble begs Jenny to tell the truth, and as the townsfolk closes in, she tearfully retracts her story. In this instance, Kimble's knowledge of children saves his life.

Episode 3

THE OTHER SIDE OF THE MOUNTAIN

Original Airdate: October 1, 1963

Teleplay by Alan Caillou and Harry Kronman. Story by Alan Caillou.

Directed by James Sheldon.

Guest Cast: Sandy Dennis (Cassie), Frank Sutton (Del Jackson), Ruth White (Grams), R.G. Armstrong (Sheriff Bradley), John D. Chandler (Quimby), Hugh Sanders (Leo), Johnny Day (Masters), Paul Birch (Police Captain Carpenter), Bruce Dern (Martin).

Prolog. *West Virginia... what used to be a town, before the coal mine gave out—a naked relic now, without future, without hope. Another dreary point in time for Richard Kimble, eight months a fugitive.*

Synopsis. After eluding a sheriff's posse, Kimble meets Cassie, a young woman who lives in the mountains with her grandmother. Cassie tells Kimble she can help him because she knows the territory. Meanwhile, Gerard heads for West Virginia after learning that Kimble's fingerprints have been identified. While Gerard and the sheriff search Cassie's home for Kimble, Cassie leads the Fugitive to an abandoned mine which has a tunnel that leads to the other side of the mountain. Cassie begs Kimble to take her along—just as Gerard and the sheriff close in.

Epilog. *Above the mountain, leaving it far below and behind him, Lt. Philip Gerard returns home without the man he had come to find and recapture. The other side of the mountain, of many mountains, a road twisting and turning into the future, without promise, without assurance for the man who must always go alone: Richard Kimble, fugitive.*

"The Other Side of the Mountain" provides us with our first extended look at the considerable detective skills of Philip Gerard. The lieutenant first suspects that Cassie's grandmother might be lying about Kimble when she says "There ain't been no young man in this house"—neither he nor Sheriff Bradley mentioned anything about a *young* man. Then while observing the wash area outside, Gerard notices that the rag near the wash bowl is completely dry. Perhaps whoever washed himself did not use the rag because he expected to use something cleaner, as though he were accustomed to drying himself with a clean towel—as a doctor would be. Clearly, Gerard isn't kidding whenever he says throughout the series, "I know Kimble."

Gerard's brilliance occasionally makes him seem arrogant and condescending, which in turn leaves him slightly open for ridicule: Bradley suggests that the lieutenant should wear Levis (instead of a suit and tie) the next time he searches for Kimble in the open country. However, according to Barry Morse, Gerard must always comport himself in a professional manner in order to remain an effective police officer. "It is very important, especially when dealing with smaller communities, as Gerard very often was, not to encourage too much closeness," Morse said. "The development of such relationships, or such feelings, may very readily lead to a restriction of his freedom of action as a police officer."

FUGE FACTS

The order in which the episodes were aired does not always reflect the order in which they were produced. This would apparently explain the Narrator's assertion in the prolog that Kimble has been on the run for eight months, when he indicated in the previous episode that it's been ten months since the escape. But in the case of this episode, "The Other Side of the Mountain" was both filmed after and aired after "The Witch." Apparently, somebody missed the reference to "eight months" in the prolog.

FUGE FOL DE ROL

Frank Sutton (Del) has a full head of hair in this episode—he's best remembered for the flat top he sported as Sergeant Vince Carter in *Gomer Pyle, U.S.M.C.*

Episodes 4 and 5

NEVER WAVE GOODBYE (Two-parter)

Original Airdates: October 8 and 15, 1963

Written by Hank Searls.

Directed by William Graham.

Guest Cast: Susan Oliver (Karen), Robert Duvall (Eric), Lee Philips (Ray Brooks), Will Kuluva (Lars Christian), Rachel Ames (Ann Gerard), Harry Bartell (Clem Parker), Paul Birch (Captain Carpenter), Henry Beckman (Passenger), Ed Holmes (Fugitive Detail Lieutenant), Bert Remsen (Skipper), William Zuckert (Navigator), Lawrence Parke (Awning Proprietor), Diana Bourbon (Yachting Wife), Tina Menard (Pedro's Wife).

(Part One)

Prolog. *Santa Barbara, California, two hours up the coast from Los Angeles. A harbor town, a fishing town, an early mission town. To Richard Kimble, temporarily using the name Jeff Cooper, it has been a sanctuary. But a fugitive knows a sanctuary becomes a trap if he stays too long.*

Synopsis. After learning of the arrest of a one-armed man for armed robbery in Los Angeles, Gerard receives permission to fly out and question the suspect—hoping that the story will flush out the Fugitive. Meanwhile in Santa Barbara, apprentice sailmaker Kimble has fallen in love with Karen, the daughter of his boss Lars Christian. Lars suffers a heart attack, and on his deathbed he implores Kimble to stay with the girl. Having seen an newspaper item about the one-armed man, Kimble tells the old man that he must visit someone in Los Angeles. If this man is the right man, Kimble will stay with Karen.

Epilog. *Richard Kimble has seen the eyes of the hunter. He knows that for Gerard the chase will never end. But his bones ache from running and he needs the love of a girl. For sanctuary, he will risk a trap. For in the long, long chase he has lost everything but hope.*

Roy Huggins originally conceived the Kimble character as a contemporary cowboy, a rootless wanderer who drifts from town to town. "The western hero is an irresponsible drifter, but he doesn't come across [as irresponsible]," he explained. "He has no family, no roots, no goals, no obligations, and no sense of guilt. He avoids commitment to people and community in a kind of willed irresponsibility, and no one seems to mind."

The contemporary cowboy of *The Fugitive* touched on a romantic lifestyle that many viewers longed to have. "Kimble was the sort of character that people wanted to sublimate themselves in," according to novelist Stephen King. "He was a drifter, he was rootless, he had no responsibilities (except not to get caught), he went to a different town every week, and he had a lot of pretty girls. I loved the way he lived [King was a teenager when the series premiered], to be able to move from town to town like that and switch jobs."

But human nature at some point leads people to settle down and establish roots ("A man cannot run forever," as the Narrator observes in this episode). Huggins knew this from the start—the contemporary cowboy would look like a bum, and American audiences would scorn themselves if they rooted for a hero who avoided the culture-induced ethic of "hard work." But his concept of a wrongly convicted fugitive addressed these issues. Kimble must remain rootless and immune from personal commitment because his life depends upon his ability to do so. The audience can accept his "irresponsibility" without feeling guilty themselves because they know in fact he is innocent.

But unlike his western counterpart, the Fugitive would gladly return to the trappings of normal life if the circumstances would allow that. In "Never Wave Goodbye," we see that the months of constant running have taken their toll. Tired and lonely, the Fugitive in this episode succumbs to his feelings. "His bones ache from running, and he needs the love of a girl," says the Narrator. Although Kimble realizes that a romantic entanglement could compromise his freedom, he also knows that he can never quell the longing for companionship (he nearly took Monica and her son with him in "Fear in a Desert City").

Despite the risks involved, Kimble allows himself to fall in love with Karen. Secure in this love, Kimble is noticeably relaxed in this episode, particularly during the early scenes of Part Two: he has momentarily cast aside the doubts that have plagued him throughout the months of running. But he cannot completely shake them—as Gerard correctly predicted in Part One, once Kimble begins to feel confident, "that is the beginning of the end." Despite his feelings for Karen, Kimble must move on without her. Although Kimble will allow himself brief moments of love in other episodes ("World's End," "In a Plain Paper Wrapper," "The Walls of Night"), until he clears his name, he cannot settle down. For a man on the run, to stand still means to die.

Part One of "Never Wave Goodbye" also demonstrates that, despite a front of police professionalism and personal fanaticism, Philip Gerard occasionally displays genuine signs of humanity. "Gerard was so weird... he had a wife, and he had a kid," observed

King. "He was always promising the kid 'We'll go fishing next week,' and then the Fugitive would show up and he'd have to chase after him, which bent his family life."

Gerard tries hard to communicate with his family. While his wife seems to accept, albeit resignedly, the reason behind Gerard's prolonged absences, his son Flip (short for "Philip Jr.") is another matter. Gerard earnestly attempts to explain the boy's latest disappointment: he can't take Flip fishing because the law is like a fishing line that must be straightened out whenever it becomes tangled. But the boy doesn't understand. "I didn't care if the line worked," he tells Gerard. "I just wanted to go fishing."

Although Gerard's family acquiesces once again in "Never Wave Goodbye," subsequent episodes indicate that the lieutenant's fixation on Kimble gradually takes its toll. Gerard's son so desperately wants to be with his father that he later stows away in a police car during a search for Kimble (in "Nemesis"), while his wife eventually suffers a nervous breakdown (in "Landscape with Running Figures").

FUGE FUN

Barry Morse called attention to one of the more noticeable casting changes in the series. "At two different points in the series, poor Gerard was issued with two totally different wives," he recalled. "I remember in one of the earlier episodes, his wife appeared very, very briefly, and an actress [Rachel Ames] was engaged, but no particular character was demonstrated. But then there was an episode much later on ["Landscape with Running Figures"] when the whole family background of Gerard became quite a crucial ingredient. And at that point, Barbara Rush played Mrs. Gerard. But nobody ever explained to the customers—the audience—that he suddenly had a totally different wife!"

Actually, Gerard would have three wives over the course of the series. In addition to Ames and Rush, an uncredited actress appeared briefly as Mrs. Gerard in the second season's "May God Have Mercy." To add further confusion, not only did Mrs. Gerard evolve from a blonde to a brunette over the years, she changed her name. In this episode, Gerard's wife was named Ann, but in "Landscape," she was known as Marie. (Perhaps her name was really "Ann Marie." Or maybe Gerard divorced Ann and married Marie...?) If that's not confusing enough, there's the matter of the lieutenant's progeny. In "Never Wave Goodbye," an uncredited actor plays Phil Gerard Jr. (in the second season's "Nemesis," Kurt Russell took over the role). However, in "Landscape," Gerard phones in and asks the baby sitter to "Say hi to the kids," so apparently he and Ann/Marie had another child in the interim—or perhaps they dumped Phil Jr. and took on a entire new brood.

(Part Two)

Prolog. *A man cannot run forever. Two hours up the coast from Los Angeles, Richard Kimble has found himself a place he thinks he is safe. Here in the early mission town of Santa Barbara, wearing the name Jeff Cooper, he has begun to put down roots. A man on the run must sooner or later become tied to a town. A look on the face of a girl, the touch of her eyes. But there may always be doubt. What has he left behind—a footprint, a careless word, a remembered image in the eye of stranger . . . a match? What can they track him with? If he is tired of running, he will put the doubt aside.*

Synopsis. Tired of running, and confident that Gerard will expect him to flee Santa Barbara, Kimble decides to trip up the lieutenant by staying put. However, after deducing that Kimble might stick around for that very reason, Gerard continues to investigate. On just a single clue (a match Kimble left behind at the Hall of Justice), Gerard traces the Fugitive to Lars' sailmaking shop, where he gets an assist from a jealous Eric. When Karen discovers that Gerard's still in town, Kimble hopes to end the search for good by faking his death in a sailing accident.

Epilog. *The road north, the road east. For the moment, to Richard Kimble, it makes no difference. The road ends nowhere.*

Hank Searls, who wrote the script for "Never Wave Goodbye," joined the Sheriff's Reserve of the Los Angeles Police Department while conducting research for a series of paperback novels he was writing back in the late 1950s. While a deputy, he became familiar with the Metropolitan Squad of the L.A.P.D., a squad of "elite" police officers that served as the basis for *The New Breed*, Quinn Martin's first series as an independent TV producer. Searls created *The New Breed* and contributed several scripts, including the pilot episode.

"Never Wave Goodbye" had its origins from Searls' background in sailing. "Quinn knew that I was a sailor, and had a 40-foot ketch that I lavished all my attention on," Searls recalled. "I was familiar with the Santa Barbara area—my wife and I sailed out of there quite a bit. It seemed like the perfect place. They had a harbor there; they had a lot of yachts there; and it seemed like a good place to have a sailmaker and all the things I wanted to get into this particular story."

The title of the episode contains a play on the word "wave." "The currents are funny down in Santa Barbara," said Searls. "After a good deal of research, I finally discovered some route by which Kimble could actually drift down the coast, and Santa Barbara was the place to set it."

FUGE FACTS

While the series writers worked hard to maintain consistency in the Kimble and Gerard characters throughout the four-year run, they occasionally overlooked a few small details—such as the exact year and date of Helen Kimble's murder. "Never Wave Goodbye" states Helen was murdered in 1960, although according to "The Judgment" the murder took place in 1961. In "World's End," the Narrator tells us that Helen was killed on September 17, but "The Judgment" gives a date of September 19. (Both dates are correct in a sense. September 17 was the date *The Fugitive* premiered on ABC in 1963, while September 19 was the date on which Roy Huggins created the series in 1960.)

Two of the key story points of "Never Wave Goodbye"—the newspaper story and the fake death—were used in later episodes. In "The Judgment," Gerard uses a newspaper account about an one-armed man in order to lure Kimble into a trap, while Kimble again fakes his death in order to deceive Gerard in "The End is But the Beginning."

Kimble saves Gerard's life in this episode. He would do so four more times before the series ends, in "Corner of Hell," "Stroke of Genius," "Ill Wind" and "The Evil Men Do."

Gerard tells us in this episode that while Kimble was married, he and Helen used to spend their summers sailing in Maine.

Episode 6

DECISION IN THE RING

Original Airdate: October 22, 1963

Written by Arthur Weiss.

Directed by Robert Ellis Miller.

Guest Cast: James Edwards (Joe Smith), Ruby Dee (Laura Smith), James Dunn (Lou Bragan), Hari Rhodes (Dan Digby), Robert F. Simon (Murphy), Harry Swoger (Wally Wilson), Richard Kemmer (Henry Stone).

Prolog. *Now 11 months a fugitive, Richard Kimble emerges from the blackness of hiding into the gray anonymity of another alias, Ray Miller. He thinks of the day when he might find the one-armed man. But, for now, Los Angeles, California offers him temporary haven.*

Synopsis. Kimble works as a cut man for boxer Joe Smith. Joe wanted to be a doctor, but he chose boxing because he felt his being black would be an obstacle in the world of medicine. Joe suffers from memory loss, and both his wife and Kimble fear that the boxing may have caused brain damage. Police detective Henry Stone (posing as a writer) is investigating Joe's manager Lou for possible mob ties, and following a tip, Stone suspects that Kimble is trying to get Joe to throw his next fight. As Kimble confronts Joe about his condition and advises him to retire from boxing, Stone uncovers Kimble's identity.

Epilog. *This was Ray Miller, cut man. Before that, James Lincoln, bàrtender. And how many weary, lonely, heartbreaking identities before that? Only if he succeeds in discovering the man who made him an outcast, can he again be Richard Kimble.*

"Decision in the Ring" was the first episode produced by Alan Armer, who had just completed a successful tenure as producer of *The Untouchables*. Armer clarified a quote attributed to him in a 1982 *Emmy Magazine* article concerning this episode. "That article said that when I saw David doing that prize fight story, I was surprised to discover that he was such a good actor," Armer said. "I had once seen him do a *Naked City*, and when Quinn first asked me about David, I remembered the *Naked City* that David had done—this was maybe two years before he ever did *The Fugitive*—and he was excellent! When Quinn asked me what I thought of David, I gave a very positive reading: I knew he was a good actor."

Martin's one fear about casting Janssen was that the actor might be too glib for *The Fugitive*. "Because David had done the *Richard Diamond* series, many people thought of him as Mr. Slick, Mr. Smooth, Mr. Sophisticated, and didn't realize that he was an actor," Armer recalled. "There are so many of these young, good-looking guys who can get away with a slick reading, but who don't have any real acting depth. David was an actor. His instincts were superb, and it stood him in good stead. He was more than just another pretty face."

FUGE FACTS

Although "Decision" was the sixth episode to be aired, it was actually the first to be filmed after the pilot, as the reference to James Lincoln (Kimble's alias in "Fear in a Desert City") in the epilog narration suggests.

Episode 7

SMOKE SCREEN

Original Airdate: October 29, 1963

Written by John D.F. Black. Directed by Claudio Guzman.

Guest Cast: Beverly Garland (Doris Stillwell), Alejandro Rey (Paco Alvarez), Pina Pellicer (Maria Alvarez), Peter Helm (Johnny Peters), John Milford (Foreman), Mort Miller (Ranger Ritter), Pepe Hern (Cardinez), Robert Contreras (Ibarra), Ed Faulkner (Jordan), Buck Young (Newsman), James Seay (Fire Chief), Stuart Bradley (Sheriff), Barry Kelley (Harry).

Prolog. *California, the Imperial Valley. Richard Kimble, now wearing the name Joseph Walker. Occupation: farm laborer. The California sun is hot. There is a strange antagonism in the eyes of the other workers. A hatred which he cannot fathom, but one which Richard Kimble tries to ignore in his effort to keep the secret of his identity.*

Synopsis. Kimble is now working as a migrant farm worker. As a forest fire breaks out nearby, Kimble realizes that Maria, the pregnant wife of fellow worker Paco Alvarez, may need a caesarean. But the fire prevents access to a hospital. Doris, the work site nurse, berates Kimble for not recognizing the urgency of the situation, and Kimble agonizes over what to do. Finally, he presents his medical credentials, offering to perform the operation. Although Doris is skeptical, Paco authorizes Kimble to proceed. A reporter's accounts of the situation are aired on nationwide television, and Gerard suspects the surgeon is Kimble.

Epilog. *There is no celebration for a fugitive. Richard Kimble moves on, his objective always the same: to find the man who alone can deliver him from execution.*

This episode was originally entitled "Fire in the Mountains." "That was one of the first shows I worked on," recalled Alan Armer. "I remember that the script needed a lot of work." Although the basic story elements remained intact, there's one significant difference between John Black's first draft and the final version—Lieutenant Gerard was not a part of the original story. Armer speculated that the decision to work Gerard into the script probably had to do with "selling the concept" of a new series. "It may have been a case where, in the early days, we wanted to keep a certain story point fresh with the audience," he said. "Since the script needed rewriting anyway, we worked Gerard into the plot to remind the viewers that Gerard was going to be a major part of the series."

FUGE FACTS

Kimble attended Cornell University Medical School, went on to advanced study at Guy's Hospital in London, then completed his residency at Memorial Hospital in Chicago. He specialized in pediatrics and obstetrics (Kimble noted in the pilot he had been a pediatrician). According to this episode, he interned in New York, although in "The Survivors" we're told that he interned at the County Hospital in Fairgreen, Indiana, where he met his future wife, a nurse named Helen Waverly.

Episode 8

SEE HOLLYWOOD AND DIE

Original Airdate: November 5, 1963

Written by George Eckstein. Directed by Andrew McCollough.

Guest Cast: Brenda Vaccaro (Joanne Spencer), Chris Robinson (Miles), Lou Antonio (Vinnie), J. Pat O'Malley (Ray), Normann Burton (Car Salesman), Jimmy Hawkins (Teenager), Melinda Plowman (Teenager), Jason Wingreen (Tim Cates).

Prolog. *Sierra Point, New Mexico. Resident population, 562. Transient population, one—Richard Kimble, who now bears the name Al Fleming. It is now more than a year since the escape.*

Synopsis. Working at a gas station in New Mexico, Kimble is taken hostage, along with customer Joanne, by holdup men Miles and Vinnie. Once on the road, Kimble pretends that he was planning to rob the garage himself and that he is on his way to a "big job." At the same time, he lets Joanne know that he is on her side—but the woman becomes terrified when she sees a newspaper headline identifying Kimble as a convicted murderer. In Los Angeles, Kimble sets up Vinnie and Miles for capture by phoning his "partner" for a meeting at a motel about the "big job." But Miles wants Vinnie to wait at the motel while he and Kimble drive off—to kill Joanne.

Epilog. *A city with 10 million lights casts a hundred million shadows, each one only a passing refuge for a man on the run—a man like the Fugitive.*

"I was working on *The Untouchables* and working with Alan Armer, whom I had also gone to college with at Stanford," said George Eckstein. "I was a casting director on *The Untouchables* when Alan gave me my initial writing assignment on *The Untouchables*, and I wrote about 10 of those. When he took over *The Fugitive*, I did a couple the first year for him, and I went on to become associate producer for the second and third years."

In addition to the 10 episodes he wrote, Eckstein helped Armer (and later Wilton Schiller) work many other scripts into shape. "Dramaturgically, *The Fugitive* was one of the most difficult shows that had ever been on television to write, because you have a protagonist whose every instinct tells him to get out, to run," said Eckstein. "You have to somehow involve him in the story in some sort of emotional sense in order to have him there, to play out the story. In most series leads, you have a man who is not himself at risk, or has a franchise to become a protagonist. But in *The Fugitive*, you have a man who is always in jeopardy, and yet still must involve himself in the troubles of someone else. And so, you have to spend maybe the first act, the first act-and-a-half, involving him emotionally to the point where he would put himself in harm's way in order to come to the aid of someone else, which is not your normal situation in a dramatic series."

Eckstein has nothing but praise for David Janssen. "Somehow, he would have the facility as an actor to make everything work," he said. "I mean, I would occasionally go to dailies, and he would make lines work that had no business working! We gave him, on occasion, some very tough things to say, and yet he managed to make everything sound credible and believable. He might toss them out, toss them aside a little bit, but he had what I thought was some sort of internal monitor that would not allow him to give a bad reading. Sometimes he would not go to the full extent of the emotion involved, but he would never be false. You would never find a moment when he was not credible. For a writer, it was a wonderful experience, because he showed you what can't work and what can work, and he would just try to do better for you."

Episode 9

TICKET TO ALASKA

Original Airdate: November 12, 1963
Written by Oliver Crawford. Directed by Jerry Hopper.

Guest Cast: Geraldine Brooks (Adrienne Banning), Murray Matheson (Morehead), John Larkin (Captain Carraway), David White (George Banning), Tim O'Connor (Steve Lund), June Dayton (Celia Decker), Gail Kobe (Ruth Wyatt), Gene Lyons (Paul Vale).

Prolog. *The freighter Alaskan Star, six hours out of Seattle, Washington, carrying a crew of 14. Accommodations for 12 passengers, one of them Richard Kimble, now wearing the name Larry Talman. Destination: Alaska, the 49th state. Objective: to earn a large sum of money in a short period of time, and thus underwrite the next phase in the search for his wife's killer.*

Synopsis. Also aboard the freighter is Paul Vale, an FBI agent searching for a Korean War criminal. Vale questions all the passengers, but seems especially interested in Kimble, George Banning (an embezzler) and his wife Adrienne. When Vale is found shot to death, the captain interrogates each passenger. When the captain discovers that Kimble's references are false, Kimble becomes the chief suspect.

Epilog. *Larry Talman, freed from the suspicion of murder, leaves the Alaskan Star. But it is Richard Kimble, still under the sentence of death, that steps ashore. He will stay in this place as long as it is safe, then he will move on. It is said there is no rest for the wicked—nor, sometimes, for the innocent.*

"Ticket to Alaska" is an old-fashioned whodunit with a clever twist on the "drawing room" element where the sleuth summons all the suspects together in order to reveal which one is the killer. Since all of the suspects in are at sea, it's unlikely that any of them can disappear for too long because there are only so many places one can hide on a ship. Writer Oliver Crawford also uses the Narrator to open each act—this is the only episode in the series that uses the Narrator this way.

Apparently, Crawford believed that Kimble's life should not be without pleasure: in addition to booking Kimble on a cruise, he got him a ticket to a baseball game in "There Goes the Ball Game." Crawford also wrote "Death is the Door Prize."

Episode 10

FATSO

Original Airdate: November 19, 1963
Written by Robert Pirosh. Directed by Ida Lupino.

Guest Cast: Jack Weston (Davey Lambert), Burt Brinckerhoff (Frank Lambert), Glenda Farrell (Mrs. Lambert), Vaughn Taylor (Crowley), Paul Langton (Sheriff), Henry Beckman (Brown), Paul Birch (Captain Carpenter), Garry Walberg (Mechanic).

Prolog. *A ride with a stranger, a friendly stranger. But a fugitive can't afford the luxury of friendship. He has to keep his thoughts to himself, weigh every word carefully. Drive carefully. Do everything carefully. From the moment you wake until you go to sleep at night—if you have a place to sleep. One false move, one little quirk of fate . . .*

Synopsis. Landing in a rural Kentucky jail following a car accident, Kimble ("Bill Carter") manages to escape with his cellmate, Davey "Fatso" Lambert. Gerard learns of Kimble's escape, and flies out to investigate. At the Lambert ranch, Kimble sees that Davey's father and his brother Frank both treat him badly. Davey explains that he burned down the old barn, although he was drunk at the time and can't remember doing it. Suspecting that Davey's brother Frank is actually responsible for the fire, Kimble decides to verify Frank's Army records at the local camp (he discovers Frank was AWOL at the time of the fire). Meanwhile, Gerard closes in.

Epilog. *A letter from an old friend. No return address, no name. A fugitive has to watch his step. Every step he takes, every hour, every minute, every second, any moves he makes might lead to death row. There's no way of knowing in advance. There's never any way of knowing.*

Executive producer Quinn Martin originally wanted Barry Morse to portray Gerard in a highly stylized manner. This concept would have accentuated not only the lieutenant's outward mannerisms, but his wardrobe as well. Gerard would have looked very much like the conventional Hollywood detective as seen in the movies, complete with trenchcoat and fedora. "As I got more confident about the way in which I thought the character ought to develop," recalled Morse, "we decided to simplify, to make less stylized, the appearance of the character."

As a result, aside from the last segment of the pilot episode, Gerard never wears the "standard" trenchcoat associated with movie detectives. This is the only episode, aside from the pilot, in which Gerard wears a fedora.

"I remember that the wardrobe department had come up with clothes based on the original concept of the series," recalled Morse. "They provided me with the standard Hollywood detective's raincoat and Hollywood detective's fedora, both of which, I thought, were quite wrong, in the light of this rather unconventional character that we were starting to aim towards. And so, I seem to remember that I threw them away behind a bush, somewhere just outside Tucson, Arizona, where we were shooting the pilot at that time. And [except for 'Fatso'], I never wore a hat or any kind of overcoat—whatever the weather, whatever the time of year, whatever the geographic location: a visual symbol of Gerard's stoical, puritanical character."

Morse himself picked out Gerard's wardrobe. "I think I only used two suits," he said. "Rather than having clothes made by some expensive tailor, I asked the wardrobe department to take me to the sort of store where Gerard would buy his clothes, ready-made, off the peg. And Quinn—good, discerning, sensitive boss that he was—supported me in these developments, and I think they did add to the somewhat unusual quality of the character, and therefore, in the end, of the series."

Episode 11

NIGHTMARE AT NORTHOAK

Original Airdate: November 26, 1963

Written by Stuart Jerome. Directed by Chris Nyby.

Guest Cast: Nancy Wickwire (Wilma Springer), Frank Overton (Al Springer), Paul Carr (Ernie), Scott Lane (Larry Springer), Doreen Lang (Anna), Harry Hickox (Charley), Barbara Pepper (Matty), Sue Randall (Jen), Bobs Watson (Milt Plummer), Charles Herbert (Cal), Ian Wolfe (Dr. Babcock), Paul Birch (Captain Carpenter).

Prolog. *This is Richard Kimble's recurring nightmare [capture by Gerard]. And each time it ends, he wonders whether he will awaken to the same nightmare of reality.*

Synopsis. A tightly-knit New England community heralds Kimble ("George Porter") for his quick action in rescuing their children from a burning school bus—particularly after he is nearly killed by an ensuing explosion. The town sheriff and his law-abiding wife nurse Kimble back from a concussion, but the Fugitive becomes restless once he discovers who his hosts are. After the sheriff's son innocently photographs Kimble for the local paper, the story of the heroic stranger hits the papers nationwide. When Gerard reads about it, he flies out to Northoak and arrests the Fugitive. But the lieutenant cannot return Kimble to Stafford until the extradition papers are processed—a three-hour period which both men anxiously endure.

Epilog. *Another city, another town. Help Wanted. Help, but there is none. Richard Kimble must live with his past and his future. His only consolation is that somewhere, perhaps here, there is a one-armed man that has nightmares of him.*

David Janssen put a lot of effort into *The Fugitive.* Although he received much of the recognition (and deservedly so) for the success of the series, Janssen had tremendous respect for the often overlooked people "behind the scenes." To him, *The Fugitive* was a team effort. "David knew the character so well that if there was something in the script that he felt was dishonest, he would get on the phone and say, 'Alan, can I talk to you?'" recalled Alan Armer. "And I'd go down to the stage, and if there was a problem in the scene, we would sit down and talk it out, and find an answer or another line that would take care of the problem."

Janssen not only contributed many ideas to writers and directors toward the development of his own character, but to the rest of the picture as well. "David was the kind of actor who read the whole script, not just his part," said Stanford Whitmore. "You know, there are scripts down here that are sent to actors, and their agents circle their roles, or every scene wherever they occur. These people do a movie, and they don't know what the movie's about because they've never read it! They just read their roles. But David was the kind of guy who would read the whole script. He knew what was going on. He *wanted* to know what was going on."

Janssen collaborated with Christian Nyby, who directed the original feature film version of *The Thing*, in the staging of the confrontation between Gerard and Kimble in Act III. Kimble awakens from his dream (a reprisal of the nightmare sequence seen in Act I) to find Gerard standing outside his cell. The camera then cuts to Gerard, shown through Kimble's P.O.V. (point of view)—from behind the bars of the cell. Then the camera cuts back to Kimble inside the cell. "It was just a thought that occurred, because Kimble wanted to see Gerard behind bars, instead of himself!" said Nyby. "A lot of how that scene was staged comes from David. He had a lot of input into the series. He'd offer suggestions in regards to things like that." (Many other episodes feature variations of this shot—i.e., filming other characters through Kimble's P.O.V.)

The dream sequences in "Nightmare" are among the few instances in the series where the scenes are overtly melodramatic. Given that Quinn Martin was known for his preference for subtle, understated drama, the nightmare scenes are extremely effective. "With a scene like the dream sequence, you go completely with it, and play it for all it's worth," Nyby explained. "You have to take what the writer [Stuart Jerome] had in mind, because if you deviated from what he had in mind with a scene like that, you might lose the point of the whole scene."

In contrast, the exchange between Kimble and Gerard—the first real confrontation between the two characters in the series—is dramatic because of its subtle presentation. "How you must hate me," utters Gerard matter-of-factly. The scene is not overplayed in any way. "It had to be a throwaway, otherwise you would lose the effect of the dream," added Nyby. "That had to be underplayed, because you can only get the audience up high occasionally. You have to taper off."

Barry Morse also put a lot of thought into this particular sequence. "This was one of the instances where my 'removal' from the U.S. perception of things gave me an objective view, which was invaluable," he explained. (Morse was born in England; he became a Canadian citizen in 1951.) "As you know, the adversarial system of the law in the U.S. is substantially different than the system which exists in Canada or in the U.K. And it made me instinctively aware that there shouldn't be in the mind of a properly trained, properly thinking police officer the 'adversarial' situation [between the law enforcement people and those whom they are pursuing], which I think is a weakness in the U.S. judicial system. It tends to set up a kind of 'payment by results' scheme, which is very bad for the interests of justice!

"In other words, Gerard has a somewhat more balanced and perhaps more mature view of what 'justice' ought ultimately to mean. Nonetheless, Gerard recognizes and accepts that he's likely to be hated by anyone in whose conviction he's taken a part. Hence, the resigned way of saying 'How you must hate me.'"

The nightmare sequence also points to a question posed by Captain Carpenter in the pilot episode. Does Gerard really believe Kimble's story? "I don't think it was really a matter of his believing," Morse said. "Whether or not he believes Kimble's story, [Gerard] would say, is an irrelevance. That is not an issue in this case—a judge and jury have not believed his story!" As Gerard understands it, his role as an instrument of the law is to carry out the jury's decision, not question it—even if it is wrong. Even a morsel of doubt could diminish his effectiveness as a police officer.

Still, it's apparent that Kimble struck a nerve with his final comment ("Your nightmare is that when I'm dead, you'll find him"): Gerard quivers his lips before making a hasty retreat. "I think anybody who is engaged in human affairs [such as police officers], if they have any sensitivity at all, will have some nightmares," said Morse of Gerard's reaction. However, given Gerard's rigid interpretation of his role as an instrument of the law, it's unlikely that the lieutenant would be troubled by that particular nightmare (and if he were, he probably wouldn't admit it). "Again, I think Gerard would say, 'This is for people other than me to decide,'" Morse continued. "The judgment as to whether or not any reasonable doubt of Kimble's innocence has been established is in somebody else's hands."

Morse fondly remembered this episode's featured guest, Nancy Wickwire (*Another World*, *As the World Turns*, *Days of Our Lives*). "She was a very distinguished actress whom I had worked with in the theater long before *The Fugitive* ever came along," he said. "She was classically trained, and we played together, for the first time, in a full-length version of George Bernard Shaw's *Man and Superman* in the mid-1950s." Wickwire died in 1973.

Episode 12

GLASS TIGHTROPE

Original Airdate: December 3, 1963

Teleplay by Robert C. Dennis. Story by Robert C. Dennis and Barry Trivers.

Directed by Ida Lupino.

Guest Cast: Leslie Nielsen (Martin Rowland), Edward Binns (Angstrom), Diana Van Der Vlis (Ginny Rowland), Jud Taylor (Floyd), Robert Quarry (Howard Pascoe), Dort Clark (Kronas), Jay Adler (Arthur Tibbetts), Tom Palmer (D.A.), Warren Parker (Lewis).

Prolog. *It doesn't matter who you are or where. Every town, every city is just like the last. A way-point on an endless road that goes nowhere. A place to stop running, to think, to hide. Another job, another name. Is that enough? It has to be. It's all you got.*

Synopsis. Working as a stock clerk in a department store, Kimble sees his boss, Martin Rowland, accidentally kill an associate in the parking lot. When Kimble ("Harry Carson") learns that a vagrant found near the scene is the prime suspect, he calls Rowland anonymously, telling him that he witnessed the incident, and that Rowland should call the police. Thinking the caller wants money, Rowland's wife Ginny enlists the store detective Angstrom to find out who is "blackmailing" Rowland.

Epilog. *When Martin Rowland accepted imprisonment for his crime, he set himself free from a prison of a guilty conscience and from a woman who had no conscience. Not so fortunate for Richard Kimble. His imprisonment remains unchanged.*

Contemporary audiences accustomed to seeing Leslie Nielsen playing deadpan comic characters will find it difficult to watch him in "Glass Tightrope" without laughing precisely because he plays Marty Rowland completely straight. But the Canadian-born actor spent years in movies (*Forbidden Planet, Tammy and the Bachelor, Harlow, Beau Geste, The Poseidon Adventure*) and dramatic television (predominantly cast as a heavy) before he became a comedy star in the *Airplane!* movies and *Police Squad!* series.

In an indirect way, Nielsen helped bring *The Fugitive* to television. While starring in *The New Breed*, Quinn Martin's first series as an independent producer, Nielsen introduced Martin to his friend Stanford Whitmore, who had recently begun writing for film and television. "Leslie knew some of my writing, and he suggested that Quinn give me a chance to see what I could do for the show," recalled Whitmore. "That was my link into Quinn." Whitmore wrote several episodes of *The New Breed* and eventually became its story editor.

FUGE FAUX PAS

Sharp-eyed viewers will notice a small glitch in Act IV in the scene where Angstrom (Edward Binns) and a police officer review wanted posters. When the camera cuts to Kimble's wanted poster, you'll notice that Kimble's birthplace is listed as Beloit, Wisconsin; all other posters used in the series clearly indicate that Kimble was born in Stafford, Indiana. As Barry Morse previously discussed, *The Fugitive* was originally set in the state of Wisconsin. Either the new posters were not available by the time "Glass Tightrope" was filmed, or the switch from Wisconsin to Indiana had not yet been effectuated.

FUGE FIRSTS

This is the first time Kimble uses two aliases in the same episode—he tells Angstrom that his name is "George Paxton."

Episode 13

TERROR AT HIGHPOINT

Original Airdate: December 17, 1963

Teleplay by Peter Germano and Harry Kronman. Story by Peter Germano.

Directed by Jerry Hopper.

Guest Cast: Jack Klugman (Buck Harmon), Elizabeth Allen (Ruth Harmon), James Best (Dan Pike), Buck Taylor (Jamie), Richard Webb (Kripps), Russ Vincent (Rufe), Richard Wessell (Charley), Doreen McLean (Mrs. Hendricks), Billy Halop (Mike).

Prolog. *The place: Utah, the hills above Salt Lake City. The project: to move a mountain. Giant machines and armies of men moving millions of tons of earth to make way for a river which one day will turn the desert into Eden. For Richard Kimble, the mountain offers protection. Here he is Paul Beaumont, timekeeper, lost among the other workers. Here he feels he can rest a while. Here he is safe.*

Synopsis. Kimble convinces project supervisor Buck Harmon to hire Jamie, a mentally disabled but physically strong young man whose family is struggling. Because the boy is an easy target for the taunts of the other crew members, Kimble becomes Jamie's protector. When Jamie is accused of assaulting Buck's wife, he becomes frightened and runs away. While Ruth lies unconsciousness, Dan Pike convinces Buck to organize a posse to hunt down the boy. Buck doesn't realize that Dan is the one who attacked Ruth.

Epilog. *Most men have some secret fear. Most men manage to live with it, to walk in the world with others and live a quiet, normal life. For one man, that is impossible: Richard Kimble, Fugitive.*

Director Jerry Hopper was scouting locations for this episode when he came across a particular construction site located on Mount Olympus in Hollywood. While negotiating with the head of the construction crew, Hopper discovered that the man was an out-of-work actor. So they struck a deal: Hopper got the crew chief a small role in the episode in exchange for free use of all the construction equipment for the segment.

Episode 14

THE GIRL FROM LITTLE EGYPT

Original Airdate: December 24, 1963

Written by Stanford Whitmore. Directed by Vincent McEveety.

Guest Cast: Pamela Tiffin (Ruth Norton), Ed Nelson (Paul Clements), Diane Brewster (Helen Kimble), June Dayton (Doris Clements), Bernard Kates (Lester Rand), Jerry Paris (Jim Prestwick), Bing Russell (Officer Westphal), William Newell (Judge), Rudy Dolan (Officer).

This is the only episode in which there is no prolog narration.

Synopsis. In San Francisco, Kimble ("George Browning") is nearly run over by a car driven by Ruth Norton, a young stewardess distraught over discovering that the man she has been seeing the past four months is married, with two children. While recuperating in the hospital, a delirious Kimble flashes back to the events leading to the night of Helen's murder. Ruth has been keeping a vigil at Kimble's bedside. When she hears Kimble utter Helen's name, she deduces he is in trouble and takes him to her apartment to recover from the accident. When Ruth remains despondent over the breakup, Kimble reveals his secret to her as a way of putting her problems in perspective. Meanwhile, Paul (Ruth's lover) appears at Ruth's apartment and becomes suspicious of her relationship with Kimble.

Epilog. *The outbound bus from San Francisco—destination known. George Browning—destination unknown. His only companion: hope. Hope for the day when he can once again become Richard Kimble.*

The Fugitive tested well during several advance screenings sponsored by ABC before the series premiered in September 1963. What the network learned most from these previews was that the audience wanted to know more about the night of the murder and of the trial. "Quinn said, 'Stan, you know more about this damn thing than anybody else, why don't you do the flashback show?'" recalled Stanford Whitmore.

But "The Girl from Little Egypt" was a far cry from the story Whitmore really wanted to do. "I was going to go in a different way," he continued. "My premise was that this guy's on the run; he's in all kinds of weather; he doesn't have good shelter; and probably his nutrition is bad. He gets pneumonia, and he gets delirious. In the delirium, the trial takes place in flashback. And so, when I did the story, I conceived him being given shelter by a Puerto Rican hooker! I then left the story with Quinn's secretary, and as soon as I got home the phone rang. Quinn said, 'Puerto Rican hooker?!?' I said, 'Look, Quinn, come on, let's get some style.... As things turned out that the Puerto Rican hooker became a stewardess, because Quinn's wife had been a stewardess."

"The Girl from Little Egypt" is one of the most popular episodes of the series because it gives the fans what they want: the background story. The episode has many great moments, such as Gerard's reaction when the judge passes sentence (Act III). Although Gerard remains silent as the camera cuts to him, a telling bit of dialogue omitted from Whitmore's pilot script enables us to determine what Gerard is thinking at this point.

In the pilot script, after discussing Kimble's whereabouts with Captain Carpenter, Gerard begins thinking aloud:

> I remember the trial. His only defense: the man with one arm... running. And at the verdict—and when sentence was passed... I remember Kimble's eyes... his eyes, and the way he stood.

> *If justice was injustice, where did he find his dignity?*

"The thing that I think bothers Gerard, that he can't get out of his throat, is the possibility that maybe Kimble *is* innocent," said Whitmore. "There is just something about Kimble that deeply bothers him. That little tinkling bell of doubt is something that bothers Gerard, and the way to get rid of it is to convince *himself* that there is no 'one-armed man.'"

FUGE FACTS

"The Girl from Little Egypt" is the only episode in which Kimble is not threatened in any way: he is neither forced out of town, nor discovered by the police. Paul does become suspicious of Kimble when they meet in Act III, and there's a slight moment of tension at the party when Kimble discovers that Prestwick is a cop (Act IV). However, in neither instance is Kimble really threatened because he holds the advantage (he knows more about Paul and Prestwick than they do about him). Kimble is not "chased" out of town, but rather leaves of his own volition.

The grey wig that David Janssen wears during the flashback sequences was designed especially for his use, according to assistant director Bob Rubin.

FUGE FAMILIAR FACES

Diane Brewster (Helen) told *TV Collector* in 1984 that she wanted to appear in more *Fugitive* episodes, particularly since she knew that Quinn Martin often reused his performers in different roles. "I would have liked to have been used on the show more frequently either in flashback or as a different character, and I couldn't do it, having played that pivotal dumb thing on the floor," she said. Brewster did, however, provide a voice-over for "The Survivors," then appeared (in flashback, of course) in the final episode, "The Judgment." She died in 1991.

Episode 15

HOME IS THE HUNTED

Original Airdate: January 7, 1964

Written by Arthur Weiss. Directed by Jerry Hopper.

Guest Cast: Andrew Prine (Ray Kimble), Jacqueline Scott (Donna Kimble Taft), Robert Keith (Dr. John Kimble), Billy Mumy (David Taft), Clint Howard (Billy Taft), James Sikking (Leonard Taft), James Nolan (Floyd), Paul Birch (Captain Carpenter).

Prolog. *Always there is the hunter, the hunted, and the trap. Traps are of many kinds: of wind, of steel, of words. But this time the trap is a city. Dr. Richard Kimble, two years a fugitive, is about to enter the trap. Why is Stafford, Indiana, a trap for Richard Kimble? Because here a thousand people know him. This city is where Richard Kimble lived for 33 years. This is the neighborhood Richard Kimble knew as a child. Here is the house in which he grew up, now in time of desperate trouble for him, a starting place within a city of danger—a city of danger because here is also the headquarters of Lt. Philip Gerard.*

Synopsis. Kimble returns home for the first time since the trial. After suffering a heart attack, his father John has donated his medical library to the University of Wisconsin and is in the process of selling the family home. Kimble blames himself for his father's heart attack, but John is more troubled about his other son Ray, who has become completely reckless since the trial. Ray believes that his life has been ruined because people see him as "Richard Kimble's brother." What's worse is that Ray also believes his brother is guilty.

Epilog. *Home is the sailor, home from the sea, and the hunter home from the hill. But for Richard Kimble, not yet. Not yet.*

"Home is the Hunted" marks the first appearance of Jacqueline Scott as Donna Kimble Taft, the Fugitive's sister. "Quinn Martin thought there was a resemblance between David and me," she said. "He said it was in the eyes. It was strange when I first heard that, because I never would have thought so.

"I remember the initial scene I filmed on my first show was the phone conversation, which was the first time in the series where Kimble's family heard from him. Because *The Fugitive* was so popular, I felt that conversation was going to be very, very important to the viewers.

"The problem was, for me, David wasn't around—he had a later call to the set that day. The plan was to shoot my scenes, and then they'd edit in David later, because David was supposed to be calling from outside somewhere. But I felt it would be better for the character, and for the viewers, if David were around when I was filming the phone conversation, so that I could actually talk to him (even though he wouldn't appear on camera with me). So I asked the director [Jerry Hopper] if we could possibly hold off filming until David arrived on the set. Jerry re-set everything to other shots and tried to delay, but he finally said 'Look, we can't stall much longer, we're gonna have to go ahead and shoot.' It's very rare, given tight television time schedules, that a director will or can make adjustments like that—that's why Jerry was such a great director.

"Just as we were about to start filming, David arrived, so I was able to 'speak to him' off camera after all. It took a little extra time to shoot the scene, but I knew it was an important scene in the series, and I think the result paid off." It certainly did—the scene is extremely poignant, and Scott's performance is excellent.

Of the family members introduced in "Home is the Hunted," only Donna and her husband Len would continue to appear throughout the series. Len would be recast twice (Lin McCarthy took the part in 1966, Richard Anderson in 1967), although as producer Alan Armer recalled, this had to do with actor availability. "You don't always have the luxury of knowing what you're going to be shooting two weeks from now," said Armer. "Sometimes you have a script, and it's the only script that's on hand that is ready. The character of Len appears in that script. So John Conwell, our head of casting, would get on the phone, call the various agents involved, and the person who had last played the brother-in-law simply wasn't available. And rather than close down and wait for him, we simply decided to go with someone else. Of course, you hope that nobody will notice, or that it won't hurt your ratings too much. But you try to be consistent."

At that point in the series, it hardly mattered who played the brother-in-law. While the Donna character would become a major driving force in the series, Len Taft never amounted to more than background material until Richard Anderson played the character in the final episode. Anderson's brooding interpretation in "The Judgment" spurred Las Vegas bookmakers to list Len as the odds-on favorite to have murdered Helen Kimble.

FUGE FAMILAR FACES

Robert Keith, the father of Brian Keith (Ed Welles in "Fear in a Desert City"), had a diverse acting career that spanned nearly 50 years. His performances have long been noted for their richly detailed characterizations, such as when John Kimble embraces his son for probably the last time (at the end of Act IV). Keith looks as if he might break down, yet he manages to remain composed—a very "Janssenesque" display of emotion.

Although John Kimble would not appear on screen again, the series refers to the character several times over the next two seasons. In "Running Scared," Kimble discovered that his father died; that episode, coincidentally, aired in early 1966, the same year that Robert Keith died.

FUGE FLIP-FLOPS

Apparently "Home is the Hunted" was filmed before the switch in locale (from Wisconsin to Indiana) went into effect. Although the Narrator clearly states in the prolog that Stafford is in Indiana, Kimble steps off a bus whose destination sign reads "Madison," which is located, of course, in Wisconsin.

Episode 16

THE GARDEN HOUSE

Original Airdate: January 14, 1964

Written by Sheldon Stark. Directed by Ida Lupino.

Guest Cast: Robert Webber (Harlan Guthrie), Pippa Scott (Carol Willard), Peggy McCay (Ann Guthrie).

Prolog. *Connecticut: green trees framing the homes of the wealthy and the near wealthy, gracious living with roots deep in the past—and without roots, interstate fugitive Richard Kimble.*

Synopsis. Newspaper heiress Ann Guthrie owns a spacious ranch in the Connecticut hills, where she lives with her husband Harlan and her sister Ruth. Ann and Ruth's father founded the *Westborne Clarion*, the newspaper which Harlan currently runs. Although Ann is the sole benefactor of her father's estate, she believes that Ruth is equally entitled to the inheritance, even though Ann stayed with her ailing father while Ruth roamed around Europe. But Ann is unaware that Ruth is plotting to do her in and claim everything for herself—including Harlan. After Kimble ("Sanford") begins to suspect them, Ruth and Harlan decide to frame him for Ann's murder.

Epilog. *Tomorrow, the Westborne Clarion will have a new editor. One of the paper's first editorials will be a plea for innocent men pursued by the Furies—men such as Richard Kimble, the Fugitive.*

"The Garden House," like the other episodes directed by actress/director/screenwriter Ida Lupino (*The Hard Way, They Drive by Night, The Light That Failed, While the City Sleeps*) emphasizes Dr. Kimble's tremendous compassion. In "Fatso," Kimble was the first person ever to offer friendship to Davey Lambert; in "Glass Tightrope," he is sensitive to the plight of the vagrant Tibbetts; and in this episode, he is the only character who doesn't prey on Ann's insecurities.

FUGE FACTS

The skeet shooting sequence in this episode brings to mind another such scene in "Ticket to Alaska," where we learned that Kimble was a champion skeet shooter in high school.

Episode 17

COME WATCH ME DIE

Original Airdate: January 21, 1964

Teleplay by Stanford Whitmore. Story by Perry Bleecker.

Directed by Laslo Benedek.

Guest Cast: Robert Doyle (Bellows), John Anderson (Cal Clement), Russell Collins (Ed Shrader), Judson Pratt (Deputy Bowers), Randy Boone (Benjy Bright), Bruce Dern (Charley Bright), David McLean (Sheriff), Virginia Christine (Cora), John McLiam (Jeff), Diane Ladd (Stella), John Harmon (Cremers).

Prolog. *Nebraska: a world of wheat, dirt roads all open to the sky, but still a silent sky. Richard Kimble has found a temporary refuge in the remote farming community of Black Moccasin. And even here, there are questions.*

Synopsis. An entire community bands together against a man named Bellows, whom they suspect of a brutal double murder. Kimble ("Ben Rogers") becomes deputized to help transport Bellows to the county seat, along with four witnesses who saw Bellows running from the scene of the crime. Although Bellows convinces Kimble that he's another victim of circumstantial evidence, the townsmen remain unswayed. Kimble rescues Bellows from an impromptu lynching. But his kindness is betrayed when Bellows escapes—and takes another farm couple hostage.

Epilog. *A walk toward the horizon: a hope that it will lead to the man with one arm. Only then will the search be over for the Fugitive.*

"Come Watch Me Die" is not the first episode in which Kimble comes to the aid of the falsely accused—he helped the vagrant in "Glass Tightrope"—but it does mark the first time he is really wrong about someone. Although Kimble learns to become more guarded with people as the series continues, he never quite turns his back on the falsely accused, as we will see in such episodes as "Scapegoat," where he testifies on behalf of a man accused of *his* murder; "Death is the Door Prize," in which he clears the security guard of manslaughter charges; and "Corner of Hell," where he comes to the defense of none other than Lieutenant Gerard.

FUGE FAMILIAR FACES

At the time of this episode, Bruce Dern (Charley) and Diane Ladd (Stella) were married to each other.

Episode 18

WHERE THE ACTION IS

Original Airdate: January 28, 1964

Written by Harry Kronman. Directed by James Sheldon.

Guest Cast: Telly Savalas (Dan Polichek), Joanna Frank (Chris Polichek), Don Keefer (Ben Haddock), Maxine Stuart (Mrs. Gaines), Connie Gilchrist (Hotel Proprietor), Miss Beverly Hills (Stripper).

Prolog. *Reno, "the biggest little city in the world." A town for all seasons, a town for all tastes. Dude ranch, divorce or dice, take your pick. For every purse, for every age, Reno has something for everyone. For Richard Kimble, fugitive, another name, another job.*

Synopsis. Lifeguard Kimble ("Jerry Shelton") finds himself in the middle of the stormy relationship between hotelier Dan Polichek and his rambunctious daughter Chris. Although Chris believes that Dan drove away her mother, the truth is that Chris' mother walked out of the marriage—and wanted nothing to do with her daughter. Unaware of the truth, Chris sets out to disgrace her father, in part by engaging herself in an affair with the reluctant Kimble.

Epilog. *Some 600 passengers will depart the Reno airport today. Some are flying on business, some for pleasure, some for urgent personal reasons. One man, as always, is flying for his life: Richard Kimble, fugitive.*

This is the only episode where Kimble travels by plane—he went by sea in "Ticket to Alaska," "Somebody to Remember," "Coralee," and "Right in the Middle of the Season." We usually find him either hitchhiking or hopping freight trains, although occasionally he can afford to pay for a bus or train ride. Kimble finds traveling by land more practical, as well as less expensive, because he can easily bail out at the first sign of trouble—something he can't do on an airplane.

David Janssen loved to fly in real life (he often flew down to his Palm Springs home during his weekend breaks from *The Fugitive*). He owned several planes, and operated (along with actor/producer/director Jackie Cooper) an air taxi service in Los Angeles. Janssen never flew without a co-pilot, however. "I'm not a very good pilot," he said in 1968. "I always felt that my participation in flying is one of enjoyment and of pleasure—I like flying in nice clear, sunny weather!"

FUGE FACTS

Working as a lifeguard is one of the first jobs that enables Kimble to use his medical skills, although he has already performed emergency duties in the past ("Decision in the Ring," "Smoke Screen").

Epidode 19

SEARCH IN A WINDY CITY

Original Airdate: February 4, 1964

Written by Stuart Jerome. Directed by Jerry Hopper.

Guest Cast: Pat Hingle (Mike Decker), Nan Martin (Paula Decker), Addison Richards (Connelly), Arthur Batanides (Wimpy), Lewis Charles (Cogen), I. Stanford Jolley (Old Man), Dennis Cross (Bus Driver), Paul Picerni (Sgt. DeSantis), Bill Raisch (The One-Armed Man).

Prolog. *Chicago. Richard Kimble has come a thousand miles on hope and the slimmest of clues in his hunt for the one-armed man. But 10 days have passed, and now hope has turned to despair. For in a city of millions, how does a fugitive go about finding a phantom?*

Synopsis. Believing that the one-armed man who murdered Helen is in Chicago, Kimble ("George Blake") contacts newspaper columnist Mike Decker, who staunchly defended Kimble at the time of the trial. Decker sees a possible Pulitzer Prize in the story, so he and Kimble organize a citywide search for the one-armed man. But Decker's under pressure. His editor wants a "Kimble" story fast, regardless of whether it's about the capture of the one-armed man or the capture of Kimble himself. When word gets out to Gerard, the lieutenant uses Decker to set a trap for Kimble.

Epilog. *Now many months a fugitive, Richard Kimble walks the night again, but no longer in despair that he is hunting only a phantom. He has seen the one-armed man, and it has given him hope. Somewhere, sometime, they will meet again.*

Although "Search in a Windy City" is not the first time we have seen Bill Raisch as the one-armed man—he appeared in a flashback in "Girl from Little Egypt"—the episode marks the first time Kimble has seen the man since nearly hitting him with his car as the one-armed man was running out of Kimble's home on the night of the murder. (In "Escape into Black," we discover that the one-armed man's name is Fred Johnson.)

The appearance on-screen of the one-armed man erases any lingering doubt as to the character's existence (except, perhaps, in the mind of Lieutenant Gerard). But while Quinn Martin never doubted that viewers would accept Dr. Kimble's story, he was hesitant about bringing the one-armed man back into the picture so soon into the series. "Quinn's concept of the one-armed man had always been this kind of ephemeral character, a kind of ghostlike, mystic—is he real/isn't he real?" explained Alan Armer. "He was stunned when I wrote the one-armed man into a script. But it really did kind of legitimize everything. It proved that there really is such a character, and that Kimble isn't a loony—he did see the one-armed man running out of the house."

Was it possible that the viewing audience might doubt Kimble's story had the one-armed man never actually appeared on-screen? "I think it's possible," Armer speculated, "although Janssen played such a legitimate character that I think the audience would have accepted his story without ever seeing an actual one-armed man on-screen."

Raisch only appeared in a handful of episodes (ten in total, but only four in the first three seasons), so the level of tension increased whenever he showed up. "He gave us a number of new dramatic opportunities, in terms of storytelling, to create suspense," said Armer.

FUGE FAMILIAR FACES

Raisch lost part of his right arm during World War II (he was badly burned while fighting a shipboard fire). A former Ziegfeld adagio dancer, Raisch moved into motion pictures after the war and eventually became Burt Lancaster's stand-in. He had a memorable fight scene in *Lonely Are The Brave* (1962) in which he nearly strangled Kirk Douglas with his empty shirtsleeve. That caught the eye of Quinn Martin and Alan Armer, who later signed Raisch to play the one-armed man.

"Quinn and Alan had been searching for an actor with an exceptional visual quality to play the alleged killer of Helen Kimble, and Bill Raisch filled that need," said assistant director Bob Rubin. "They had been looking for someone who could make a memorable impact on the audience. Hiring Bill worked perfectly. Even though we would only caught a glimpse of him frantically escaping the Kimble home that night, Bill looked so menacing that he was unforgettable."

FUGE FACTS

Gerard dismisses Paula's declaration of Kimble's innocence as a "purely emotional" reaction. "A number of women have felt that way about him," he tells her. However, both male and female viewers were captivated by the character, and particularly David Janssen's performance. This, according to Barry Morse, is the greatest testimony to Janssen's tremendous appeal as an actor. "David had an uncanny power of invoking sympathy from all sorts of people," said Morse. "Not only the mostly sex-driven sympathy which he obviously did evoke from ladies who wanted to hide him under their bed, or perhaps in their bed, but also immense sympathy from the most macho of men who regarded him as a male 'ill done by.'"

In this episode, we learn that three jurors held out for Kimble's acquittal, but according to "The End Game," four jurors held out.

Episode 20

BLOODLINE

Original Airdate: February 11, 1964

Teleplay by Harry Kronman. Story by John Hawkins and Harry Kronman.

Directed by John Erman.

Guest Cast: Nancy Malone (Cora Bodin), John Considine (Johnny Bodin), George Voskovec (Max Bodin), Parley Baer (Lee Borroughs), Dan Barton (Lt. Sampson), Lew Brown (Sgt. Hackett).

Prolog. *["No more running today, huh?" says Kimble to the dog.] For you, either, if your name is Kimble. No more running today, or perhaps tomorrow, or for maybe a few weeks, with luck. You've found yourself a place to rest. Another name, another job. Your name, Dick Lindsay. Your job, handyman at the Bodin Russet Kennels.*

Bodin Russet Kennels: For thirty years breeding America's finest Irish Setters. Prize-winning animals, closely guarded. Protected from the outside world by lock and key. For what reason, then, would a member of the Bodin family take Colleen, one of the kennels' most valued animals, and deliberately turn her loose in a field to run away? Why?

Synopsis. Max Bodin, who breeds prize-winning show dogs, is putting his kennel up for sale. He doesn't know that one of his champion Irish Setters has developed hip dysplasia, which means that all dogs in the bloodline will likely inherit the condition and be worthless as show dogs. Max's son and daughter-in-law know that the market value of the kennel would drop if word leaked about the dysplasia, so they scheme to keep the truth from Max—and live off the sale. But when Kimble stumbles onto the condition (and their plan), they have him investigated.

Epilog. *You took a chance for someone, and it worked out for him. Someday, perhaps, it will work out for you—somewhere, in some far off city, at some far off time. But this is now, and you are still running. You are a fugitive.*

The final scene of the pilot episode—Kimble stops to pet a stray kitten—established another recurring motif of *The Fugitive*: Dr. Kimble's affinity for animals. Although he was trained as a pediatrician ("The only thing I know about dogs is that I like them"), Kimble recognizes that the special kind of love, care and attention an animal needs is not far removed from that required of a child. In some cases, such as the stray kitten he befriended in the pilot or the goldfish he freed in "Shadow of the Swan," Kimble identifies very closely with animals.   While this theme has been featured in other episodes this season (the pilot; and briefly in "Fatso," where Kimble calms the horse), "Bloodline" is the first episode where the Fugitive's affinity for animals plays a key role in the story. Kimble quickly develops a bond for the dogs, particularly with Colleen. He runs after the Setter when he sees her wander off the premises, then frees her leg from the barbed wire once he finds her in the woods. Despite Max's order to shoot Colleen ("You can't give in to your feelings; you can't run a kennel on sentiment"), Kimble spares the dog and nurses her back to health. Colleen returns the favor at the end of the story by saving Kimble's life. Even though she finds Kimble in the woods after following his scent, she recognizes the Fugitive as the man who rescued her, and obeys his command to go away.

"Bloodline" features several other tender moments, such as the scene in Act I where Kimble and Max discuss the dying breed of fathers and sons who work together. Kimble really likes Max, and for a brief moment he opens up to the old man. "I always thought I'd be working with my father," Kimble says wistfully. "It didn't turn out that way."

Episode 21

RAT IN A CORNER

Original Airdate: February 18, 1964

Teleplay by Sheldon Stark and William Morwood. Story by William Morwood. Directed by Jerry Hopper.

Guest Cast: Warren Oates (Herbie Grant), Virginia Vincent (Lorna Grant), Malachi Throne (Santelli), Tommy Farrell (Lt. Ryan), Glen Vernon (Sharp), Stewart Bradley (Police Sergeant), Gerald Gordon (Policeman), Barbara Perry (Woman in Hall), John Mayo (Technician), Ruth Packard (Woman in Post Office).

Prolog. *Countless weeks and months of running, endless running, endless searching for the man with one arm, pausing only for a job like this to stay alive. Richard Kimble, fugitive: Dan Crowley, clerk.*

Synopsis. Herbie Grant, a second-rate hood, is shot in the leg while trying to rob the liquor store where Kimble works. Thought to be the same man who killed two other liquor store owners, Herbie hides in the store car and later takes Kimble hostage. After reluctantly agreeing to help Herbie, Kimble is summoned to the police station, where he meets Herbie's sister Lorna. She recognizes Kimble from her job at the post office, and threatens to report Kimble if he turns in her brother. Kimble stays quiet, but Herbie is later arrested after a hotel maid recognized his picture in the newspaper. Believing that Kimble doublecrossed him, Herbie reports Kimble to the police.

Epilog. *Somewhere, a destination for this truck. But for Richard Kimble, no destiny. And even asleep there are shadows, shadows that haunt a man on the run: a fugitive.*

The newspapers seen in this episode indicate that Kimble is probably somewhere in Ohio. In Act I, *The Bolton Chronicle* carries the headline about the liquor store killer, while in Act III we see a headline from *The Youngstown Chronicle.*

Santelli tricks Herbie into ratting on Kimble by pretending there's a $5,000 reward for Kimble's capture. No reward would exist until the fourth season, when *The Stafford Chronicle* established a $10,000 reward in "Ten Thousand Pieces of Silver."

Episodes 22 and 23

ANGELS TRAVEL ON LONELY ROADS (Two-parter)

Original Airdates: February 25 and March 3, 1964

Written by Al C. Ward. Directed by Walter Grauman.

Guest Cast: Eileen Heckart (Sister Veronica), Albert Salmi (Chuck Mathers), Sandy Kenyon (Sheriff Morris), Ken Lynch (Lt. Craig), Shary Marshall (Sherie), Jason Wingreen (Al Friar), Rodolfo Hoyos (Manuel), Burt Douglas (Sgt. Lane), Percy Helton (Hobo), Bill Zuckert (Officer Mesta), Ruta Lee (Janet), Lane Bradford (Sheriff Anderson), John Durren (Clete), Thomas Hasson (Lossie).

(Part One)

Prolog. *A "miracle" is defined as an effect on the physical world which surpasses all known human powers. For Richard Kimble, however, this has become a world of stark realities, a world where life is lived in inches—each one possibly the last.*

Synopsis. On the run from the Nevada State Police, Kimble ("Nick Walker") meets up with Sister Veronica, a nun travelling to Sacramento, where she plans to renounce her vows. After fixing her car, Kimble agrees to travel with Veronica only to the nearest train station. But Veronica believes that Kimble has been sent to her as an act of providence, and insists that the Fugitive accompany her to the end of her pilgrimage.

Epilog. *Two fugitives: one who has lost faith in her strength to cross a mountain, the other who must cross it in order to live. Sister Veronica turns to Richard Kimble for help. But the road is long, and the mountain is high.*

"David had a wonderful sense of humor, a kind of David Niven sense of humor," said Alan Armer. "'Angels Travel on Lonely Roads' gave him a chance to play this lovely, reactive humor of his, where he reacted to the events that happened because of Sister Veronica's presence. Part of the fun of that two-parter was just his delightful reactions to all of the miraculous things that happened."

Indeed, some of Janssen's reactions in "Angels Travels on Lonely Roads" are priceless, such as when Kimble first meets Veronica early in the first segment. After hearing Veronica tell him that she believes Kimble was sent "from the highest authority," Janssen knits his eyebrows, nonplussed. Another instance occurs early in Part Two, after Veronica scares off Clete and Lossie ("You're nothing but two overgrown boils that need a lance on the face of life, and if you spend two weeks in my school, I'd be the one to give it to you"). After quietly observing, Kimble remarks, "You're a fraud, Sister. You said you were going to renounce your vows because you couldn't communicate with people—you couldn't get through to them." The Fugitive then motions to where the boys were standing. "Those two sure got the message," he smiled. (So will those viewers who have experienced first-hand Catholic school nuns like Sister Veronica.)

(Part Two)

Prolog. *Richard Kimble, alias Nick Walker, had called it "a car looking for a quiet place to die." But this ancient vehicle, held together by faith and rusty wire, has come halfway across the mountains carrying two fugitives: Sister Veronica, a fugitive from God on her way to Sacramento to renounce her vows; and Richard Kimble, fugitive from injustice, now wearing the name Nick Walker, borrowed from a wallet which he had found in Lincoln City. Two fugitives moving through a dragnet which straddles two states, one unaware that the other is the object of the intensive manhunt.*

Synopsis. Veronica and Kimble continue their journey to Sacramento. But the state police have determined their location and set up roadblocks throughout the area. Meanwhile, Veronica learns Kimble's identity through a televised news report.

Epilog. *Two fugitives: one having found a resting place, the other continuing to step off his inches on the scale of life. For him, the future will be no less precarious. But, somehow, he won't feel quite so alone.*

Eileen Heckart (Veronica) won an Oscar in 1972 for Best Supporting Actress (*Butterflies are Free*). Fans of *The Mary Tyler Moore Show* will recognize her as Mary's cantankerous Aunt Flo. Heckart starred as Eleanor Roosevelt in 1976 (*Eleanor*, a one-woman play), and also played the former First Lady three years later in the mini-series *Backstairs at the White House*. Heckart and Janssen both appeared in the Debbie Reynolds film *My Six Loves* (1963).

Heckart was the only *Fugitive* guest star who returned to play the same character in a later episode (she reprised Veronica in the fourth season's "The Breaking of the Habit").

Episode 24

FLIGHT FROM THE FINAL DEMON

Original Airdates: March 10, 1964

Written by Philip Saltzman. Directed by Jerry Hopper.

Guest Cast: Ed Nelson (Steve Edson), Carroll O'Connor (Sheriff Bray), Ellen Madison (Linda), Don Dubbins (Deputy Horton), Rudy Solari (Joey), John

Duke (Bus Driver), Guy Wilkerson (Desk Clerk), Kathleen O'Malley (Telegraph Clerk).

Prolog. *Richard Kimble's hands once eased the pain, ministered the illness, even saved the lives of countless children. Now the hands are as fugitive as the man to whom they belong.*

Synopsis. Steve Edson, who works with Kimble ("Al Dexter") at a health club, helps Kimble escape from Sheriff Bray, a lawman with political aspirations. However, Kimble doesn't realize that Steve is a fugitive of conscience: five months earlier, Steve was acquitted of a murder he actually committed, and now he cannot live with the fact that his crime went unpunished. Kimble reluctantly allows Steve to travel with him. But Steve has been leaving behind clues that soon put Bray back on their trail.

Epilog. *For almost two years, Richard Kimble has lived the life of a fugitive. How many times in his despair has he thought he would gladly trade places with any man on earth. Now Richard Kimble knows: any man, except one.*

"It was easier to write for *The Fugitive* than other programs at that time because there were so many built-in givens on the show. All you had to do was come up with the premise," said Philip Saltzman. "I was into psychological drama at the time, so I just came up with a one-line premise. The Fugitive pairs up with a man who has truly committed a crime, and because he's guilty in getting away with it, he really wants to get caught! So the man leaves a trail because, psychologically, he can't go on, and he somehow makes all these dumb moves which will ensure his getting caught, and the Fugitive will get caught with him. So I paired the innocent who's accused and the guilty who's not accused."

The result of this pairing is a short course on the "science" (as Steve puts it) of how Kimble stays on the run while avoiding detection. Kimble lives by a few basic rules, each of which are illustrated in this episode:

1. Whenever possible, travel by bus or train. The frequent turnover of passengers makes it difficult for the driver (and thus the police) to keep track of you.

2. If you are driving a car, always observe the speed limit (unless someone is chasing you). A speeding ticket or a car accident will attract the police.

3. Never cash a check. An out-of-town check requires a phone call to your home branch, which could also attract the police.

4. If you're staying at a hotel, never make a long distance phone call. By checking the phone records, the police could discover your next destination, or uncover information about your past (girlfriend, family, etc.). (Kimble usually makes his calls from a pay phone.)

5. If you have another person's I.D., memorize every detail about that card before you use it. (Kimble provided the telegraph clerk with Steve's birthdate.)

6. Always have an alias ready in case you need one on the spot, as Kimble did with Joey (he came up with "Paul Edson")—and always remember which name you're using.

7. If you confide in people, be sure they never call you by your real name. In a tight spot, a slip like that could make a difference.

8. Whenever possible, always travel alone: traveling with others could lead you open to complications (such as Steve's psychological demons) that could tie you down at a critical moment (such as when the police are outside your hotel room).

FUGE FAMILIAR FACES

Earlier in 1964, Carroll O'Connor (*All in the Family, In the Heat of the Night*) and Barry Morse starred in "Controlled Experiment" on *The Outer Limits*.

Episode 25

TAPS FOR A DEAD WAR

Original Airdate: March 17, 1964

Teleplay by Harry Kronman. Story by Harry Kronman and Merwin Gerard.

Directed by William Graham.

Guest Cast: Tim O'Connor (Joe Hallop), Lee Grant (Millie Hallop), Flip Mark (Kenny Hallop), Noam Pitlik (Sgt. Bert Keefer), Nick Nicholson (Bar Owner), John Zaremba (Druggist).

Prolog. *These have been desperate months for Richard Kimble, running in fear. Someday, somewhere, someone will recognize him. Who? When? That's what he lives with.*

Synopsis. Back in the Korean War, Kimble was nearly killed by an exploding grenade. Rendered unconscious by the explosion, and surrounded by confusion, he never learned that the man who saved his life that day was a soldier named Joe Hallop. The incident not only permanently disfigured Joe's face, it left him psychologically scarred. Joe has long followed Kimble in the newspapers. When he recognizes the Fugitive (as "Bob Davies"), Joe plots to murder him with one of his war mementos—a live grenade.

Epilog. *For Richard Kimble, it must always be this way. Until he finds the man with one arm, the one man in the world who can help him walk in the light again, Richard Kimble must find his way in the dark—a fugitive.*

In "Taps for a Dead War," we learn that Kimble was a corpsman in Korea, although he has previously alluded to his war experience—he told Joe Smith in "Decision in the Ring" about treating a soldier whose arm was shattered by a grenade. Unlike his TV counterpart, however, David Janssen was stateside during the Korean War. He was in Special Services, booking entertainment acts for Fort Ord, California. "I certainly didn't want to go to Korea," he told *TV Guide* in 1972. "I knew there were people over there who were going to shoot at me." After the war ended, Janssen returned to Fort Ord to film *The Girl He Left Behind* (1956), with Natalie Wood and Tab Hunter.

Episode 26

SOMEBODY TO REMEMBER

Original Airdate: March 24, 1964

Written by Robert C. Dennis. Directed by Jerry Hopper.

Guest Cast: Gilbert Roland (Gus Priamos), Madlyn Rhue (Sophie), Alan Baxter (Local Detective), Peter Mamakos (Pete), Peter Coe (Micky), Paul Birch (Captain Carpenter), Robert Millar (Airport Ticket Agent), Maura McGiveney (Travel Agency Clerk), Gus Trikonis (Young Boyfriend).

Prolog. *For Richard Kimble, a thousand names, a thousand jobs. Here he is Johnny Sherman, warehouse worker, and as always for a fugitive, the load is a heavy one.*

Synopsis. Gus Priamos, who has only six months to live, hopes to aid the Fugitive with a scheme designed to convince Gerard that Kimble has fled the country. But when Gus's jealous girlfriend Sophie suspects Kimble of trying to murder Gus, she notifies Gerard.

Epilog. *The past two years have been an endless procession of names, most of them forgotten. But one name will be remembered. For a fugitive is a lonely man, and Gus Priamos has been a friend.*

Gerard defends Kimble after Sophie suspects the Fugitive of murdering Gus. The Lieutenant explains that while Kimble has been spotted before, he has never killed anyone. Barry Morse referred to incidents such as this one when he discussed his character's scrupulous nature. "Regarding the exact way of referring to [Kimble], it seemed to me that there must have been instances where Gerard made it clear that the word 'killer' might not be appropriate," he said.

FUGE FACTS

"[The Fugitive] must stay in this country," wrote Roy Huggins in 1960 as part of his original concept of *The Fugitive* (see Appendix 1). "Here he is one American among nearly 200 million Americans. Outside our borders passports are required, questions are asked; he is the conspicuous stranger."

This episode underscores Huggins' point. Kimble explains to Gus that he cannot fly to Greece himself because he would stand out like a tourist in a foreign land.

Episode 27

NEVER STOP RUNNING

Original Airdate: March 31, 1964

Written by Sheldon Stark. Directed by William Graham.

Guest Cast: Claude Akins (Ralph Simmons), Joanna Moore (Helen Simmons), Wright King (Dave Simmons), Michel Petit (Jimmie), Paul Comi (Deputy Sheriff), Patrick McVey (Sheriff), Peggy Stewart (Mrs. Franklin), Buck Young (Mr. Franklin), Ray Kellogg (Truck Driver), Jason Johnson (Druggist), Maya Van Korn (German Farm Woman), Jane Barclay (Nurse), Carl McIntire (TV Announcer).

Prolog. *Never in one place too long. That's the first rule for a fugitive. Always keep running, always with the nightmare fear that one day the chase will catch up with him. One day. Perhaps now.*

Synopsis. "Doc" Kimble becomes an unwilling party to the kidnapping of a young hemophiliac. When Kimble discovers that the boy has been bruised, he must smuggle the boy past the kidnapers and to the nearest hospital—or else the boy will die of internal bleeding.

Epilog. *Another path, another road. Roads that twist and wind nowhere. Richard Kimble: Fugitive.*

The best part of "Never Stop Running" appears in the epilog. Kimble skips stones into a creek, then slides down the hill and makes his way over the water, just before the final fade to black. In contrast to the usual closeout sequences in the series—which often depict Kimble hovering in a corner, or walking pensively, or hopping a freight train, or simply running for his life—here we see him enjoying a brief respite from running, searching and hiding.

FUGE FACTS

"Never Stop Running" contains another instance of Kimble's remarkable resourcefulness. Using what appears to be a cigarette, he manages to turn on the ignition of the German woman's truck. *MacGyver* would be proud.

Episode 28

THE HOMECOMING

Original Airdate: April 7, 1964

Written by Peter Germano. Directed by Jerry Hopper.

Guest Cast: Shirley Knight (Janice Pruitt), Richard Carlson (Allan Pruitt), Gloria Grahame (Dorina Pruitt), Warren Vanders (Floyd Warren), Walter Woolf King (Judge Parker), Mary Jackson (Ellie Parker), Eddie Rosson (Seth's Boy), James Griffith (Seth Crowley).

Prolog. *The Pruitt family home—the Tidewater, South Georgia—in antebellum years a home graced by gracious women. And even after cotton was no longer king, the Pruitt women were gentle and well-bred. Richard Kimble, fugitive, pauses here in his endless flight. For as long as he dares, he will be David Benton, research technician.*

Synopsis. Janice Pruitt has spent the past year in a sanitarium recovering from a nervous breakdown she suffered after witnessing a vicious dog attack that took the life of a young boy under her care. She returns to her home in Georgia to find that her father Allan has remarried. Hoping to drive Janice back to the sanitarium for good, her stepmother Dorina uses a neighbor's dogs to convince Janice that the attack dogs that killed the boy are still alive (when everyone else knows that those dogs were put to sleep). After Kimble also hears the dogs one night, Dorina asks the sheriff to investigate him.

Epilog. *Someday, someday, Richard Kimble will be settled, when he can take his own name again, when he finds the man who killed his wife. Until then, he must be what he is now: a fugitive.*

"The Homecoming" was one of the many *Fugitive* episodes directed by Jerry Hopper, one of the first directors to make the successful transition from motion pictures (*The Atomic City, Blueprint for Robbery*) to television (*Cheyenne, The Untouchables, Naked City, The Rifleman, Burke's Law*). "Not very many of the directors who had been doing films were able to cope with TV because they had to shoot a lot faster," said Dorothy Hopper, his widow. "Jerry was very much in demand, as a director of both. He directed almost 600 TV episodes." Jerry Hopper died in 1988.

One of Janssen's first films was *The Private War of Major Benson* (1955), which Hopper directed. "Jerry really liked David, and he was very upset when David died," Mrs. Hopper said.

Episode 29

STORM CENTER

Original Airdate: April 14, 1964

Written by George Eckstein. Directed by William Graham.

Guest Cast: Bethel Leslie (Marcie King), Dennis Patrick (Harry Montjoy), Robert Fortier (First Officer), Clay Farmer (Second Officer), Craig Duncan (Skipper).

Prolog. *Webers Landing, Florida. A thousand miles from the state prison where Richard Kimble was scheduled to die. Tonight, it will seem closer.*

Synopsis. Five years ago, Marcie King asked Dr. Kimble to perform an abortion, but Kimble refused. Although Marcie went through with the operation, because of complications she can no longer bear children—and she holds Kimble responsible. Now amidst a hurricane, Marcie and her embezzler boyfriend recognize Kimble ("Larry Phelps") and threaten to expose him unless he drives them to safety.

Epilog. *A long night for Richard Kimble. But for a fugitive, the nights are always the longest.*

A unique visual effects team was recruited to create the "hurricane" sequences in "Storm Center." The project, known as "Operation Dunk," required the construction of a 700-gallon tank that sank beneath the surface of the Goldwyn Studios soundstage where *The Fugitive* was filmed. The tank had a false bottom which was triggered to drop the water several feet below the studio. Rollers agitated the water, while wind machines generated "gales" of 50 miles per hour. This is how the team generated the violent waves and gusts of wind that battered David Janssen and guest star Bethel Leslie.

"Production values contribute to the success of the series," Janssen told *TV Guide* in 1964. "Most shows would use some kind of a model boat in a tank and that's exactly what it would come out looking like."

FUGE FUN

Kimble's strongest character asset is his tremendous moral integrity, but sometimes he seems just too good to be true. By poking fun at Kimble in this episode (Marcie calls him a "two-legged breathing ethic"), George Eckstein grounds the character just a little bit. But Kimble has a sense of humor about his image. "The land of the self-righteous isn't all that bad," he chides Marcie.

Episode 30

THE END GAME

Original Airdate: April 21, 1964

Written by Stanford Whitmore. Directed by Jerry Hopper.

Guest Cast: John McGiver (Jake Devlin), John Fiedler (Sam Reed), Joseph Campanella (Lt. Spencer), Martine Bartlett (Street Walker), Christopher Connelly (J.J. Watson), Chick Hearn (TV Newscaster), Stuart Margolin (Jimmy), Lee Krieger (Vendor), Richard Chambers (Photographer), Gil Frye (Officer), Martin Garralaga (Gardener), Ted Bensinger (Man at Road Block).

Prolog. *This is the instrument [a camera], and this its operator. The subject: newlyweds, and a day to remember, always.*

This is the Fugitive, and as fate would have it, he is the target. And this is the sound [camera clicks] like that of a trigger, of a trap.

This is the picture which vanity, not fate, discards.

But fate is not finished with Richard Kimble: it is only a matter of time and place. This is the place, and with the common ordinary act of a man buying cigarettes, now is the time. And fate is swift and sure.

Synopsis. A discarded photograph leads Gerard to Chicago, where he manages to trap Kimble within an eight-block radius. While the lieutenant slowly closes in, Kimble finds refuge in the home of two men who have long argued over his innocence.

Epilog. *The end game he has won—but for how long? Another night and another road, and still the deadly game goes on. And so must he. North, south, east, west, a man alone: the Fugitive.*

The last episode to be filmed that year, "The End Game" plays very much like a finale, particularly when you consider that it pre-dates the era of television series filming "deliberate" conclusions. That trend wouldn't begin for another three years, following the lead of "The Judgment." But "The End Game" has a definite sense of climax, particularly in some of Gerard's remarks (one of his final lines is "so this is how it ends"). The very title of the episode is an allusion to "the end"—writer Stanford Whitmore lifted it from *Endgame*, a play by Samuel Beckett, the 20th century dramatist who often wrote about "the last things." As it happened, though, the cast and crew knew that they would be returning for another season. "It really wasn't a question of maybe we won't get renewed," Whitmore recalled. "Quinn knew it was going to be renewed for another entire season."

Like the Beckett play, the title of this episode refers to the closing moves of a chess game. With most of the pieces eliminated, the end of the contest is clearly seen, to be resolved with a few stylized moves. Once Gerard cordons off the neighborhood where Kimble is hiding, the Fugitive's elimination appears certain. Also like the play, three of the characters (Kimble, Devlin and Reed) are "paralyzed" insofar as they remain inside the house during most of the second half. Whitmore deftly balances the tension of the looming dragnet with several light moments, most of which evolve around the interplay of Janssen and guest stars John Fiedler (Mr. Peterson of *The Bob Newhart Show*) and John McGiver (*My Six Loves*). But the script also allowed Barry Morse to play off the humor generated in the scenes with Christopher Connelly ("After meeting you, I hope he makes it") and Martine Bartlett (the street walker who blows cigarette smoke in Gerard's face after he called her a dupe).

Gerard, however, remains driven as ever in this latest game of wits. In a revealing bit of dialogue, he explains that he must stay an even course because "emotion's my enemy as much as it is Kimble's. If either one of us gets overeager, anxious, rattled, that one's going to be the loser, no matter how long it takes." But Gerard does allow himself an occasional moment of quiet confidence (such as during the roadblock sequence), which harkens back to another comment he made about Kimble in this episode—confidence is fatal. The same applies to him.

Gerard clearly becomes angry as his low-key operation gives way to the "Roman holiday" atmosphere that increasingly benefits the newspeople and the roadside vendor, all of whom hope to capitalize on it. Despite the laws of free enterprise (as the vendor argues), Gerard believes that no one has the right to "cash in" on events where someone's life hangs in the balance—even if that someone is Richard Kimble, convicted murderer.

"I thought this was a very enlightened piece of writing," recalled Morse. "It's one more example that Gerard had a rather better view of the United States system of justice than apparently most U.S. citizens do! It always used to surprise me that people didn't get that point, that the exploitation for immediate personal greed of the hot dog vendor was not in any way assisting the U.S. system of justice. And that those sort of people who seek to capitalize on whatever sensational values there may be in other people's miseries, are really not to be encouraged.

"And in that respect, you would think the average American citizen would say, 'Good on ya, Phil!' But they never did," he continued. "It always seemed to me to be a quite praiseworthy kind of response. It's the exactly the sort of response that I would have made."

Morse cited this scene as another instance where the character was shaded slightly by Morse's perspective as a non-U.S. citizen. "Probably the degree of intensity with which I played it might have been a contribution of my own. I have always been of the opinion that the degree to which the legal system ultimately contributes to justice in the U.S. of A. is, shall we say, 'susceptible to improvement.' That's about as tactful as I can be! But that necessarily colored my way of handling things.

"The vehement way in which I played that particular incident is a very interesting example of the way I thought such a right-minded and scrupulously honest (which he is, I think!) character as Philip Gerard would have responded in that circumstance—with a certain amount of revulsion."

Barry Morse's point is well taken. The legal system *is* susceptible to improvement —this ultimately is what *The Fugitive* is about. The system (which Quinn Martin defined in *The Producer's Medium* as government, justice and society) can work, provided it is tempered with the compassion to accept human expectations and failures. When the system fails, as it did with Dr. Kimble, ordinary citizens must call upon themselves to correct the distortion. Ironically, in the case of the hot dog vendor, Gerard addresses the situation by momentarily letting go of his unyielding reliance upon the law and speaking out on Kimble's behalf—as a fellow human being.

FUGE FAREWELLS

"The End Game" turned out to be Whitmore's final contribution to the series he helped shape. "*The Fugitive* was really one of the better experiences of my life in Hollywood," he said. "I've been with a number of actors and actresses, and they always give you the impression that, well, okay, you've done your work and now they'll take over. David was quite the opposite. David had great respect for writers and directors—it was a team effort as far as he was concerned. And he was every bit the professional. I'm sorry he's not with us."

EPILOG: FIRST SEASON

The End Game" concluded an extraordinarily successful first season for *The Fugitive.* Shortly before this episode aired, *TV Guide* named it the Best New Show of the 1963-64 season. With an average of 21 million viewers tuning in each week, *The Fugitive* quickly established itself as one of ABC's most popular shows, along with *The Donna Reed Show*, *The Patty Duke Show*, *Ben Casey* and *Doctor Kildare.* With the network still struggling to remain competitive, *The Fugitive* provided the network with a much needed boost.

Although *The Fugitive* did not rank among the top twenty series of 1963-64, it consistently won its time period, despite such formidable opposition as *The Garry Moore Show* (CBS, 1958-64). When Moore closed out his long-running popular variety series at the end of the season, *The Fugitive* laid claim to Tuesdays, 10:00 p.m. for the next three years.

David Janssen's consistently engaging performances won him the first of three Emmy nominations. Unfortunately, he faced stiff competition in a category incredibly broad—Outstanding Continued Performance by an Actor in a Series (he lost out to Dick Van Dyke). Perhaps realizing the disparity of having four dramatic leads (Janssen, Dean Jagger, George C. Scott and Richard Boone) competing in the same category with a comedy lead (Van Dyke), the Television Academy the following season separated the Lead Performer category into separate awards for comedy and dramatic series. Ironically, Janssen did not receive an Emmy nomination for 1964-65. Janssen fared much better with the readers of *TV Guide*, who named him Best Dramatic Actor in the magazine's Annual Poll, and of *TV Radio Mirror*, who named him Best Male Star of 1964. *The Fugitive* also won *TV Guide*'s Silver Bowl Award for Best New Series.

David Janssen, wrestles with Michael Witney, Earl Holliman and Bruce Dern in *The Good Guys and the Bad Guys.*

Ron Howard.

Kurt Russell.

Ed Begley.

Claude Akins.

Angie Dickinson.

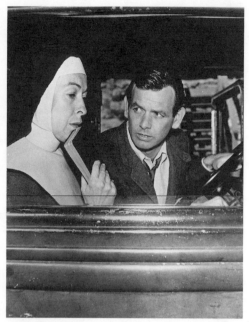

Eileen Heckart.

Shirley Knight.

Ruth White.

David with Susan Oliver in *Never Wave Goodbye.*

David with Jacqueline Scott who played his sister, Donna Kimble Taft.

THE EPISODES

SECOND SEASON, 1964-1965

PRODUCTION CREDITS

Starring David Janssen as The Fugitive
Also Starring Barry Morse as Lt. Philip Gerard
and William Conrad as The Narrator

Executive Producer: Quinn Martin
Created by Roy Huggins
Producer: Alan A. Armer
Associate Producer: Arthur Weiss
Assistant to the Executive Producer: Arthur Fellows

Director of Photography: Meredith Nicholson, A.S.C.
Production Manager: Fred Ahern
Music: Peter Rugolo
Assistant to the Producer: John Conwell
Post-Production Supervisor: John Elizalde
Art Director: Serge Krizman
Film Editors: Jerry Young, John Post, Robert L. Swanson, Marston Fay
Assistant Directors: Read Kilgore, Wes McAfee, Lloyd Allen, David L. Salven, Jack Barry
Property Masters: Irving Sindler, Don Smith
Chief Electrician: Vaughn Ashen
2nd Cameraman: Joe August Jr.
Special Photographic Effects: Howard Anderson
Music Supervisor: Ken Wilhoit
Set Decorator: Sandy Grace
Makeup Artist: Jack Wilson
Costume Supervisor: Elmer Ellsworth
Costumer: George Harrington
Hairdresser: Lynn Burke
Assistant Film Editors: Tom Neff, Jr., Carl Mahakian, Harry Kaye
Script Supervisor: Richard Chaffee
Sound: The Goldwyn Studio
Production Mixer: John Kean
Sound Editor: Chuck Overhulser
Re-Recording: Clem Portman

PROLOG: YEAR TWO

The *Fugitive* continued to enjoy its extraordinary success throughout its second season. Taking a cue from the fans, whose enthusiastic response to the episodes that either brought Kimble home ("Home is the Hunted") or provided background information ("The Girl from Little Egypt") was enormous, producer Alan Armer and his writers created several other stories that returned the Fugitive to his past, such as "World's End," "The Survivors," and "May God Have Mercy."

Of particular interest this season is the outstanding "Escape into Black," in which Kimble must return to his past in order to regain his memory after an accident renders him amnesiac. David Janssen delivers a powerful performance in this episode, especially in the sequence where Kimble struggles to recover his identity amidst an onslaught of oral recollections of the trial.

The second season is marked by an entirely new opening title sequence. Each segment begins with a short clip (called a "teaser") from the episode, then segues into a silhouette—taken from a still frame from the episode "Nightmare at Northoak"—of Kimble running into an dark alley. The silhouette would become a sort of logo for *The Fugitive* for the remainder of the series. A timpani drumroll accompanies the silhouette, followed by William Conrad's booming delivery of the most famous run-on sentence in television history:

"*The Fugitive*, a QM Production, starring David Janssen as Dr. Richard Kimble, an innocent victim of blind justice, falsely convicted for the murder of his wife, reprieved by fate when a train wreck freed him en route to the death house; freed him to hide in lonely desperation, to change his identity, to toil at many jobs; freed him to search for a one-armed man he saw leave the scene of the crime; freed him to run before the relentless pursuit of the police lieutenant obsessed with his capture."

This sequence incorporated still photographs taken from such episodes as "The Girl from Little Egypt" (the train wreck, plus the close-ups of Diane Brewster as Helen Kimble and Bill Raisch as the one-armed man); "World's End" (Kimble running); and "Fear in a Desert City" and "Smoke Screen" (the Fugitive toiling at two of his many jobs). The close-ups of Barry Morse as Gerard were also lifted from "Nightmare at Northoak."

American audiences continued to watch *The Fugitive* in record numbers. By the end of the 1964-65 season, *The Fugitive* ranked number five among the top 25 programs in network television. "It often seemed that there wasn't anybody on this planet [back then] who wasn't watching *The Fugitive*," recalled Barry Morse. The public recognition was enormous, enormous! Of course, when travelling, I was exposed all the time to the responses of the public, and very fervent they were. People responded, of course, quite predictably, with hostility to me personally! Sometimes, if it got too awkward, I would revert to my own native English accent, and even exaggerate it a bit, and say things like, 'Oh, no, no, I'm not that television actor! No, you've—I'm actually an academic! I'm over here doing a course of instruction at your university—Yale—and I'm just on my way back to England. But I do understand that there is an actor on television—uh, B-Barry something—who bears some resemblance to me, but I'm not him!' I would do a bit of a performance like that to simply get out of it if people had been too demanding, or too aggressive, which they quite often were."

With David Janssen, of course, the public recognition was quite the opposite. "David and I were very close friends," recalled post-production head Arthur Fellows. "As a matter of fact, I got married the first year of *The Fugitive*, and when we finished it, David and his wife went with us on our honeymoon. We went through the Caribbean, and crowds of people would be yelling, 'Hey, *El Fugitivo! El Fugitivo!* People really liked him, and liked that show."

"People would walk up to me and ask me 'How's your brother,'" added Jacqueline Scott. "I'd say, 'I haven't got a brother or sister—I'm an only child'—and then the nickel dropped. I got used to that."

Episode 31

MAN IN A CHARIOT

Original Airdate: September 15, 1964

Written by George Eckstein. Directed by Robert Butler.

Guest Cast: Ed Begley (G. Stanley Lazer), Kathleen Maguire (Nancy Gilman), Robert Drivas (Lee Gould), Gene Lyons (McNeil), Dort Clark (Sgt. Pulaski), Walter Brooke (Moderator), Harold Gould (Eller), Stewart Moss (Judge Tyler), Peter Duryea (Paul Mitchell), Edward Madden (Dr. Gary).

Prolog. *The man is Richard Kimble, and not surpisingly, the man is tired. Tired of looking over his shoulder, the ready lie, of the buses and freight towns. Richard Kimble is tired of running.*

Synopsis. Kimble ("Frank Borden") happens onto a televised debate in which once-renowned attorney G. Stanley Lazer claims that he could reverse Kimble's conviction if the case went back to trial. After Kimble enlists his help, Lazer decides to test his theory by staging a mock trial, using his law students and the real transcript of the case.

Epilog. *Another town, another name. The search continues. And Richard Kimble now knows beyond any doubt that it must continue. There is no resting place for a fugitive.*

"That was the show that really won us the Emmy in 1966," said Alan Armer of "Man in a Chariot." "When the TV Academy said that *The Fugitive* had been nominated, they asked us to send an episode to run for their Blue Ribbon Judging Panels. 'Man in a Chariot' was the episode we sent."

Armer considers "Man in a Chariot" one of the best segments in the entire series. "That was an episode I personally liked a lot," he continued. "That was George Eckstein's script—and a lovely, lovely script. Just so good, and very rich." In fact, Armer, who currently teaches screenwriting at California State University/Northridge, often uses scenes from "Chariot" to demonstrate certain principles of screenwriting.

Eckstein recalled another compliment he received for this episode. "I met and talked with Ed Begley, Jr. about ten years ago," he said. "I had never met him. I introduced myself to him, and told him that I had written that script for his father. And he said that his father had kept the speech—the final summation he delivered at the close of Act IV—in his wallet. I was very flattered to hear that."

FUGE FACTS

Eckstein named the Nancy Gilman character after a friend of his from Kansas City.

According to this episode, the docket number for *The People of the State of Indiana v. Richard Kimble* is Case No. 33972 in the Stafford County Superior Court.

Episode 32

WORLD'S END

Original Airdate: September 22, 1964

Written by Stuart Jerome. Directed by Robert Butler.

Guest Cast: Suzanne Pleshette (Ellie Burnett), Carmen Matthews (Ada Burnett), Dabney Coleman (Sgt. Keith), Henry Beckman (Keller), Woodrow Parfrey (Farmer Newlin), Paul Birch (Captain Carpenter), Peter Brocco (Hotel Clerk), Robert Gibbons (Inn Manager), Jess Kirkpatrick (Mortician), Sallie Brophy (Mrs. Newlin).

Prolog. *Another dreary town, another shabby street. Another weary pause on Richard Kimble's search for the man with one arm, his only real hope for escaping a life of fear. [Kimble reads the newspaper.] No front page. Richard Kimble turns directly to the classified section. Here are the things that really matter: a room, a job, a way to stay alive. But tonight, something else: "Personal to R.K. Have information regarding September 17th. Phone me at home. Urgent. E.B." September 17 was the night Richard Kimble's wife was murdered.*

Synopsis. Kimble answers a classified ad from Ellie Burnett (the daughter of his former defense attorney). They arrange to meet in Kansas City to discuss the information she received about a one-armed man from the private detective hired by her father. Gerard has also seen the ad and knows who wrote it. Because Gerard's family is close with the Burnett family, he knows that Ellie has fallen in love with Kimble, and so he investigates her. Ellie finds out moments before Kimble arrives that this one-armed man was killed in a fire. The news devastates Kimble, but he decides to verify the matter for himself. After Kimble leaves, Ellie's private investigator returns with more news—the one-armed man who died was actually in prison when Helen was murdered. Kimble's one-armed man is still alive! But Ellie, realizing this may be her only chance at a life with Kimble, withholds the truth.

Epilog. *Where will Richard Kimble go? Wherever the bus is going. Wherever the Fates will take him. Wherever there is hope of finding the one-armed man. And now, once again, there is that hope.*

Suzanne Pleshette is renowned worldwide for her success on the Broadway stage; her starring roles in important motion pictures (*The Birds, Nevada Smith, If It's Tuesday, This Must Be Belgium*); her numerous guest appearances on television; her memorable, Emmy-nominated performance as Leona Helmsley in *The Queen of Mean*; and, of course, her six seasons as Emily Hartley on *The Bob Newhart Show*. In "World's End," she makes the first of her two outstanding *Fugitive* guest appearances (she also starred in "All the Scared Rabbits").

"It was wonderful to see 'World's End' again, because I hadn't seen that show since I did it back in '64," Pleshette said after screening the episode in early 1993. "David was so good! You could see the promise of the actor he had the courage to become fully later on.

"David was a natural—ahead of his time in many ways. His talent was so great that he made it look seamless, and effortless. He was a skilled professional who never really received the kind of appreciation as an actor that he truly deserved.

"As wonderful a performer as he was while he was starring in *The Fugitive*, David became even better once he stopped trying to be what he thought was a conventional Hollywood leading man. Once he let go of that mentality, and put forth his heart and his skills and allowed himself as an actor to be naked before the camera...that's when he began to be wonderful. Just wonderful. He was doing really excellent work, particularly in movies for television, during the last 10 years of his life.

"David and I were about to do a series together just before he died," Pleshette continued. "One of the networks was creating something for us. That would have really been wonderful...but instead of playing opposite him, I wound up delivering the eulogy at his funeral, and my husband Tom Gallagher was one of the pallbearers. We both miss him every day of our lives."

Episode 33

MAN ON A STRING

Original Airdate: September 29, 1964

**Written by Barbara and Milton Merlin and Harry Kronman.
Directed by Sydney Pollack.**

Guest Cast: Lois Nettleton (Lucey Russell), John Larch (George Duncan), Patricia Smith (Amy Adams), Malcolm Atterbury (Sheriff Mead), Cyril Delevanti (Old Timer), Russell Collins (Doc Phillips).

Prolog. *The road is endless for Richard Kimble. Endless, uncertain.*

Synopsis. Kimble ("Joe Walker") comes to the aid of Lucey Russell after he discovers that her car has broken down; in gratitude, she provides him shelter for the night. But the police soon find the dead body of Lars Adams, a man with whom Lucey had been having an affair, only a few feet from where her car was parked. Lucey becomes the prime suspect. Lars' wife Amy knows that her husband was killed accidentally, but she wants Lucey to take the rap. Kimble can vouch for Lucey, but testifying for her could jeopardize his own freedom.

Epilog. *Always new people, always new places. Only one thing is constant for Richard Kimble: at the end, there is always the road. Richard Kimble is a fugitive.*

"David was very considerate, and very protective of me," remembered Lois Nettleton. "I was rather new to the business at the time and wasn't familiar with all the technical things that go on in television. One of the crew members went up to me after we finished shooting and told me that I have to learn how to watch the key light and all that. Well, David overheard him, and he went up to the guy and said 'Don't tell her that stuff! That's the director's job to tell her if she misses her mark. Just let her act—she's great!'"

Nettleton enjoyed working with Janssen, and that certainly comes across in all of her episodes. "Well, I did have a crush on him once," she said. "He was such a darling man to work with. I liked him a lot." Nettleton, who also starred in "In a Plain Paper Wrapper" and "Death is the Door Prize," later won Emmy Awards for *The American Woman: Portraits of Courage* (1977) and *Insight* (1983). She has starred in *Accidental Family*, *All That Glitters* and *In the Heat of the Night*.

FUGE FACTS

This is the first time Kimble repeats an alias: he went by "Joe Walker" in the episode "Smoke Screen." Kimble would use the name "Thomas Barrett" in two fourth season episodes ("Passage to Helena," "Death of a Very Small Killer").

Kimble the mechanical marvel strikes again. First he gets the car engine to start (although he admits that opening the air filter and twisting it is a pretty standard trick). Then in the epilog, he fixes the wheel of a little boy's skateboard.

FUGE FEATURE FILM MAKERS

Sydney Pollack, who won an Emmy in 1965 for Outstanding Directorial Achievement in Drama ("The Game," a segment of *Bob Hope Presents the Chrysler Theater*), went on to become a prominent director of motion pictures. His films include *The Slender Thread*, *This Property is Condemned*, *Castle Keep*, *They Shoot Horses Don't They*, *Jeremiah Johnson*, *The Way We Were*, *Three Days of the Condor* and *Tootsie*. Pollack appeared as an actor in *War Hunt*, the 1962 film written by Stanford Whitmore.

Episode 34

WHEN THE BOUGH BREAKS

Original Airdate: October 6, 1964

Teleplay by George Eckstein. Story by James Griffith and George Eckstein. Directed by Ralph Senensky.

Guest Cast: Diana Hyland (Carol Hollister), Lin McCarthy (Malleson), Royal Dano (Preacher), June Vincent (Laura Pearson), Don Briggs (Whit Pearson), Robert Hogan (Sgt. Barrett), Alex Gerry (Dr. Kisen), Sue Randall (Ruth Fisher), Marge Redmond (Norma), Jo Helton (Woman on Street), Eddie Guardino (Eddie), Jud Taylor (Joey).

Prolog. *Grand Forks, North Dakota. It is 26 months since the escape, and still another city has become a blind alley for Richard Kimble. The man with one arm, the author of the crime for which Kimble was to die, remains elusive, and again it is time to move on.*

Synopsis. A disturbed young woman whose newborn child died a year earlier abducts another baby—and mistakes Kimble ("Pete Broderick") for her late husband.

Epilog. *Another town with its thousand faces. Examine them well, for somewhere among them tonight, tomorrow, next week, will be one face that will tighten in recognition. And for a fugitive, the running will begin again.*

By choosing pediatrics as Richard Kimble's medical speciality, series creator Roy Huggins provided executive producer Quinn Martin with a gateway to exciting story ideas that Martin fully exploited. "Our hero had to be an educated man and his profession immediately established him as a college graduate and more," said Martin in 1964. "He had to have warm, human sympathies, and a good sense of values. What easier way to put this across than to make him a doctor who deals with children?"

Martin then cited "When the Bough Breaks" as one of many story ideas for *The Fugitive* that were created as a result of Kimble's medical background. "Because Kimble is a doctor, he recognizes that the woman on the train (the Diana Hyland character) has a medical problem," he explained. "It is all so subtle that most men would have arrived at an entirely different conclusion."

Episode 35

NEMESIS

Original Airdate: October 13, 1964

Written by Harry Kronman. Directed by Jerry Hopper.

Guest Cast: Kurt Russell (Phil Gerard Jr.), John Doucette (Sam Deebold), Slim Pickens (Hank Corbin), Bing Russell (Matt Davis), Adrienne Marden (Mrs. Deebold), Paul Birch (Capt. Carpenter), Garry Walberg (Jaeger).

Prolog. *A trout hatchery high in the mountains—made to order for Richard Kimble, fugitive—far off the main road. A lonely job, too lonely for most men.*

Synopsis. Kimble works at the Evergreen Fish Hatchery, where the local sheriff recognizes him. Meanwhile, while traveling through the mountains with his son Phil Jr., Gerard phones headquarters and discovers he is approximately 200 miles from where the sheriff spotted Kimble. Gerard decides to investigate with the sheriff and arranges to have Phil Jr. stay with the sheriff's wife—but the boy manages to sneak into the sheriff's station wagon and hide in back. Kimble discovers Gerard and the sheriff arriving at the hatchery and slips out the back door. Kimble drives off in the sheriff's car—unaware that Phil Jr. is still inside.

Epilog. *For Richard Kimble, another shabby room, another lonely night, another reaching out to touch someone he has met along the way. That is how it is. That is how it must remain: Richard Kimble is a fugitive.*

"Nemesis" adds a few new wrinkles to Gerard's character. The lieutenant actually looks relaxed as we see him driving his son at the start of the episode. That changes, of course, once he discovers Kimble's location. Gerard the father must become Gerard the instrument of the law once again.

Phil Jr.'s inadvertent involvement with the Fugitive puts the lieutenant in a difficult situation. While he is definitely concerned for his son's safety, Gerard cannot show it because any sign of emotion could curtail his effectiveness as a police officer. Yet, because Gerard knows Kimble so well, he can rest assured that Phil Jr. will remain unharmed. The Fugitive cares too much for children to abandon Phil Jr., regardless of who his father is. "I know Kimble," Gerard tells Sheriff Deebold. "He'll feed the boy." Gerard's instincts, both as a detective and as a parent, are correct—Kimble indeed stops long enough to feed Phil Jr.

Meanwhile, Phil Gerard Jr. shows that he is every bit his father's son: he leaves behind clues that will lead Gerard to him, such as a trail of football cards (although this is stopped once Kimble confiscates the cards), and a sweater that he folds in the shape of an arrow (that points toward the cabin). Again, Gerard the father helps Gerard the detective ("Phil never folded a sweater that neatly before in his entire life").

FUGE FAMILY TREE

"I had always hoped that we might to able to investigate further the 'private life' (if you want to call it that), or the inner mind of Philip Gerard," said Barry Morse. "But we didn't do it, to any substantial extent. No doubt, we would have gotten around to it, if time had allowed....But if there were ever a sort of Elysian extension of the series, it would be interesting to find out how and why he married his wife, what his parents did, and so forth. And I always (at least in the back of my mind) tried to prepare some kind of biographical background, because you never know when something may turn up that might prove an opportunity to indicate that your father was either a stockbroker, or a tinsmith, or a road sweeper, or a Republican senator, or whatever! It's useful to have some background in your mind. Although, inevitably, [the character's background] does develop as the weeks and the months go by."

FUGE FACTS

In this episode we learn Gerard's address: 934 South Maple Avenue, Stafford, Indiana.

Episode 36

TIGER LEFT, TIGER RIGHT

Original Airdate: October 20, 1964

**Written by William Link and Richard Levinson.
Directed by James Goldstone.**

Guest Cast: Leslie Nielsen (Harold Cheyney), Carol Rossen (Irene Cheyney), Jeanne Bal (Laura Pryor), John Lasell (Mike Pryor), David Sheiner (Lt. Hess), James Noah (Doug Warren), Richard Bull (McIntire), Paul Sorensen (Radio Operator), Tim Stafford (Glenn Pryor), William Keene (Dr. Garber).

Prolog. *Those who run need sanctuary, a time and a place to catch their breath and plan ahead. On the estate of a wealthy couple, Richard Kimble has found his temporary haven.*

Synopsis. Kimble ("Frank Jordan") works as a gardener on the estate of a wealthy couple, Mike and Laura Pryor. The Pryors' son Glen is very fond of Kimble because he shows him more attention than his own father. Harold Cheyney, a war veteran, lost the use of his legs after he was hit by a truck owned by Mike's company. After a company lawyer got him to sign papers relieving Mike of liability, Harold wrote several times asking for work but none of the letters was answered. Harold and his wife Irene decide to get even by kidnaping Mike and holding him for $100,000. Unfortunately, Harold has never seen Mike. After observing Kimble's interaction with Glen, Harold kidnaps the Fugitive by mistake.

Epilog. *The life of a fugitive is seldom downhill. Richard Kimble moves on, the hunter and the hunted, free now to continue his search.*

Carol Rossen traveled across the country in order to work on this episode. "I was living in New York and doing Broadway at the time (*Nobody Loves an Albatross, The Glass Menagerie*)," she said. "In those days, they would send you a script if they were ahead on their writing, and you would come out and do it (most TV was made in L.A.). Working with David Janssen was a particular pleasure.

"First of all, I thought David was a neat person, and he had great humor. He didn't blow himself up. He was someone who understood what he had to do, and he worked real hard. My experience was that he would always rehearse. He never played the bored exhausted star—you know, they were working real hard in those days, and those hours on any series show, now or then, are just outrageous. And in those days, sometimes [the stars] wouldn't get out of their trailer to rehearse. But David had real respect for the work, and he had respect, at least when I was working with him, for the rehearsal process. There was no nonsense about that.

"Then, personally, I just liked David a lot, and he liked me," Rossen continued. "I just thought he was a wonderful person. I loved his sensibility, I loved his humor, and thought he was very human. I think it's that humanity which still comes through the stylized manner of *The Fugitive*—that makes it still appealing.

"I don't know that there was anyone that didn't like David. He was really a wonderful guy, and decent, and hard working."

As hard as the cast and crew worked on *The Fugitive*, they also made room for levity. "That set was available for that kind of tension-breaking 'intrusions,' where something funny could happen, and people could go with it," Rossen continued. "We played a trick on Leslie Nielsen in that show ['Tiger Left, Tiger Right']—I think we were all locked in a room somewhere, and at some point somebody's supposed to come to the door, the cops, I think...And we played the scene, and the knock came at the door, and Nielsen went to the door to open it. It wasn't the cops. It was Marty Landau, dressed as an American Indian, coming off another set!"

Rossen has fond memories of *The Fugitive*. "I think of it with great, great affection, and I think of it as the best of real, good, solid, workmanly commercial television," she said. "They were good people, and it was good to work there because the people were respectful of each other, and good to each other, and loyal to each other. And those are virtues and values that are not exactly described often in Hollywood, and they're always appreciated when you run into them as a professional. You remember that more than [why this episode's title] is 'Tiger Left, Tiger Right.'

"I mean, I don't remember a story line—you can tell me a story line, and I will recall it or certain actors that I worked with. But, essentially, what I recall, when I think about experiences, is the spirit of the set, and the 'soul' of the set. And that was a very sweet, sweet place. Good people. And I think of David with great love, and caring, and I'm terribly sorry he's not with us anymore. I mean, that's how I feel. That's my memory. That's how I feel."

FUGE FACTS

This is the only episode in which Kimble allows himself to be photographed.

Episode 37

TUG OF WAR

Original Airdate: October 27, 1964

Written by Dan Ullman. Directed by Abner Biberman.

Guest Cast: Arthur O'Connell (Samuel Cole), Don Gordon (Morgan Fallon), Harry Townes (Art Mallet), Earl Swenson (Service Station Proprietor), John Harmon (Al), Jon Lormer (Pastor), Katie Sweet (Patty Mallet).

Prolog. *The farm hand who likes his work lives a wholesome, uncomplicated life—unless he is Richard Kimble, fugitive. The quiet country road is a road to danger, the peaceful village or farm a potential trap.*

Synopsis. Kimble ("Paul Kelly") is captured by two lawmen—one an aging sheriff, the other a cocky young deputy—who wage a battle over his arrest.

Epilog. *How much further must a fugitive go before he can stop and rest? North or east, or west or south, one direction is as good or bad as another, if you're Richard Kimble—fugitive.*

"*The Fugitive* was one of my favorite series, mainly because of David Janssen," said script supervisor Dick Chaffee. "It was a shame that David passed away at so young an age. He was a great guy. He kept the crew laughing all the time, and everybody just loved working with him. He was friendly with everybody, and he didn't think he was above anybody else. He just mingled with the whole crew. That's what I liked about him."

Years later, Chaffee discovered that Janssen remembered one of Chaffee's old work habits. "I had a bad reputation of driving my car to location on *The Fugitive*, which you weren't supposed to do because of the company's contract with the Teamsters," he recalled. "Everybody knew that I was driving to location. So years later I did a Movie-of-the-Week with David up in Washington (*High Ice*), and I hadn't seen David for about 10 years. Our first shot was up on top of this mountain, and we had to be airlifted up there by helicopter. When everybody was assembled up there, the director introduced David to the crew. And David said to me, 'How'd you get up here—did you drive your car?' I was amazed that he remembered that."

Episode 38

DARK CORNER

Original Airdate: November 10, 1964

Written by Harry Kronman. Directed by Jerry Hopper.

Guest Cast: Tuesday Weld (Mattie Braydon), Elizabeth MacRae (Clara Braydon), Paul Carr (Bob Matthews), Crahan Denton (Sam Denton), John McLiam (Sheriff Grover), James Seay (Bus Driver), Rudy Dolan (1st Deputy), Dave Armstrong (2nd Deputy).

Prolog. *You travel at night if you're on the run. The dark is a shield against curious eyes, against questions, against talk. Haunted by what lies behind; as always, fearful of what lies ahead.*

Synopsis. Kimble ("Jim Russell") finds refuge from the police in a farm house, where he meets Mattie Braydon, a sculptress who suffers from hysterical blindness. Mattie protects Kimble from the police and begins using him as a model. But once the Fugitive determines that Mattie is possessive and manipulative, he realizes that his freedom is in danger.

Epilog. *Richard Kimble still travels in the dark, waiting, hoping for the day when he can prove his innocence. Until then, it must remain night for him. Until then, Richard Kimble must be what he is: a fugitive.*

"If a method acting school ever gets a script of 'Dark Corner,' it will set their curriculum back a dozen years," said Tuesday Weld in a 1964 interview. "A method actor would have to run quite a gamut to portray Mattie's emotions, and ask herself quite a few questions, like 'At the start, am I really a nice person? Do I fall in love with Kimble? Do I change because he rejects me? Would his rejection change me into a vicious person gradually or rapidly?'"

Weld noted that of all the women she played on television (including Thalia Menninger on *Dobie Gillis*), she could not recall any character more mixed up than Mattie Braydon. "At the start of 'Dark Corner' I am a blind girl and a sympathetic character," she said. "When David Janssen takes refuge with my family, we become friends. I enjoy the special privileges which come through family sympathy. I dominate my dad, my sister and her boyfriend."

Once again, Kimble's medical background enables him to recognize the problem. Mattie's affliction can be corrected, but the manipulative girl does not want that to happen. "At first Dr. Kimble is very attentive but he changes when he begins to understand my motivation," Weld said.

FUGE FIX-ITS

The resourceful Kimble has basic mechanical expertise—he impresses Sam and Bob with his ability to fix their car's engine (he had also fixed cars in "Angels Travel on Lonely Roads" and "Man on a String").

Episode 39

ESCAPE INTO BLACK

Original Airdate: November 17, 1964

Written by Larry Cohen. Directed by Jerry Hopper.

Guest Cast: Betty Garrett (Margaret Ruskin), Ivan Dixon (Dr. Towne), Maxine Stuart (Nurse Proctor), Bernard Kates (Lassoe), Donald Barry (Checker), Tom Troupe (Dr. Block), Herb Vigran (Marty), Paul Birch (Captain Carpenter), Bill Raisch (Fred Johnson).

Prolog. *Another stopping place at the end of another road. If your name is Richard Kimble, you're guilty of escape and flight. You have no future unless you can find the past: the night of September 17, two years ago. You saw the man who killed your wife that night. The face was there for only a moment, but you'll never forget it, and you keep looking. Today, a truck driver mentions a one-armed man in Decatur: the description fits.*

Synopsis. On the verge of closing in on the one-armed man, Kimble is rendered amnesiac after a freak gas explosion at a roadside diner. While the Fugitive fights to regain his memory, a struggle ensues between a social worker who believes in his innocence and a doctor who thinks he's guilty. Meanwhile, the one-armed man (whose name is revealed to be Fred Johnson) slips away—but not before reporting Kimble to the police.

Epilog. *Some will believe him, some will not. Some will change their beliefs. But most importantly, he again believes in himself. He again has the will to run. And for a fugitive, this instinct is survival.*

"In this episode, 'Escape into Black,' it becomes firmly established that I know that Kimble is after me, and I'd better not let our paths cross," said Bill Raisch in 1964.

To this point in the series, the viewers have been given no clue as to how the one-armed man felt about the situation. "I am established as a man who gets out of the way quickly when anyone looks up," Raisch continued. "In the two previous shows I've been in ['The Girl from Little Egypt,' 'Search in a Windy City'] I made fast getaways. But it wasn't clear to me that I was running especially from Dr. Kimble. I even go so far as to blow the whistle on Kimble and give the police an anonymous tip he can be found at a certain hospital, a victim of amnesia."

Raisch then discussed some of the reactions he got from viewers as to his role on *The Fugitive*. "I am amazed at the number of persons who now recognize me on the street," he said. "Some of my fan letters even declare [I should be] innocent. They want Kimble to give himself up and take the heat off me."

FUGE FACTS

Kimble's mother was named Elizabeth; she did not appear, nor was she mentioned at all, in the first season episode "Home is the Hunted," where we met Kimble's father. However, at the very end of "The Judgment," Len Taft asks Donna to leave their sons with "your mother," so apparently Elizabeth Kimble is rather shy and wishes to stay away from the limelight.

Bernard Kates (Lassoe) had previously appeared as Lester Rand, the attorney who prosecuted Kimble in the flashback episode "The Girl from Little Egypt."

Writer Larry Cohen created *The Invaders* for executive producer Quinn Martin.

Episode 40

THE CAGE

Original Airdate: November 24, 1964

Written by Sheldon Stark. Directed by Walter Grauman.

Guest Cast: Joe De Santis (Joe Valdez), Brenda Scott (Carla Valdez), Tim O'Connor (Dr. Davis), Richard Evans (Miguel), John Kellogg (Officer Chrisman), Rodolfo Hoyos (Tonino), Richard Angarola (Pete), Joe Dominguez (Pablo), Julian Rivero (Old Man at Party).

Prolog. *Little fishing villages that dot the coastline are like the sea that sustain them: capricious, sometimes cordial, sometimes angry, dangerous. Tonight, the village of Puerto Viejo will be festive. Handyman Jeff Parker rooms in the warehouse loft. He's had a pleasant month here, but he's made no commitments—for it's only a matter of time before he has to move on. Parker is a fugitive.*

Synopsis. When a dockside community in Mexico is beset with a plague epidemic, Kimble has the area quarantined. But he soon finds himself trapped when the local doctor suspects his true identity.

Epilog. *Far ahead in the distance, and time, lies a harbor of many names—Safety, Love, Security, Peace. Meantime, the only haven for Richard Kimble is to move, and remain, a fugitive.*

"*The Fugitive* was a much less escapist show than most prime-time series," observed TV scholar David Thorburn. "Although the plots were often melodramatic, the circumstances, physical spaces, and forms of labor presented in the series were ordinary and realistic ones with which many people in the audience could identify."

Viewers took to *The Fugitive* partially because they could identify with the helplessness felt by Kimble over his false accusation. But Thorburn, who interviewed Quinn Martin in 1978 for his research on the history of prime time, believes the series also struck another collective nerve. "Martin was very aware of the extent to which he was tapping into broad implicit resentment of the professional classes," he said. "I think he felt that the audience enjoyed watching this rich doctor being forced to live out an ordinary, working-class life. That sort of 'bringing' low of the doctor figure was part of the show's appeal."

Kimble had encountered the kind of resentment Thorburn discusses in past episodes ("Smoke Screen," "Somebody to Remember"). However, the only rancor Kimble experiences in "The Cage" comes not from the working class, but from a member of his own standing. Dr. Davis (Tim O'Connor of "Taps for a Dead War") believes that Kimble is guilty, and that his only motive for saving the town is to make up for the life he took. But Davis misses the point. "Kimble is a doctor," Thorburn continued. "He is forced to hang around longer than he should because someone needs him or because the moral or honorable thing to do is to risk personal danger in the service of his obligations as a healer." The workers in this episode apparently grasp this truth. Once they discover Kimble is a doctor, they raise him up to an almost reverent status.

FUGE FIRSTS

This episode marks Kimble's first visit to Mexico while on the run.

Episode 41

CRY UNCLE

Original Airdate: December 1, 1964

Written by Philip Saltzman. Directed by James Gladstone.

Guest Cast: Edward Binns (Josh Kovaks), Brett Somers (Miss Edmonds), Ronny Howard (Gus), Donald Losby (Sean), Diane Ramey (Kathy), Steve Ihnat (Officer Hasboro).

Prolog. *After a while, one town is much like any other. And even a man running from the law must pause occasionally for the routine of everyday life. But for Richard Kimble, everyday life is anything but routine.*

Synopsis. After finding refuge in an orphanage, Kimble ("Pat Thomas") becomes entwined in the plight of a troubled teenager who passes him off as his uncle.

Epilog. *For Richard Kimble, there is still no end to his flight. It could come tomorrow, or next year—or never. But tonight, Richard Kimble is almost content—for having found a home, and an end to running, for another fugitive.*

Writer Philip Saltzman based "Cry Uncle" on his experience with Vista Del Mar, a Los Angeles home for orphans and troubled children that Saltzman discovered while driving home from work one day. "I used to wonder about the kids in that place, and then the idea started about putting the Fugitive in a situation of having a kid who had no real family, and all he had was an uncle who'd hasn't written or talked to him in all those years, and the Fugitive becomes a kind of prisoner of these teenagers," he recalled. "Of course, if they're in a place like this, they must be incorrigible, and they're on the edge of going to reform school...That became a kind of vehicle, and so you had a very emotional scene—you know, here's the kid who says, 'My uncle, who you all said didn't love me and didn't think about me, has shown up [in the person of Dr. Kimble], and this is my uncle.' In a way, he's shaming the Fugitive, but on the other hand, the Fugitive has to act a part and play a part. And he does—before he leaves, he turns the kid around."

"Cry Uncle" is a powerful episode that fully exploits Kimble's relationship with children. Saltzman believes that the character's bond with children can be drawn from two factors—his medical background and his innocence. "In 'Cry Uncle,' he lived with kids, but he was helping them," said Saltzman. "He cares about [young] people, being a pediatrician, and it showed in a more honest manner. It was easier for him to relate to them, and their innocence."

FUGE FAMILIAR FACES

Donald Losby (Sean) played Mark Welles in "Fear in a Desert City." Brett Somers (Miss Edmonds) was once married to Emmy Award-winning actor Jack Klugman (*The Odd Couple, Quincy, M.E.*). Edward Binns previously starred in "Glass Tightrope."

Ronny Howard (Gus) is known for his TV roles as Opie Taylor *(The Andy Griffith Show)* and Richie Cunningham *(Happy Days)*; today he is a successful film director (*Splash, Cocoon, Parenthood, Backdraft*). Howard's brother Clint also appeared on *The Fugitive*, in "Home is the Hunted" and "Set Fire to a Straw Man."

FUGE FOL DE ROL

"Cry Uncle" is the only episode in which we see Kimble doing his laundry. Although he worked in a laundromat in "This'll Kill You," we never saw him wash any of his own clothes.

Episode 42

DETOUR ON A ROAD GOING NOWHERE

Original Airdate: December 8, 1964

Teleplay by Philip Saltzman and William D. Gordon. Story by Philip Saltzman. Directed by Ralph Senensky.

Guest Cast: Lee Bowman (Ted Langner), Elizabeth Allen (Louanne Crowell), Phyllis Thaxter (Enid Langner), Don Quine (Sandy Baird), Frank Marth (Hornbeck), Warren Vanders (Andy), Barry Cahill (Bus Driver), Walter Brooke (Jess Platt), Steve Bell (Bob Street), Lana Wood (The Doll).

Prolog. *Never chase a thief... not if your own fear of capture is probably greater than his. Even in the fashionable remoteness of Indian Lake Lodge, that fear haunts this clerk who calls himself Stu Manning. At other times, Richard Kimble might have enjoyed vacationing here. But there is no vacation for a fugitive.*

Synopsis. Kimble's work as a hotel steward is cut short when he's accused of lifting funds. He tries to escape via the hotel bus, but becomes trapped when the bus breaks down and the other passengers discover his secret.

Epilog. *The difference between good and bad, between love and hate, is often elusive. The difference between life and death, for Richard Kimble, is always simply his freedom to remain a fugitive.*

This episode "detours" slightly from the standard weekly format of *The Fugitive*. "A lot of times, in these episodes, the Fugitive is able to help people," said Philip Saltzman. "He's a problem-solver in certain respects. It wasn't a new device, but it was a very useful one. *Shane* was that way. You don't know much about him, he doesn't tell much about himself, but before he leaves he solves everybody's problems."

But Kimble can't really do anything about the problems of the people he encounters in "Detour on a Road Going Nowhere" because his hands, quite literally, are tied. The Langners' marriage, troubled for 16 years, will likely remain troubled. Kimble doesn't change Louanne's fear of intimacy, either—she recognized the biggest part of the problem herself when she realized that she could never be the woman to whom Kimble was reaching out the night before. The only "problem" he solves in this episode is the immediate matter of escape. After his hands are freed, Kimble disarms the most dangerous member of the group (Sandy) and after taking a calculated risk that Enid would not shoot him, leaves the gun behind and departs.

Kimble knows too well that love and hate—like life and death—are often separated by a thin line which he doesn't always have time to ponder. The burden he carries as a fugitive is that the urgency of his situation does not allow him the time to ponder that difference. Louanne's apology for her behavior clearly touched Kimble, but with the police closing in, the Fugitive never had the opportunity to respond. Until he clears himself, the possibility of love remains elusive.

FUGE FORMER AND FUTURE ELLERY QUEENS

Lee Bowman is the second former television *Ellery Queen* to guest star on the series in as many seasons (Lee Philips was the first, in "Never Wave Goodbye"). In 1968, David Janssen co-starred with Jim Hutton in *The Green Berets*—Hutton would later play Ellery Queen in the 1975-76 TV version.

Episode 43

THE IRON MAIDEN

Original Airdate: December 15, 1964

Teleplay by Paul Lucey and Harry Kronman.
Story by Peter R. Brooke and Paul Lucey.
Directed by Walter Grauman.

Guest Cast: Stephen McNally (Jack Glennon), Nan Martin (Congresswoman Snell), Richard Anderson (Colonel Lawrence), Christine White (Susan Lait), Paul Lambert (Solomon), Jason Wingreen (Photographer), John McLiam (Alec Neal), Dennis Cross (Victor), Ed Deemer (Crewman), Richard Schuyler (Sheriff).

Prolog. *Here in Southern Nevada, man is changing the bleak face of nature. With his machinery, he is carving a shaft deep into the unriveting rock and sand. A missile launching silo. When the job is finished, the Air Force will take over. But for now it is a civilian crew that tunnels under the desert crust—a crew of deep and abiding loyalties. One of its newest members, a fugitive—Richard Kimble, working now as laborer and first aid man. The name he has taken: Parker.*

Synopsis. An explosion seals a government construction crew (including Kimble), along with a strong-willed Congresswoman, inside an underground worksite in Nevada. When his identity becomes uncovered, Kimble faces a double threat: the Congresswoman threatens to expose him, while Gerard stands waiting above.

Epilog. *Richard Kimble eats alone. For him, all roads are lonely, all seasons dangerous. Until the day when he can prove his innocence, Richard Kimble must remain a fugitive.*

You certainly have to feel sorry for Gerard by the end of this episode. How could Kimble possibly slip away this time? But just as G. Stanley Lazer observed about Kimble in "Man in a Chariot," a certain chemistry works against Gerard whenever he comes close to apprehending the Fugitive. Sometimes the circumstances are beyond his control, such as the train wreck, or in this episode when Susan innocently tells Kimble that "his friend is here to see him." But in other instances, Gerard's impetuous nature betrays him. Glennon's plan would not have worked had Kimble not anticipated Gerard going down the shaft. But the most important element of the equation is something that Gerard could never quite grasp—Kimble's ability to convey his innocence to strangers and thus compel them to help him.

Gerard does seem a little overconfident in this episode, although given these circumstances, one could hardly blame him. But the lieutenant ought to know better—he observed in "The End Game" that emotion is as much his enemy as it is Kimble's. Or to repeat another Gerardism (from "Never Wave Goodbye"), confidence is fatal to the both of them.

FUGE FAMILIAR FACES

"The Iron Maiden" marks the first of Richard Anderson's six *Fugitive* appearances (Dabbs Greer also appeared in six shows). Best known for his roles on *The Six Million Dollar Man* and *The Bionic Woman*, Anderson acted in many Quinn Martin shows, including a co-starring role opposite Burt Reynolds on *Dan August*. "Quinn had what you call the old-fashioned 'stock company,' Anderson said. "There were actors that he specifically liked, and I had worked on a show (I can't remember which one) originally, and they put me on the list. That's how that happened. I worked in all his shows...I was working for other people, too, but I would get calls from Quinn Martin when I wasn't able to do the shows because I was working on something else."

Episode 44

DEVIL'S CARNIVAL

Original Airdate: December 22, 1964

Written by William D. Gordon. Directed by James Goldstone.

Guest Cast: Philip Abbott (Charles Edward Schachter), Warren Oates (Hanes McClure), Madeleine Sherwood (Marybeth Thompson), Strother Martin (Shirky Saulter), Dee Pollock (Tad Thompson), George Mitchell (John Petri Allsup), David Kent (Little Jim), Steve Harris (Bead Hallock), Ronnie Haran (Sue-Ann Crayton), Robert Sorrells (Jud Tormey), Matt McCue (Cook), Woodrow Parfrey (Cleo Potter).

Prolog. *This is a man who must keep moving—pursuing, pursued. He is not a man of solitude, but often the friendless, open road is his only alternative to death by execution. Richard Kimble: he travels a lot by thumb, makes many a long, lonely hike between rides.*

Synopsis. Kimble unwittingly hitches a ride with Hanes McClure, a bad seed out to settle the score with his hometown. After Hanes lands the both of them in jail, Kimble must endure the spectacle the town makes of the double arrest.

Epilog. *The things a fugitive turns away from are sometimes evil, sometimes good—and difficult to leave. Everything left behind is dangerous. There is no safety for him anywhere, but if he can keep moving, there is hope.*

Strother Martin steals the show as Shirky Saulter, the conniving capitalist; a few years later, Martin became permanently ingrained in popular culture by virtue of one line in the Paul Newman film *Cool Hand Luke* (1967): "What we have here is failure to communicate."

Philip Abbott starred as Assistant F.B.I. Director Arthur Ward, the immediate superior to Inspector Lewis Erskine (Efrem Zimbalist Jr.) on the long-running, highly successful Quinn Martin series *The F.B.I.* (ABC, 1965-74).

Madeleine Sherwood was best known for her role as the Mother Superior on *The Flying Nun*; Sue Randall played Miss Landers, Beaver's teacher on *Leave It to Beaver*.

Episode 45

BALLAD FOR A GHOST

Original Airdate: December 29, 1964

Teleplay by George Eckstein. Story by Sidney Ellis and George Eckstein. Directed by Walter Grauman.

Guest Cast: Janis Paige (Hallie Martin), Mark Richman (Johnny Haywood), Paul Fix (Dan Martin), Noam Pitlik (Davey), Hugh Sanders (Sheriff Larson), Anne Helm (Nora Martin).

Prolog. *At a job several miles south of Salisbury, Ohio, Richard Kimble, wearing the name "Pete Glenn," grows restless now. He's worked here two months, long enough at one place—perhaps too long. Time to move on.*

Synopsis. Kimble's about to leave his job at a roadside lodge until he discovers that the next scheduled performer is Hallie Martin, a singer who bears an uncanny physical resemblance to his late wife Helen.

Epilog. *A chance meeting. A thousand ghosts are stirred. And a fugitive wonders how long before they'll be at rest.*

Quinn Martin hired the best writers available. In fact, in Martin's set-up, the producers were essentially "story editors," focusing their attention on the scripts while Arthur Fellows concentrated on post-production aspects of the show. "I would say 70% of what I did was work with writers, developing stories, trying to steer them in appropriate and imaginative directions," said producer Alan Armer.

Martin's scheme gave Armer and his writers a lot of leeway in terms of creating new ideas for the series. "The first two seasons [before he became a producer himself], I would pitch the idea to Alan," said George Eckstein. "In those days, the writer usually came up with the idea 90% of the time. The different writers would come in and pitch to the producer ideas they had for the series. Depending on the writer's credits, or the originality of the idea, they would be given a story assignment, and then depending on the status of the writer, either the story assignment and script without a cutoff, or just the story assignment. You would have a variety of freelance writers coming in and pitching ideas."

Haunting Kimble with the ghost of his wife was a great idea, and "Ballad for a Ghost" is well executed, from Janis Paige's excellent performance to Walter Grauman's strong direction. The only problem is that, aside from a slight resemblance, Paige doesn't look anything like Diane Brewster (who played Helen in "The Girl from Little Egypt").

FUGE FACTS

Eckstein named the characters Hallie and Nora after his own two daughters. He also wrote the music and lyrics to Hallie's song "Just One Road I Travel," which was also the original title of this episode.

The Narrator tells us in the prolog that Kimble has worked in Salisbury for "two months, long enough at one place—perhaps too long. Time to move on." This harkens back to series creator Roy Huggins' suggestion that Kimble adopt an arbitrary rule of never staying in any given locale for longer than six weeks.

Episode 46

BRASS RING

Original Airdate: January 12, 1965

Written by Leonard Kantor. Directed by Abner Biberman.

Guest Cast: Angie Dickinson (Norma Sessions), Robert Duvall (Leslie Stevens), John Ericson (Lars), Phillip Pine (Lt. Gavin), Karl Swenson (Morgan), Buck Young (Police Sergeant), James Tartan (Doctor), Sandra Gregg (Girl on Pier).

Prolog. *The southern coast of California, where the land ends and an amusement pier juts out into the sea. A place where strangers meet, where a new face is not suspect. The fingerprints are still Dr. Kimble's, but the name is now Ben Horton.*

Synopsis. Norma Sessions hires Kimble to care for her brother Leslie, who has a physical disability. Kimble doesn't realize that Norma (along with her boyfriend Lars) is plotting to murder Leslie to collect the insurance money. When Norma suspects that Kimble is hiding from the police, she decides to pin the crime on him.

Epilog. *Save up a lot of loneliness, and you're out to spend it somewhere. This time, on a lonely pier, livened only by the sound of an ancient calliope. And a brass ring caught by a fugitive will only give him another brief ride to nowhere.*

The cast and crew spent an average of four days out of every seven shooting days "on location"—away from their home base, sound stages #1 and #2 at the Goldwyn Studios in Hollywood. "We often used the term 'shooting on location,' but to us that really meant shooting (nearby, but physically) outside the studio walls," said assistant director Bob Rubin. "Distant location is where you're housed overnight. Due to travel time and distance, it may well be neither functional nor economical to return everyone to the studio each night, so it becomes more practical to 'go on distant location'—and provide accommodations, meals, per diem, and transportation—complete the necessary filming, and then return to L.A. For us, shooting on distant location was only necessary for a couple shows each season.

"Thus, with an objective of having each episode take place in a state of the U.S. different from the state portrayed in the previous episode, production-wise, being based in L.A. was ideal. We had options.

"Except for the pilot, which was actually filmed in Tucson, Arizona, in truth our *most* remote filming location wasn't very remote at all. Within two hours of the studio were snowcapped mountains, vast lush forests, endless desert sunsets, miles of horse farms and citrus groves, or an elegant $10 million estate in Beverly Hills. In Hollywood, there's virtually everything a creative production team such as ours could possibly have ever hoped to have immediate access to—including the obvious state-of-the-art talent, crews, facilities, equipment, and weather. For a filmmaker, Southern California is a visual paradise—with an ocean view. In black-and-white or in color, *The Fugitive* was always visually interesting."

FUGE FAMILIAR FACES

Angie Dickinson (*Rio Bravo, Ocean's 11, A Fever in the Blood, The Killers, The Chase, Point Blank, Police Woman*) also starred with David Janssen in the TV-movie *A Sensitive, Passionate Man* (1977).

Robert Duvall won the Best Actor Oscar for *Tender Mercies* (1983), and later returned to television for the miniseries *Ike* (1979) and *Lonesome Dove* (1989).

Episode 47

THE END IS BUT THE BEGINNING

Original Airdate: January 12, 1965

Teleplay by George Fass and Arthur Weiss. Story by George Fass. Directed by Walter Grauman.

Guest Cast: Barbara Barrie (Aimee Rennick), Andrew Duggan (John Harlan), Frank Maxwell (Lt. Garlock), Robert Yuro (Sam), Paul Birch (Capt. Carpenter).

Prolog. *A man who has to run to survive finds respite sometimes in desolate places. For the moment, this man is Steve Younger: for the moment, a truck driver. Yet today, within the hour, Steve Younger has a rendezvous with death.*

Synopsis. A tragic car accident may bring hope for the Fugitive. By assuming the identity of the dead man, Kimble tries to convince Gerard of his own demise—and bring an end to the running.

Epilog. *Now indeed, Steve Younger is dead. But the thin thread which binds Richard Kimble winds back into the fingers of Lt. Philip Gerard, who will follow it—and cut it, if he can.*

"As well as I've come to know Richard Kimble," observes Gerard to Aimee Rennick (Barbara Barrie), "the only thing about him that I have never understood was that quality of him that made sensitive, intelligent strangers want to help him." Gerard never manages to understand that "quality" because his role as instrument of the law prevents him from doing so. "Having been alongside my brother [Len, a London policeman] for such a long time, I began to realize that it was no part of his job to make personal judgments—and he was an immensely humane guy," said Barry Morse. "That was somebody else's business. That was the judge and jury's job. What Gerard had to do was to assemble the evidence which was to go before the judge and jury. And if that is what is meant by 'obsessive,' than that's what you have to be. You have to adhere to the rules of the law. If somebody wants to change the rules of law, that's the business of the electorate. But for the time being [Gerard would say], in the job that I do, I must adhere to the rules established by whatever local jurisdiction I work in."

This is the only episode in which Gerard admits his obsession with Kimble. "The word [obsession] was tacked on, almost like a name, because it was a very convenient way of describing him for the customers,"said Morse. "But the word 'obsession' troubles me a little bit. Obviously, it did seem, to people who didn't have Gerard's view of things, that this was an 'obsessive' matter which had developed in him. But, I think he would say—you must always try and work on the inner perspective of the person whom you're playing—that his 'conviction' (perhaps that's the best word) in this particular case, arose entirely from the fact there had been a 'conviction' in another sense of that word, in which the laws of his country, and of his state, had made a pronouncement; that it is not for him to question the operation of that law. It is his duty, his sworn duty, to uphold the demands of that law.

"That, in turn, has impact on why Richard Kimble is so important to him. A man with such high standards (as I hope it was quite clear he had), such inflexible, such demanding—some people would say *impossible*—standards, would naturally feel the person who represented to him a kind of failure, a kind of falling below his highest code, was immensely important. The cases that are resolved, the cases that are successfully carried through, from a law enforcement point of view, are simply matters for the file. But something which is outstanding, in the way that the Kimble case was, naturally becomes much more important, because it represents, until it *is* solved, a shortcoming to *him*."

Kimble would certainly attest to Gerard's standards. In another instance of the characters' mutual respect for each other, he commends the lieutenant's abilities while he prepares Aimee for her confrontation with him. "He's brilliant," says Kimble of Gerard. "He knows me maybe better than I know myself."

Meanwhile, Aimee Rennick provides a worthy opponent for Gerard, never dropping her guard until once the lieutenant has driven away. Not only does Gerard admit his obsession to her, he pays her a compliment ("You're a stimulating woman"). Barbara Barrie *(Breaking Away)* turns in an outstanding performance.

FUGE FACTS

This episode marks one of the few instances in which Kimble expresses doubt in himself: he muses to Aimee that he may have deliberately caused the accident that killed the trucker.

Kimble closes out a letter to his father with "Love to Doug and Sis." While "Sis" obviously refers to Donna, it is unclear who "Doug" is—according to "Home is the Hunted," Kimble's brother is named Ray, and his brother-in-law Len.

FUGE FAMILY

Berniece Janssen (David's mother) appears in this episode—she's seen accompanying a gentleman as Kimble tries to sneak back into his hotel room. Berniece, a former Ziegfeld showgirl who appears occasionally in such TV shows as *Cheers* and *Murder, She Wrote*, also has a role in the motion picture version of *The Fugitive* (1993).

"I played the court reporter during the trial scene," she said. "I had a ball! I have a small part, but everybody treated me like a queen! I had my picture taken with Harrison

Ford—he's such a gentleman, and he's a great actor. He does an outstanding job playing Richard Kimble. I know that David would be proud."

Episode 48

NICEST FELLA YOU'D EVER WANT TO MEET

Original Airdate: January 19, 1965

Written by Jack Turley. Directed by Sutton Roley.

Guest Cast: Pat Hingle (Sheriff Joe Bob Sims), Mary Murphy (Thelma Hollister), Dabney Coleman (Floyd Pierce), Tom Skerritt (Neeley Hollister), Curt Conway (Mr. Hollister), Dabbs Greer (Mayor Duncan), Chet Stratton (Driver), Burt Mustin (Charley), Kevin Brodie (Johnny), Read Morgan (Highway Patrolman).

Prolog. *Bixton, Arizona—small, quiet. For some, a good place to live. But for Richard Kimble, fugitive, it's only a stopover between rides—a stopover he will not soon forget.*

Synopsis. A politically ambitious sheriff arbitrarily arrests Kimble ("Richard Clark") and subjects him to slave labor. After Kimble witnesses the lawman murder another prisoner, he soon finds his own life in danger.

Epilog. *In the aftermath of violence, there must always come a moment of peace, a time for healing and a time to restore the delicate balance of life versus death. But for a fugitive, there can be no moment of peace. He must travel the road of the hunted. And for Richard Kimble, that road apparently has no end.*

Quinn Martin's most lasting contribution to television, according to TV scholar David Thorburn, was the development of a visual style for dramatic television that adapted the complexities of feature film making to the confined space of the small screen. "He was one of the central figures in developing a visual style for dramatic programming that was as complicated in an audio-visual sense as movies were," said Thorburn. "You can recognize a distinctive visual texture in all QM series, interesting camera angles, a visual complexity, that aim to create a kind of visual excitement and energy."

"Nicest Fella You'd Ever Want to Meet" stands out from all other episodes of *The Fugitive* precisely because it is the most visually complex segment of the series. Director Sutton Roley certainly understood Martin's approach to the medium: much of Roley's television work is marked by his stylish and often innovative use of the camera. Roley knew how to create excitement: not surprisingly, he directed many episodes of *Mission: Impossible.*

Roley's use of the camera in "Nicest Fella You'd Ever Want to Meet" not only enhanced the action and tension of the story, it established the most important facet of the antagonist's character. "The Pat Hingle character was written as a flamboyant sheriff," Roley explained. "But I think we made him more complex than that simply by making him off-centered and by playing a lot of subtext. Subtext is the most important tool a filmmaker has. For example, we did things like the marble platform for the first scene in the park [Act I], so Hingle could stand high as the master of his universe and talk down to his multitudes. Anytime you can motivate elevations, it gives you a reason to shoot angles. So long as the angles are motivated and not done simply for effect, they make a film interesting. Conversely, the standard master close-up and over-the-shoulder shots can become boring and make the film ordinary. That's why I use angles."

Roley also adapted himself to the confines of the small screen. "First of all, you're shooting for television, and everything is shot tighter (or it should be) than a motion picture," he said. "To me, the only way you can open that box is in depth. Let's look back at that jail cell sequence in Act II where Tom Skerritt was way in the foreground. I used a wide angle lens to keep everything in sharp focus, both in the foreground *and* background. So when Pat Hingle walked up the hall to the cell, he and Skerritt and

Janssen were all in sharp focus. That's the way you can open up the television set: shooting in depth, as opposed to the stage, where you stage for the proscenium (in width, rather than in depth). In my opinion, film should be always be staged in depth."

Flamboyant by his own admission, Roley sometimes got into trouble with other producers who thought he was "difficult" to work with. "They say if you're off-centered, you're difficult," he laughed. "Film (motion pictures) is a director's medium, and television is a producer's medium. When you go in to direct an hour television show, you're simply a guest for two weeks, nothing more, and you're not always a welcome guest! Not many television directors make waves, and that's why most shows look like they come out of the same cookie cutter. Unfortunately, that's what most TV producers want.

"Nevertheless, I always say to actors, 'Hey, we're doing an hour show here, but I shoot it like it's *Macbeth*!' And I think that's the way you have to care: you get enthusiasm going, you get juices running, you get some excitement on the set, and it's not just boom-boom-boom-boom, cut-and-print, and in and out. You work a lot harder, and it only shows a little bit, but it's more fun doing it that way. And, more than just that, the end result is always a hell of a lot more gratifying."

FUGE FACTS

Roley used a 12' x 10' mirror to shoot the scene in which Hingle drives into the camera. "You use a mirror with stanchions on both sides [as a frame], so it would sit upright on the road," he explained. "You get off with the camera at an angle and you shoot into the mirror, at the car. Then you let that car drive directly into the mirror—by doing that, you can bring the car right to you. Then you cut the film just before the point of impact."

The "Apache Park" scenes for this episode were filmed at the Corrigan Ranch in Simi Valley, California.

Episode 49

FUN AND GAMES AND PARTY FAVORS

Original Airdate: January 26, 1965

Written by Arthur Weiss. Directed by Abner Biberman.

Guest Cast: Katherine Crawford (Joanne Glenn), Mark Goddard (Dan Holt), Joan Tompkins (Madge Glenn), Anthony Call (Paul Andrews), Peter E. Deuel (Buzzy), Thomas Hasson (Joe), James Davidson (Dave), Tom Palmer (Charles Glenn), Gerald Hamer (Warren), Joe Perry (Police Sergeant).

Prolog. *Two years ago, this man was Richard Kimble, doctor of medicine. Today, he is Douglas Beckett, employed in the hills above Los Angeles. He is a trusted chauffeur and gateman. He is also still a fugitive.*

Synopsis. Kimble now works as the chauffeur for a wealthy couple whose daughter is secretly dating a pool cleaner. While chaperoning a party for the girl's friends, Kimble throws out an unruly young man who tries to crash the party. Unfortunately, the boy turns out to be a detective buff—who recognizes his picture from a police magazine.

Epilog. *The world in which young people get married and share love and build dreams is a thousand miles from the world in which Richard Kimble walks: the world of pursuit and fear, the world of a fugitive.*

"Fun and Games and Party Favors" was filmed in six days, as opposed to the normal seven days it took to complete an episode. Producer Alan Armer believes the shortened schedule may account for the show's frenetic pace. "We were terribly overbudget at that time," he said. "I think that was the only show we shot in six days, trying to save a little money. It showed, apparently."

FUGE FAMILY AFFAIR

"Fun and Games" was a family affair of sorts. Katherine Crawford (Joanne) is the daughter of series creator Roy Huggins; and director Abner Biberman cast his son Tom in a small role.

Episode 50

SCAPEGOAT

Original Airdate: February 2, 1965

**Teleplay by William D. Gordon. Story by Larry Cohen.
Directed by Alexander Singer.**

Guest Cast: Dianne Foster (Janice Cummings), John Anderson (Justin Briggs), Harry Townes (Ballinger), Don Quine (Vin Briggs), David Macklin (Roy Briggs), Whit Bissell (Gibson), Tom Reese (Norman), Bill Zuckert (Scales), Doreen McLean (Landlady), Russ Bender (Timekeeper), R.L. Armstrong (Curry), Ted Gehring (Bar Patron), Bill Erwin (Bar Patron).

Prolog. *The name on the time card is Hayes. A name is easily changed, dropped and forgotten. Every identity Richard Kimble has borrowed has vanished for good when he moved on...*

Synopsis. A man recognizes Kimble ("Bill Hayes"/"Eddie Frey") from the Fugitive's recent stay in South Dakota—and is surprised to see him alive. After learning that the townspeople believed he was murdered by his former employer, Kimble faces a moral dilemma: should he return to the town and clear the man convicted for his murder?

Epilog. *He will use many other names, and move through many other places searching for Richard Kimble, dreading each backward look, as long as he must remain a fugitive.*

It makes sense for Kimble, every once in a while, to bump into someone whom he'd met while using a previous alias ("Eddie Frey"). As careful as Kimble is about visiting the same place twice, the country is only so big. As much as he travels, he's bound to come across some former acquaintance along the way.

FUGE FACTS

Doreen McLean (Landlady), who also appeared in the episode "Terror at Highpoint," was for many years the casting secretary for QM Productions.

Episode 51

CORNER OF HELL

Original Airdate: February 9, 1965

**Teleplay by Jo Helms and Francis Irby Gwaltney.
Story by Jo Helms and Zahrini Machadah.
Directed by Robert Butler.**

Guest Cast: R.G. Armstrong (Tully), Bruce Dern (Cody), Sharon Farrell (Elvie), Sandy Kenyon (Kyle), Dabbs Greer (Sheriff), Edward Faulkner (Roy), James Griffith (Dispatcher), Nick Nicholson (Truck Driver), Paul Birch (Captain Carpenter).

Prolog. *A man on the run, convicted on circumstantial evidence of a murder he did not commit, calling himself Paul Hunter, driving relief for InterSouth Freight. This is his first trip. It is to be his last. He's only a few miles away from a grim encounter with truth—and irony.*

Synopsis. In the backwoods of Louisiana, Kimble finds himself in the unlikely role of protecting Gerard from a lynching after a moonshiner accuses the lieutenant of assaulting his daughter.

Epilog. *It is a never ending pattern: buy a ticket, catch a bus, east or north, south or west. Destination: Anytown. This time, maybe he'll be there, the man with one arm—and for Richard Kimble, the never ending pattern will be ended.*

Originally entitled "This Place Belongs to Another People," this story initially focused on the sadistic nature of Tully's police-hating community. In the first draft of the script, for example, Gerard is completely humiliated: not only do Tully's people relieve the lieutenant of his gun, they strip him of his shoes and socks, so that when he is returned from the woods after his escape attempt, his feet are badly cut and bruised. The story originally took place at night, which made Gerard's ordeal more harrowing—in the darkness, he is attacked by thousands of cargo spiders, and later runs into a swarm of bees. And before Gerard is "sentenced," he endures a shower of beer, cigar burns on his leg, and numerous kickings and beatings.

Apparently, the authors realized that the torment was excessive, because Gwaltney made a handwritten note at the end of the first draft to "emphasize the trial more," particularly in the fourth act. The end result is, as the Narrator puts it, "a grim encounter with truth and irony" for both Kimble and Gerard. The Tullys, like the South Dakota townspeople in "Scapegoat," use circumstantial evidence as the basis of ridding themselves of a man they simply do not like. Gerard finds himself thrust into the same nightmare which Kimble has faced for over two years (the script describes Gerard's flight into the woods as "an insane parody of the beginning of the series"), and Kimble finds himself in a position to save Gerard once again. Despite the personal torment the lieutenant has caused him, Kimble continues to rescue his adversary because he needs him alive. Just as Kimble represents a failure to Gerard, Gerard represents a failure to Kimble because the lieutenant insists that the one-armed man is a fantasy. To keep the moral order straight (as well as clear his own name), the Fugitive needs Gerard as much as he needs Fred Johnson.

While Kimble has shown a facility to blend in with people of other factions, Gerard's understanding of his role as instrument of the law binds him to actions that fall within the perimeters of his duty. While this belief certainly protects Gerard from answering direct questions concerning Kimble's innocence, it also causes a tunnel vision which occasionally (as in this episode) gets him into trouble. Gerard cannot conceive of circumstances where "the law" would allow for exceptions like the Tullys, because enforcing "normal" standards would prove less practical and more expensive. Because he cannot relate to anything he doesn't know (not surprisingly, Elvie calls him a foreigner), Gerard hides behind what he knows best. If Gerard is guilty of any crime in this episode, it's a crime of arrogance—an arrogance that masks a fear of the unknown.

As a result of his ordeal, Gerard learns compassion for Kimble. However, because he is an instrument of the law, he cannot allow himself to show it. Regardless of what Gerard may feel, the incident does not change one cold hard fact. "The truth is, still, you're guilty before the law," Gerard says as he leaves Kimble at the end of the episode.

FUGE FACTS

At the beginning of this episode, in order to escape the roadblock, Kimble bails out of the moving truck and races into the woods. Remarkably enough, Kimble emerged without a scratch. "That's because David didn't quite 'jump' out of the truck—the truck was only moving at two miles per hour," explained assistant director Bob Rubin. "We undercranked—that is, we adjusted the camera's variable speed motor to the slowest possible number of frames per second while we filmed that sequence. When projected at normal film speed (24 frames per second), it appeared more dangerous to the viewer than it actually was.

"Besides, we needed David all-in-one-piece for the next episode—so what do you expect?!"

Episode 52

MOON CHILD

Original Airdate: February 16, 1965

Written by Dan Ullman. Directed by Alexander Singer.

Guest Cast: Murray Hamilton (Mel Starling), June Harding (Joanne Mercer), David Sheiner (Sheriff Mack), Virginia Christine (Alma Mercer), Dean Stanton (Randy), Mort Mills (George Mangus), Val Avery (Burns), Burt Douglas (Johnny North), Helen Kleeb (Miss Cloud), Charles Thompson (Mr. Duffield), Jim Goodwin (Benny).

Prolog. *Enter a town for the first time and, if you're a fugitive, you will try to determine where the danger is. Most often, it will come from the police—but not always.*

Synopsis. A small town vigilante group mistakes Kimble ("Bill Martin") for a serial killer who strangles his victims with a clothesline. A mentally retarded girl soon befriends the Fugitive and shelters him in the basement of her home.

Epilog. *The night is over. The town that held a gun to Kimble's head is many miles behind, already becoming part of the dizzying procession of towns through which a fugitive must pass, searching for the man who can mean his salvation.*

Viewers who remember the old Folgers Coffee commercials of the 1960s and 1970s will get a laugh at the scene in Act III where Joanne's mother (Virginia Christine) pours coffee for Mel Starling and Sheriff Mack. Christine poured a lot of coffee in these commercials—she played Folgers spokesperson "Mrs. Olsen." She also played Natalie Wood's mother in *Splendor in the Grass* (1961).

Dean Stanton—also known as Harry Dean Stanton—is known for his roles in such films as *Repo Man* (1984) and *Paris, Texas* (1984). Murray Hamilton (Mel) played Katherine Ross' father in *The Graduate* (1967) and the Mayor in *Jaws* (1975); he also guest starred in many of executive producer Quinn Martin's other series, including *Barnaby Jones* and *Cannon*.

Episode 53

THE SURVIVORS

Original Airdate: March 2, 1965

Written by George Eckstein. Directed by Don Medford.

Guest Cast: Ruth White (Edith Waverly), Louise Sorel (Terry Waverly), Lloyd Gough (Ed Waverly), Richard Devon (Police Sergeant), Burt Metcalfe (Phil Corbin), Herb Ellis (Frank), John Newton (Larry).

Prolog. *This is where it began—Fairgreen, Indiana. Here, ten years ago at the county hospital, Richard Kimble completed his internship. Here, he met a nurse named Helen Waverly, and here they resolved to get married. Now, he's come back to a town when people have reason to remember him—perhaps some more than others.*

Synopsis. After reading about his father-in-law's pending bankruptcy, Kimble returns to Fairgreen, Indiana—the town where he met Helen as an intern ten years before. He finds an ally in his sister-in-law, Terry—but nothing but contempt from his mother-in-law, Edith, who still clings to Helen's memory.

Epilog. *A man tries to arm himself against the lonely night, for he knows that at this time and place there can be no homecoming for a fugitive.*

One of the best episodes of the series, "The Survivors" introduces the audience to another important element of the Kimble tragedy: the reactions of Helen's family. "We thought that we should get back to the roots at some point, and see where those people are," said George Eckstein.

Not only was it appropriate to return to the past, it was fitting that Eckstein should write the story. By this point in time, Eckstein had gradually become more involved in the writing of the show: by the third season, he became the series' associate producer. "George Eckstein is an incisive, creative talent," said assistant director Bob Rubin. "He and Alan Armer were the two people who not only really, really cared, but they 'knew' *The Fugitive*—and they knew it better than anyone else. As bosses, as producers, as writers, and as executives, Alan and George were a creative, idea-generating team—with class."

In many respects, "The Survivors" parallels the previous "homecoming" episode, "Home is the Hunted." Like Stafford, Fairgeen poses a special danger for Kimble because all the townspeople know him. Both the Waverly family and Kimble's own family have mixed reactions about seeing him. A newspaper item draws Kimble home in both episodes; each story features a deeper emotional conflict (Ray's resentment, Edith's grief) which Kimble feels compelled to resolve before he leaves. Even the closing narratives echo each other. Compare this episode's epilog with the Narrator's summation in "Home is the Hunted:" *Home is the sailor, home from the sea, and the hunter home from the hill—but for Richard Kimble, not yet.*

FUGE FEATURES

This is one of the few episodes in which Kimble wears dark glasses (he also wore them in "Terror at Highpoint"). Other than hair dye, he uses no other means to alter his appearance. While this may seem odd at first, consider that one of the keys to Kimble's survival is his ability to avoid detection. Wearing dark glasses would tend to attract the attention of the police, so by not wearing them Kimble is more likely to blend in with other people. On an aesthetic level, the use of dark glasses would rob the viewers of one of David Janssen's strongest assets as a performer—his ability to communicate emotion to the audience through his eyes.

Episode 54

EVERYBODY GETS HIT IN THE MOUTH SOMETIME

Original Airdate: March 9, 1965

Written by Jack Turley. Directed by Alexander Singer.

Guest Cast: Jack Klugman (Gus Hendrick), Geraldine Brooks (Lucia Mayfield), Michael Constantine (Ernie Svoboda), G.B. Atwater (Cleve Logan), Jimmy Stiles (Jimmy Mayfield), Tracy Stratford (Lucy Mayfield), Kathleen O'Malley (Receptionist), John Mayo (Mr. Williams), K.L. Smith (Pete), Marlowe Jensen (Sgt. Fontaine), James Devine (Gas Station Attendant).

Prolog. *The road of escape has led Richard Kimble to a new sanctuary. The work: dispatcher for Bullet Trucking Company. No questions asked, no references required. A good job for a fugitive.*

Synopsis. Now a truck driver for a small freight company, Kimble ("Bill Douglas") discovers that his boss, who is being blackmailed by his late partner's wife into paying her bills, plans to hijack one of his own trucks.

Epilog. *Justice can be delivered by a final act of violence, or it can be elusive and taunting as it has become for Richard Kimble. For him, justice hides around the next bend in the road, beyond the next mountain, on the bus that is just pulling out. Somewhere, sometime, he will find it, and so he moves on.*

"Everybody Gets Hit in the Mouth Sometime" shows us that even Dr. Kimble's patience has its limits. After Lucia's bratty son nails him with a slingshot, the Fugitive turns around and spanks the kid on the rear end (and adds a twist to the Narrator's remark that "justice can be delivered by a final act of violence"). Allowing Kimble to display his temper on occasion kept the character grounded in reality, according to producer Alan Armer. "It was so heartwarming to see that kid get his and to see Kimble doing something other than patting a kid on the head," he told *Emmy Magazine* in 1982. "When you get a character that noble, you say 'Oh, come on, let's keep him human.'"

Episode 55

MAY GOD HAVE MERCY

Original Airdate: March 16, 1965

Written by Don Brinkley. Directed by Don Medford.

Guest Cast: Telly Savalas (Victor Leonetti), Carol Rossen (Anne Leonetti), Norman Fell (Lt. Cermak), Maggie Pierce (Nurse Stockwell), Jud Taylor (Toby Warren), Abigail Shelton (Gloria), Noah Keen (Dr. Becker), Mary Jackson (Nurse Oberhandy), Don Eitner (Intern).

Prolog. *A man on the run assumes many identities, each one reflecting in some way the life he has left behind. Thus, Dr. Richard Kimble, now known as Harry Reynolds, works as an orderly in a Michigan hospital. Once a respected pediatrician, he finds a hint of security in the familiar hospital routine. But no man, not even a convicted murderer, can completely abandon his past, nor can his past abandon him.*

Synopsis. Victor Leonetti, who holds Kimble responsible for his daughter's death, turns in the Fugitive after recognizing him as a hospital orderly. Upon learning that Kimble was trying to contact a specialist at the time of the girl's death, Leonetti tries to make amends—by confessing to the murder of Helen Kimble. Meanwhile, an incapacitated Kimble, recovering from a gunshot wound sustained during an escape attempt, awakens to find Gerard standing at his bedside.

Epilog. *The death sentence comes in many forms, affecting each man in a different way. For some it means an end to pain, for others it becomes a challenge to live. For Richard Kimble, the challenge is repeated with every new turn of the road.*

"May God Have Mercy" was the first of five scripts contributed by Don Brinkley. "In each episode, you try to bring out some facet of the characters that hasn't been developed or projected before," he said. "Especially with Gerard. You'd like to show just an element of compassion, because over the years he became such a dark force that you wanted to show that there was a little more to him than that. Whenever possible, I tried to do that."

In "May God Have Mercy," Brinkley provides the lieutenant with a touch of realism. To this point in the series, Gerard has shown that he will drop everything to follow any lead with even the remotest possibility of finding Kimble. But when he's awakened by the phone call in Act II, he hesitates running off on "a wild goose chase" without receiving a positive identification from the Michigan police. Although the lieutenant immediately reconsiders and books a flight out, it's refreshing to see Gerard act skeptical once in a while.

"That was a human reaction," commented Brinkley. "You can't make a puppet out of the man: every time he hears 'Kimble,' he drops everything and rushes out the door. The man has to have some rational approach to his job. Somewhere down the line, he'd been handed some false leads, and he had to at least accept that fact and realize it's possible that this might not be Kimble. After all, it wasn't as if he was just going down to the corner drug store to pick the guy up—he's going to another state [this episode takes place in Michigan]. So, he would be a little skeptical, just in terms of reality. You try to make the characters as human and real as possible."

FUGE FAMOUS FATHERS

Carol Rossen's father was legendary Hollywood motion picture producer/director/screenwriter Robert Rossen, who won the Academy Award for Best Screenplay for *All the King's Men* (1949), which also won the Oscar for Best Picture. Robert Rossen's other films include *The Roaring Twenties*, *The Treasure of Sierra Madre*, *Body and Soul*, and *The Hustler*.

Episode 56
MASQUERADE

Original Airdate: March 23, 1965

Written by Philip Saltzman. Directed by Abner Biberman.

Guest Cast: Norma Crane (Mavis Hull), Edward Asner (Sheriff Cliff Mayhew), John Milford (Leonard Hull), H.M. Wynant (Pinto), Rayford Barnes (Bo Jenkins), Wayne Heffley (Grub), Ross Elliott (Desk Deputy), James Doohan (Deputy #1), John Dennis (Deputy #2).

Prolog. *If you are a fugitive, you travel a lot, most often by hitching a ride with a stranger. And always you ask yourself, "Who is he? What kind of man hides behind that face?"*

Synopsis. In an unlikely turn of events, Kimble finds himself protected by the police after a marshal mistakes him for Leonard Hull, an important government witness scheduled to testify against a big-time racketeer.

Epilog. *For a man named Blackburn, justice will be done. But for Richard Kimble, that day has not yet come. And so he moves on, searching.*

Writer Philip Saltzman nearly became associate producer of *The Fugitive*. "I had a meeting with Quinn Martin during the second season, and he said that Alan Armer was leaving the show, and was to become his personal assistant, and that George Eckstein, who was associate producer, was going to move up to producer," he recalled. "He asked would I come in and be story editor, or associate producer. I said, 'Wonderful, I love the idea of working on the show.' That was on Friday. On Monday, the deal fell apart! My agent told me because Alan Armer decided not to become the assistant, he wanted to stay with the show. He then remained with the show, and the job dried up."

Saltzman eventually began producing several of Martin's programs, beginning with *Twelve O'Clock High*, then later the long-running series *The F.B.I.* and *Barnaby Jones*.

Episode 57
RUNNER IN THE DARK

Original Airdate: March 30, 1965

Written by Robert Guy Barrows. Directed by Alexander Singer.

Guest Cast: Ed Begley (Dan Brady), Richard Anderson (Barney Vilattic), Diana Van Der Vlis (Claire Whittaker), Peter Haskell (Bob Sterne), Nellie Burt (Mrs. Ferguson), Vaughn Taylor (Mayor Penfield), Bing Russell (Sgt. Eggins), Irene Tedrow (Maude Keller), Don Lamond (TV Emcee), Don Ross (Officer).

Prolog. *No job for Richard Kimble is anything more than a means to an end: survival. The dignity of his profession is a memory, and a hope. He can never know what unexpected shift of fate will send him running again, perhaps in pursuit of the one-armed man, perhaps in flight for his life.*

Synopsis. Kimble ("Tom Burns"/"Phil Mead") seeks refuge at a home for the blind. One of the residents is Dan Brady, a veteran lawman who remains bitter for having lost his position as police chief to the more educated, but less experienced, Barney Vilattic.

When Dan suspects Kimble's true identity, he sees an opportunity to reclaim his former job.

Epilog. *Free once again, with the rootless freedom of the hunted, anonymous in a world in which he must dread the sound of his own name, Richard Kimble continues running, searching—a fugitive.*

Although he has played many comedy and musical roles (*Mama, Hit the Deck*), Richard Anderson is most often associated with playing authoritative roles, such as government agent Oscar Goldman on *The Six Million Dollar Man.* "I don't think you go too far away, in a sense, from how they perceive you," he said. "I think, possibly, when I got into a part where I had an opportunity to play a commander, or an authoritarian, or person in charge, there's probably a side of me that's easy to do."

Anderson believes his ability to play such characters is more a behavioral facet than an acting facet. "I think a side of you that maybe you do more naturally tends to lead you into a lot of work," he said. "It's called 'behavioral' acting. A perfect example of that was Humphrey Bogart—he was a behavioral actor. The parts he played most of his life were things that were out of his behavior."

Could the same be said of David Janssen? "It's hard to know," said Anderson. "I knew David fairly well. I don't know where his schooling was, but he was a well educated man, from books. It cured his mind to read a great deal: I could see some of that when I worked with him...David was two people. First of all, he had a delightful sense of humor. Witty. And I think a natively bright man. On the other hand, we had this very dark and neurotic character that he played, and how much that was close to him, I don't know. But I suspect there must have been a lot of pain there in his life, and anger, although I don't know too much about his early life. But that is the extent of what I surmise about David. I liked David. I liked him. He was a very, very nice guy, which is probably the highest compliment you can pay anybody. He's a nice guy."

Given the amount of thought and care that Janssen put into his performances, not only on *The Fugitive* but in his other roles, he would have to be considered a "behavioral" actor. "David Janssen was real; Richard Kimble was real," added assistant director Bob Rubin. "David had been through personal and career adversity; Kimble was *living* adversity. In David's past there was success as a talented actor; Kimble had enjoyed success as a talented doctor. Then, while on the run, Kimble lived like a homeless person does today—struggling day to day to survive. David likewise had been up and down—he had been broke and he had prospered—more than once (before and after his hit *Richard Diamond* series). David, like all successful people, knew what it's like to fail, to be down and out—that's why he remained so self-effacing about his celebrity, even though *The Fugitive* had propelled him into TV superstardom and into a household name.

"As far as playing Richard Kimble was concerned, David knew there was a part of his diverse past that he could directly draw from as he continued to build, develop, mature, and play the character. David Janssen became Richard Kimble.

"One of the messages of *The Fugitive* is that Kimble *never* gives up hope that he'll succeed (in clearing himself), even though the odds are overwhelmingly against him. David Janssen knew what 'getting up off the floor' really meant."

Episode 58

A.P.B.

Original Airdate: April 6, 1965

Written by Dan Ullman. Directed by William D. Gordon.

Guest Cast: Paul Richards (Neil Pinkerton), Lou Antonio (Matt Mooney), Shirley Knight (Mona Ross), Fred Beir (Lt. Peterson), Virginia Gregg (Mrs. Ross), Claudia Bryar (Housekeeper), Hugh Sanders (Sheriff), Jim Nusser (Smiley), Hal Riddle (Dispatcher).

Prolog. *One community appears much like any other to a man who travels a lot. To Richard Kimble, fugitive, some are friendlier than others, some are more colorful. But they all have one thing in common: danger.*

Synopsis. Kimble ("Ed Morris") hops a freight train and stumbles onto a trio of escaped convicts. One of the prisoners dies from gunshot wounds, while another—a professional killer named Pinkerton—forces Kimble to treat him. The convicts continue to hold Kimble hostage as a safeguard against police, then take over the home of a young woman and her mother.

Epilog. *As a doctor, Richard Kimble was sworn to the preservation of human life. Now, years later, as he travels the lonely path from city to city and state to state, the life he is searching to save is his own.*

"One of the exciting parts of making *The Fugitive* was all the stunt work," noted assistant director Bob Rubin. "So many dozens of stunt men and stunt women were resourceful in helping us stage *and* execute the high-speed chases, fist fights, or just conveniently hopping off or on the nearby moving train. Our production staff, of course, always worked to anticipate and/or prevent *any* kind of accident from happening to *anyone*—the cast, the crew, or simply by-standers—on the set inside the studio, or outside on location.

"But, let's face it...if something serious were to happen to David Janssen...we were all out of work. Thus, we did our best to protect David from any potential on-camera risk-taking by utilizing one of several of the best Hollywood stunt men or trade (double) David in any of the dangerous 'messes he had gotten himself into.'   Guys like Bill Hickman, Troy Melton, Fred Stromsoe, Glen Wilder, Dick Dial, and Carey Loftin did a great job performing dangerous stunts for David. Whenever you view any of the 120 episodes, it is virtually impossible to discern that wasn't *really* David driving at 95 miles-an-hour on that mountain road."

Rubin also pointed out another set of people whose important contribution to the entire production are often overlooked. "Each season, we used hundreds of background atmosphere players in the shows," he said. "These men and women (known as 'extras') who perform the non-speaking parts certainly always enhanced the viewers' believability of the overall scene. On camera, although often unnoticed (as individuals), they are usually hard at work in the background of the scene. Whether tourists exiting the hotel lobby in 'The Chinese Sunset;' carnival patrons having fun in 'Approach with Care;' or visitors to the L.A. Zoo in Part One of 'The Judgment'—they (thanklessly) make quite a contribution.

"Also, while each shot is being lighted under the guidance of the D.P. (director of photography), working with the lighting director (chief electrician, or 'gaffer'), the key grip, and their people...we utilized another type of 'extra' called a stand-in. These are women and men who are paid to watch the actors rehearse their parts; then they relieve the actors and 'stand in' the actors' position while the lighting process takes place. Stand-ins are used so that the actors can take advantage of this 'down time' to have their make-up touched up, or review the dialogue with each other or with the director, until the D.P. informs the assistant director to bring in the director and the 'real' actors... called the 'first team'...for the final rehearsals before actually filming. Several key and valuable stand-ins worked on *The Fugitive*, saving the cast a lot of time so that they, too, could be even better. Reliable folks like Buddy Mason, Virginia Kennedy, Carol Byrd, and Joe D'Angelo worked very hard at this. David Greene and Jim Crowell both 'stood in' for David and 'stunt-doubled' him several times, as well.

"The stunt doubles, the stand-ins, and the extras were all part of the great team that Quinn Martin had assembled, directly and indirectly, to score touchdowns every Tuesday night at 10 o'clock."

Episode 59

THE OLD MAN PICKED A LEMON

Original Airdate: April 13, 1965

Written by Jack Turley. Directed by Alexander Singer.

Guest Cast: Celeste Holm (Flo Hagerman), Ben Piazza (Blaine Hagerman), Michael Davis (Paco Flores), Rodolfo Hoyos (Raphael Flores), Jean Hale (Lisa), Jan Shutan (Lois), Armand Alzamora (Ernesto), Rafael Lopez (Pedro), Rico Alaniz (Carlos), Byron Morrow (Leland Hagerman), John Clarke (Bill), Lawrence Montaigne (Sheriff), Warren Parker (Minister), Penny Kunard (Marjorie).

Prolog. *Encinas County, California. For the common laborer, a haven of perpetual harvest. For Richard Kimble, a sanctuary. But here on this fertile land, where the miracle of life stands in rich abundance, Kimble has watched the hand of death reach out and twist fate to its own purpose.*

Synopsis. Kimble's ("Jim Wallace") refuge on a California citrus ranch is disrupted when the owner suddenly dies and his sadistic son arrives to stake his claim.

Epilog. *Death brings with it a jolting shock of reality. No man can live or die in this world without in some way affecting the lives of others. Richard Kimble flees the aftermath of tragedy, a tragedy of which he was not the maker, of which he will share the guilt. This is the burden of a fugitive.*

John Conwell discussed the process of selecting the guest stars for *The Fugitive*. "In those days, it was very easy, because it was just between a couple of us, and the networks were not involved in any way in the casting," he said. "We could do what we wanted, and I think we did a better job of it than years later, when the networks began to intervene."

While there were some instances where a character was written with a particular performer in mind (Ed Begley in "Man in a Chariot," Suzanne Pleshette in "World's End"), for the most part the casting decisions reflected whichever actor was right for the part and available for the episode. Conwell usually leaned toward those leads who worked on the East Coast. "In those days, a lot of the really talented and wonderful actors came from New York," he said. "I had been an actor myself and I knew and had acted with many of these people, so that when I went into the production end, I quite often hired them because I knew they were terrific, and I knew that they were right for the part.... Brenda Vaccaro was somebody who came from New York; Lou Antonio, who now is a big director; Burt Brinckerhoff, whom I had acted with in New York, and now is a director; Jack Weston; Celeste Holm; these are just some New York names."

The Fugitive owes part of its success to Conwell's excellent casting decisions, according to George Eckstein. "John was a supreme casting director, and knew the show as well as anybody," he said. "The casting was excellent, particularly the secondary parts. It was very solid throughout, and it gave the series that heightened sense of reality."

FUGE FAMILIAR FACES

Celeste Holm would return for the fourth season's "Concrete Evidence." Ben Piazza *(Love of Life)* would play an equally despicable character in "Double Jeopardy," a 1975 episode of *Harry O* that reunited David Janssen with two other *Fugitive* guest stars: Will Kuluva and Kurt Russell.

Episode 60

LAST SECOND OF A BIG DREAM

Original Airdate: April 20, 1965

Teleplay by George Eckstein. Story by John Eastman.
Directed by Robert Butler.

Guest Cast: Steve Forrest (Barry Craft), Laurence Naismith (Major Fielding), Milton Selzer (Lou Cartwright), Robert Karnes (Sheriff Ralls), Marlowe Jensen (Al), James Sikking (Bert), Don Spruance (Desk Deputy), Ed Long (Bus Driver).

Prolog. *Fifty-five miles outside of Lincoln, Nebraska, wild animals in cages bring the curious to Major Alan Fielding's Jungleland. Richard Kimble, wearing the name Nick Peters, has found work here. The job began this morning. It is destined to end tonight.*

Synopsis. Kimble finds work tending to the animals at Major Alan Fielding's Jungleland. But he soon becomes the main attraction after Barry Craft, Major Fielding's scheming partner, stumbles onto his true identity.

Epilog. *One man's dream ends, while another man's nightmare merely continues. Richard Kimble is free. He has room—for tonight.*

People from all walks of life used to submit story ideas for the series, according to producer Alan Armer. "We used to receive scripts from little old ladies and high school students and grocery clerks from all over the country," he said. Although Armer and George Eckstein appreciated the input from the viewers, they weren't able to use many of these ideas. However, "Last Second of a Big Dream" was an exception. "This episode came from a man in Michigan [John Eastman]," Armer said. "He worked for an advertising agency in Michigan. We asked him to come out. We liked his ideas, and did some rewrites with him. That was one of the few story ideas that ever came to us from the outside."

The episode was partially filmed at the TV animal compound known as Jungleland in Thousand Oaks, California.

EPILOG: SECOND SEASON

T*he Fugitive* ended its second season as the number five-rated program on television, with an overall Nielsen rating for the season of 27.9. Translated, nearly one out of every three American households owning TV sets that year tuned in every Tuesday night to watch *The Fugitive*.

A rating is one of two measurements used to determine a TV show's popularity; the other is known as a "share." The difference between ratings and shares: a rating reflects the percentage of "TV households" (that is, household with television sets) that are watching a particular program, while a share reflects the percentage of TV households whose sets are in use while the program is on. If you asked ten people who owned TVs if they watched *The Fugitive* last Tuesday night, and five said yes, you would register a rating of five out of ten, or 50%. But if two of those five people watched the program at a third person's house, that means only eight of those ten TV sets were actually in use at 10 o'clock. If three of those eight sets were tuned in to *The Fugitive*, you would have a three out of eight share, or 37.5%. While the ratings figure may sometimes look more impressive, the share is generally considered the more reliable measurement.

Although an established hit going into the season, *The Fugitive* benefitted from the popularity of *Peyton Place*, the program that immediately preceded it. *Peyton Place* aired twice a week on ABC (Tuesdays and Thursdays at 9:30 p.m.), and the Tuesday night segment ranked 20th among the Top 25 programs, with an average rating of 24.6. (The Thursday night show did even better—it scored 9th, with a 26.4 rating.)

The Fugitive's incredible popularity was not confined to the United States—the program was broadcast in 70 countries worldwide. David Janssen was recognized as an international symbol of hope and freedom; fittingly, the Hollywood Foreign Press Associated in 1965 awarded Janssen the Golden Globe Award for Best Male Television Star of the year.

Kimble confronts his wife's killer, the "one-armed man" played by Bill Raisch.

Leslie Nielsen and Carol Rossen in *Tiger Left, Tiger Right.* Below, Carol Rossen today.

THIRD SEASON, 1965-1966

PRODUCTION CREDITS

Starring David Janssen as The Fugitive
Also Starring Barry Morse as Lt. Philip Gerard
and William Conrad as The Narrator

Executive Producer: Quinn Martin
Created by Roy Huggins
Producer: Alan A. Armer
Associate Producer: William B. Gordon, George Eckstein
Assistant to the Executive Producer: Arthur Fellows

Director of Photography: Meredith Nicholson, A.S.C.
Production Manager: Fred Ahern
Music: Peter Rugolo
Assistant to the Producer: John Conwell
Post Production Supervisor: John Elizalde
Location Manager: Bud Brill
Art Director: James Vance
Film Editors: Robert L. Swanson, Marston Fay
Assistant Directors: Lloyd Allen, Wes McAfee, Jack Barry, Lou Place, Robert Rubin, Russ Haverick
Property Masters: Irving Sindler, Don Smith
Casting: Meryl Abeles
Chief Electrician: Vaughn Ashen
2nd Camera Operator: Joe August Jr.
Special Photographic Effects: Howard Anderson
Special Effects: Si Simonson
Music Supervisor: Ken Wilhoit
Set Decorator: Sandy Grace
Makeup Artist: Jack Wilson
Costume Supervisor: Elmer Ellsworth
Costumers: Stephen Lodge, Karlice Hinson
Hairdresser: Lynn Burke
Assistant Film Editors: Harry Kaye, Tom Neff Jr.
Script Supervisors: Richard Chaffee, Kenneth Gilbert
Editorial Consultant/2nd Unit Director: Carl Barth
Sound: The Goldwyn Studio
Production Mixer: John Kean
Sound Editors: Chuck Overhulser, Chuck Perry, Eddie Campbell
Re-Recording: Clem Portman

PROLOG: THIRD SEASON

A banner year for *The Fugitive.* "The third year, we won a number of awards—an Emmy Award for Best Dramatic Series, and several others," said Alan Armer. "That's very gratifying."

Not only did the Television Academy bestow the Emmy, its highest honor, on *The Fugitive*, other producers began flattering the series by creating similar programs, each featuring a wandering protagonist who helps the people he encounters. The trend actually began in early 1964 with *Destry*, a western series with John Gavin as a loner who searches for the men who framed him for embezzlement. January 1965 saw the debut of *Branded*, another western about an Army captain dishonorably discharged after the Army mistakenly believed he abandoned his troops during an Indian attack—the captain (played perfectly by Chuck Connors) roams the country looking for a witness who can help him restore his honor.

By Fall 1965, three more similar series appeared on the networks: *The Man Called Shenandoah*, with Robert Horton as an amnesiac who searches for clues to his identity; Rod Serling's *The Loner*, featuring Lloyd Bridges as a disillusioned Union soldier who quits the Army after the Civil War; and *Run for Your Life*, created by Roy Huggins, starring Ben Gazzara as an attorney who travels the world helping people after learning he himself has only two years to live. Of these three series, only *Run for Your Life* caught on with the viewers—it enjoyed a successful three-season run.

Aside from a new associate producer (George Eckstein replaced William Gordon) and an occasional variation in format (in some episodes, the Narrator's prolog does not occur until several minutes into Act I), the only noticeable change in the third season is the disappearance of Police Captain Carpenter (Paul Birch), Gerard's commanding officer. No explanation was ever given for Carpenter's departure, and since the character was little more than a mouthpiece for two years (occasionally asking for the viewers' sake what Gerard really thought about Kimble), none was really required. However, Carpenter's presence did create the sense that Gerard couldn't just run around willy-nilly following up on every reported sighting of Richard Kimble: the lieutenant had to answer to someone. The elimination of the police captain in effect makes Gerard a more formidable opponent precisely because he no longer has to answer to a superior officer. "There was never any question: Gerard was the Indiana detective in charge of Richard Kimble. That was his only job," added novelist Stephen King.

The Fugitive hits its peak this season with the excellent two-parter "Landscape with Running Figures." The overall level of writing begins to decline slightly after this episode. The downward spiral continued with the departures of Armer and George Eckstein at the end of this season, although the writing is resuscitated after Eckstein returned during the fourth season.

Episode 61

WINGS OF AN ANGEL

Original Airdate: September 14, 1965

**Teleplay by Don Brinkley. Story by Don Brinkley and Otto King.
Directed by William A. Graham.**

Guest Cast: Lin McCarthy (Warden Maddox), Greg Morris (Mickey Deming), Lane Bradbury (Janet Kegler), Harold Gould (Dr. Willis), Sue Randall (Nurse Thompson), Ned Glass (Lee Troy), Val Avery (Jerry Kulik), Bing Russell (Officer #1), Ted Gehring (Fogarty), Joe Perry (Joe Robbins), Anne Loos (Miss Jay), Dave Armstrong (Officer #2), John Ward (Guard at Gate).

Prolog. *When a man has the law at his heels, every stranger becomes a potential enemy, every incident takes on sinister proportions. Dr. Richard Kimble has eluded his pursuers for more than two years. He knows that his freedom depends largely on luck, and that sooner or later that luck must run out.*

Synopsis. An escaped felon takes a young woman hostage in an attempt to ward off the police. Kimble disarms the man, but is stabbed during the struggle. The police transport Kimble ("George Eagen") to the nearest hospital—which happens to be on a prison ground. When two inmates recognize Kimble, they threaten to expose him unless he assists them in their drug smuggling scheme.

Epilog. *When a man is on the run, every stranger is a potential enemy, every friend a surprise. For Richard Kimble, the only real friend is the darkness, and the road that has no end.*

"The great advantage to doing *The Fugitive* was the fact that your hero was involved emotionally just by waking up in the morning," said Don Brinkley. "One of the problems with the shows, especially back in those days, was that all the heroes were cardboard characters. They never made any mistakes, they were never in trouble, and they were always right. One of the problems we had was getting them emotionally involved. That's why so many cop series have shows in which their sisters were raped, and their brothers were killed, and their cousins were embezzled, and that kind of thing. But with *The Fugitive*, you had a protagonist who woke up in the morning, and he was involved emotionally—he was in trouble just by being there! That gave the writer a great advantage, because he didn't have to go through all kinds of contrivances to build some emotional involvement for Kimble."

In "Wings of an Angel" Kimble must decide whether saving the lives of the men who are threatening him is more important than saving his own. "From time to time, you have to show that Kimble will do things that are against his moral values, simply because he has to survive," said Brinkley. "He didn't actually steal the morphine: he just broke the seal and transferred saline into the bottle..."

FUGE FLUBS...?

Greg Morris (Mickey), one year away from *Mission: Impossible*, figures in a small debate over an apparent flub that occurs in Act II. Mickey tells Kimble that he's not involved in the blackmail scheme because his parole hearing is pending. Because Morris was filmed with his back to the camera for most of the scene, part of his speech is muffled, so it sounds like one of his lines in this sequence begins, "Now, Dave, my parole hearing comes up in exactly two weeks..." But a closer hearing, and several rewinds of the VCR, indicates that Morris does not say "Now, Dave." He says, "Now, *dig*," which is in character with Mickey's hip lingo—Morris peppers a lot of his dialogue with phrases such as "dig it," "cats," etc.

Episode 62

MIDDLE OF THE HEAT WAVE

Original Airdate: September 21, 1965

Written by Robert Hamner. Directed by Alexander Singer.

Guest Cast: J.D. Cannon (Sheriff Todd Collison), Carol Rossen (Laurel Harper), Sarah Marshall (Sheila Pettie), John Lasell (Frank Pettie), Paul Comi (1st Deputy), James Doohan (Doctor), Mimi Dillard (Waitress), James Johnson (2nd Deputy).

Prolog. *Lake City, New York. A roadhouse hideaway outside of town. Music, a few drinks, and sometimes a momentary escape into a private world for just two people. For Richard Kimble, escape is always momentary, and two people are one two many in a private world already crowded with pursuers.*

Synopsis. Laurel Harper, distraught after Kimble ("Jim Owen") breaks off their affair, disappears into the night. The next day she is found on an abandoned road, unconscious and badly beaten. Her suspicious sister convinces the police to hold Kimble for questioning.

Epilog. *Another place, another memory to follow him, another escape through the night—always the way of a fugitive.*

Aside from the apprehension ABC executives initially had over Dr. Kimble's murder conviction, *The Fugitive* stayed clear of controversy during its network run. The pilot episode removed any doubts as to Kimble's character, while the series avoided any claims of subversiveness by affirming faith in the judicial system and improving the understanding of better law enforcement. Considering how quickly they had to create stories, producer Alan Armer and his writers were concerned more with the practical side of meeting a deadline with a quality script than with stirring any political feathers.

"Middle of the Heat Wave" contains one of the few instances of controversy in the series. Contemporary viewers watching this episode for the first time will probably be angered by Laurel's comments during the epilog about her assault. Without meaning to discourage any debate over the sexual politics in the episode, it should be noted that the resolution of the story, while considered passe by current standards, should be understood in the context of the networks' 1960s protectionist mentality faced as they were with the social revolution.

Laurel Harper's statement ("I led him on, 'til I decided time's up") essentially lets her brother-in-law Frank off the hook for the charge of rape and puts the onus on herself. While Laurel decided to pick up the first man she saw, she was acting out of the anger and hurt resulting from the breakup with Kimble. Blurred by emotion, she could not think clearly, and was thereby vulnerable until much too late. Frank's attack is doubly heinous because of its incestuous overtones. Certainly, if this story were written today, Frank would have been held accountable, and rightly so. Laurel may have "enticed" him, but she never consented (she decided "time's up"). A woman always maintains the right to say no.

However, it would be wrong to project any other controversy onto this episode because it was simply the product of another time. "Middle of the Heat Wave" was written during a more naive era of network television which considered certain topics taboo. Consider that the episode never uses the terms "rape" or "sexual assault" to describe what happened. The attack is inferred: after Kimble asks if Laurel suffered only cuts and bruises, the sheriff simply replies "I wish it were."

Carol Rossen, who is excellent as Laurel, agrees that the conclusion of "Middle of the Heat Wave" has to be understood in the context of network anxiety. "To tell you the truth, I thought it was a dopey ending at the time, but I was paid to say my words, not to cause trouble," the actress recalled. "So, I tried to put a character's twist on the words 'I led him on'—the explanation of an embittered woman commenting on the sexual attitudes of her world: a Barbie Doll mentality. I doubt that I was successful, but I gave it my best effort."

After watching the episode recently, Rossen thinks that the actors' interpretation of this story clearly indicated that the then-current network perceptions of women (embodied by such TV icons as Donna Stone and June Cleaver) were hangovers from the 1950s on their way out. "I watched my characterization of Laurel very carefully, and this girl was a very manipulated woman, but they picked me to play her," she said. "I was an actress with a very strong quality, I was always cast for that quality. So, clearly what they wanted from me was somebody who would give it a bite, instead of just playing an ingenue who 'kinda' got drunk and 'kinda' found herself in this terrible position. They didn't want a straight ingenue who projected 'What do you mean, you're leaving me? Oh my God, no!' and then unconsciously gets involved and says 'Oh! I led him on and oh my God!' That's not the way it's played."

Rossen's delivery of her final lines ("You either go to pieces or you grow up") bears this out. "I never did go to pieces, and I don't think anybody ever wanted anybody to think that she had, otherwise the director would not have allowed me to play it that way," she continued. "I was really trying to give it another twist, which was to say 'I'm stuck, dammit, you people! I'm stuck in this situation. I'm not going to rat on the guy. I'm not going to screw up my sister's life. I'm not going to do these things, but I'm mad.' And if you see the way I play it and you see the brevity of that—I whipped through those words. I wouldn't whip through anything unless I felt that doing so represented a point of view.

"I tried to give it the twist that she was well aware of the hypocrisy—that's even confirmed in the writing of the first scene that I have with David, where she says 'Oh, I've heard that stuff before.' It's not fully explored and they certainly only tip-toe through a challenge to that mentality. But it's there, and I was playing it, and if I wasn't inordinately successful, it was because there weren't enough words to support me."

Ironically, "Middle of the Heat Wave" is difficult to watch not because of its potent subject matter, but because it is incredibly slowly paced. Perhaps in order to appease the network's anxiety over the rape issue, the story in its final form has hardly any teeth at all. The episode suffers from slowly paced direction, a flat script, and a fourth act that makes little, if any, sense. Why would Laurel's sister even consider hiding Kimble after baiting him for three-quarters of the show? Although ultimately disappointing, "Heat Wave" is worth watching because of the efforts of the actors to deliver the necessary punch to the story. "Even J.D. Cannon in it endlessly uses the word 'honey,' and he uses it sardonically as an actor," Rossen pointed out. "I can hear him—I know J.D. That's not the way people talk unless they were trying to make a point. The epilog 'tack-on' was clearly for the network."

Episode 63

CRACK IN A CRYSTAL BALL

Original Airdate: September 28, 1965

Written by William Link and Richard Levinson. Directed by Walter Grauman.

Guest Cast: Larry Blyden (Sal Mitchell), Joanna Moore (Joan Mitchell), J. Pat O'Malley (Mr. McBride), Nellie Burt (Mrs. Daniels), Frank Maxwell (Lt. Bliss), Walter Brooke (Wilcox), John Crawford (Sergeant), Pitt Herbert (Motel Manager).

Prolog. *A highway has a life of its own. Each car brings a new face. And for Richard Kimble, working now in a midwestern gas station, the next might be the face of danger.*

Synopsis. After recognizing Kimble ("Joe Warren") at a nearby filling station, a phony mentalist hopes to cash in on some quick publicity. While his wife lures Kimble into a false meeting with the one-armed man at a park 200 miles away, he appears on television—and "predicts" Kimble's appearance at the same location.

Epilog. *An anonymous room, another town. For Richard Kimble, the day has ended. But there's little time to rest. Tomorrow, his search continues.*

Trust and honesty are the major themes in this second contribution from the writing and producing team of William Link and Richard Levinson (*Columbo, Murder, She Wrote, Murder by Natural Causes, The Execution of Private Slovik*). Always vulnerable to betrayal, Kimble never reveals anything about himself to people until he feels he can trust them. The Fugitive admits that he has "lost the habit" of accepting people at face value, but he must remain cautious: one slip could mean the end. Although he never lets up in his suspicion of Joan, Kimble has to trust her because she may be telling the truth. Although Kimble was correct to suspect her, at least Joan has a conscience—she offered Kimble a way out ("This has been no joy ride for me, either"). Levinson and Link also wrote the second season episode "Tiger Left, Tiger Right."

Episode 64

TRIAL BY FIRE

Original Airdate: October 5, 1965

Written by Philip Saltzman. Directed by Alexander Singer.

Guest Cast: Charles Aidman (Capt. James Eckhardt), Frank Aletter (Burton Green), Jacqueline Scott (Donna Taft), Tommy Rettig (J.J. Eckhardt), Marion Ross (Marion Eckhardt), Booth Colman (Les Donaldson), Chris Alcaide (Lt. Holvak), Ed Deemer (Sgt. Rainey), John Durren (Eddie Bragg).

Prolog. *Occasionally, a fugitive must make contact with reality, to escape the loneliness of flight, to preserve his sanity. For Richard Kimble, contact with reality consists of an occasional telephone conversation with his sister. Tonight's call, however, could mean a great deal more.*

Synopsis. Donna summons Kimble home with a possible break in the case: a letter from James Eckhardt, an Army captain who also saw the one-armed man on the night of Helen's murder. Eckhardt's story appears solid enough to clear Kimble, until a tip from a prison inmate who once sold the captain morphine enables Gerard to discredit his testimony.

Epilog. *A witness has seen the one-armed man. Richard Kimble has had confirmed what he had almost begun to doubt himself. And a phantom seen by two men can be seen again.*

Once again, a small part of Kimble's story is legitimized—a witness has seen the one-armed man. "I remember saying, 'What would happen if we ever came to trial, and the Fugitive found a witness—someone showed up who actually saw the one-armed man, and knows the Fugitive didn't do it,'" said Philip Saltzman. "So, working from that premise, I had the sister call Kimble and say, 'My God, we found a witness, he's an Army officer, and he's great, and you've got to come in for a hearing'—I did a lot of research on the writ of corum novis—and Kimble had to come in.

"And Gerard's nature was so distrustful: he had to make sure that the witness was truly a witness. So, here you have this nice guy [played by Charles Aidman] and, of course, what you find out is that the officer, who had been wounded, was undergoing treatment and was taking drugs at the time because of the pain—he was taking some kind of opium drug. So he could be discredited on the stand. And the Fugitive has to find that out. And here you have, at the last moment, Gerard's waiting, the press is waiting, and everybody's waiting, and the bus comes into town, and it empties, and he's not on the bus, because he knew the witness wouldn't work, and he has to go on. He's running again." (Of course, in "The Judgment," the Fugitive uncovers an even better witness: the man who actually saw Johnson murder Helen Kimble.)

While Captain Eckhardt is not without skeletons, his testimony is solid enough to present a reasonable doubt. Gerard knows this. But unless he clings to the possibility that the jury would perceive the captain as a "junkie," the lieutenant's all-consuming faith in "the law" would crumble. "If you go back to Javert, in *Les Miserables*, he commits suicide because his whole reason for living is to track down Valjean," said Saltzman. "When he finally finds him, Javert realizes that his life has been exempt of anything else. Likewise, Gerard's got nothing else to live for. He has to believe that Eckhardt is guilty, otherwise he has wasted all these years, because the captain's testimony could clear Kimble, which in turn would mean that the law was wrong."

"Trial by Fire" also marks Jacqueline Scott's second appearance as the Fugitive's sister. "I just wrote Donna the way I saw her, without having to change her too much," said Saltzman. "And I knew Jackie, too, which helped. When I was a young bachelor living in Hollywood, she and her husband were friends of another writer I knew, and we used to see Jackie and her husband a lot, so I knew what she sounded like and what she looked like—which helps in the writing of a character. It's much more honest than when you're writing without a cast in mind. You pick a figure, and the figure emerges when you have an actor to match that."

Writing for Donna requires understanding the moral dilemma she takes on by supporting her brother. "What you take into consideration is the relationship between the brother and the sister, and what is at stake for Donna by supporting Kimble," added Don Brinkley, who wrote the episode "Running Scared." "She has a family to deal with, and there's a certain amount of risk involved there. There's a dilemma that she's undergoing—the fact that by merely supporting her brother, she's putting herself and her family in some form of jeopardy. And yet, she has this love for her brother, and feels dutybound to help him.

"You have to consider all those things, and deal with them—that's what makes the character interesting. If it were just a cut and dry situation where she was either a good guy or a bad guy ('Yes, I'll help you/No, I won't help you'), she's a very dull character. But the fact that she has to deal with some very specific moral dilemmas makes her more interesting."

FUGE FAMILIAR FACES

Marion Ross (Marion) is also known as Mrs. Cunningham on *Happy Days* and Sophie on *Brooklyn Bridge*.

Episode 65

CONSPRACY OF SILENCE

Original Airdate: October 12, 1965

Written by William D. Gordon. Directed by Jerry Hopper.

Guest Cast: Donald Harron (Major Christopher Beck), Malachi Throne (David Jones), Bill Gunn (Avery), Wesley Addy (Price), Robert Cornthwaite (Pickett), Mort Mills (Murchison), Byron Morrow (General Orvan Fredericks), Lawrence Montaigne (Section Leader), Dick Wilson (Berger).

Prolog. *High Desert Inn, 62 miles from the town of Reeseburg, Arizona. It's a vacation spot for the very rich. Tycoons and statesmen come to spend long weekends here, relaxing incommunicado. For one man, depleted by the terrible pace of running for his life, it is a vital oasis, a needed place to pause and recruit his energy—and hope.*

Synopsis. Kimble ("Fred Tate") is unaware that the desert resort where he works is really a secret government test site for chemical weapons. He is then mistaken for a spy by Major Beck, the head of the project. When several project members (including the staff physician) suffer from the resulting exposure of a chemical explosion, Kimble is pressed into service—unaware that Beck still plans to turn him in.

Epilog. *All secrets are safe with this man, because none is as deadly to him as his own. His secret is that he is Richard Kimble.*

Robert Cornthwaite (Pickett) portrayed the mad scientist in the original motion picture version of *The Thing* (1950). Dick Wilson, who played Berger—the bartender who drank too much—often played an inebriate on *Bewitched*; he was also known as Mr. Whipple in the "Please don't squeeze the Charmin" TV-ad campaign.

FUGE FACTS

The hotel in "Conspiracy of Silence" was originally known as the White Prairie Lodge, and the chemical company Banhauser-Lister.

Episode 66

THREE CHEERS FOR LITTLE BOY BLUE

Original Airdate: October 19, 1965

Teleplay by Chester Krumholz and Harry Kronman. Story by Chester Krumholz. Directed by Walter Grauman.

Guest Cast: Richard Anderson (George Forster), Edward Asner (Roy Malinek), Fay Spain (Mona Keel), Milton Selzer (Ben Willoughby), Vaughn Taylor (Arvin Keel), Doris Singleton (Janet Willoughby), DeForest Kelley (Charlie), Amy Douglas (Aunt), Jason Wingreen (Jack), Byron Foulger (Clerk), Woodrow Parfrey (Mort Graham).

Prolog. *He used to be a doctor of medicine. He's a chauffeur now, driving his employer home to the small midwestern town where he was born. Home: for the man at the wheel, it is only a word, because there is no home for him. Not now, because he's Richard Kimble, a fugitive.*

Synopsis. Kimble ("Tom Nash") chauffeurs George Forster, a successful contractor who returns to his midwestern hometown with big plans for the community. While the homecoming is greeted by overall apathy and resentment, Kimble discovers that one of the townspeople is threatening to kill George.

Epilog. *Darkness and silence and flight into fear. Richard Kimble has made this journey before. He will make it again. Until he proves his innocence, he remains a fugitive.*

Richard Anderson particularly enjoyed this episode. "Well, you can't go home again," he said, alluding to Thomas Wolfe. "No matter how you try to go back there and reacquaint yourself, you can't, because the people envision you differently, and you're the same when you go back, but the town's not. I liked this episode because that was quite a literate point of view, what happens about going back. You can't go back, and you can't live in yesterday. That's why that script interested me."

Episode 67

ALL THE SCARED RABBITS

Original Airdate: October 26, 1965

Teleplay by William Bast and Norman Lessing. Story by William Bast. Directed by Robert Butler.

Guest Cast: Suzanne Pleshette (Peggy Franklin), R.G. Armstrong (Marshal Matt Peters), Liam Sullivan (Dean Franklin), Debi Storm (Nancy Franklin), Nancy Rennick (Ann), Robert Sorrells (Deputy), Meg Wyllie (Mrs. White), Garry Walberg (Lt. Wilson), Steven Bell (Mechanic), Edward Faulkner (Sheriff), Susan Davis (Mona), Hal Lynch (Sergeant).

Prolog. *The ad in the newspaper reads "Wanted: Someone to drive." For a fugitive anxious to move on, it is apparently an ideal answer. Apparently.*

Synopsis. Kimble ("Joe Taft") is hired to drive Peggy Franklin and her daughter Nancy to California. Kimble doesn't realize that Peggy has abducted Nancy from her ex-husband, pathologist Dean Franklin. Nancy innocently removes a rabbit from Dean's research laboratory— but the rabbit has meningitis. When Nancy contracts the sickness, Kimble must risk his freedom in order to save her.

Epilog. *For a few moments, Richard Kimble became a doctor again, and memories were stirred of another time, and another world. But this is now, and he is again a fugitive searching for the end of a perilous road.*

The onscreen electricity generated by Suzanne Pleshette and David Janssen is the highlight of the outstanding episode "All the Scared Rabbits." The actors' first scene together in Act I particularly sparkles.

"I'd known David since I was a kid, and aside from being friends who loved each other deeply, we also had the same approach to work," said Pleshette. "We were always on the same wave length, and the ease with which we worked came out of respecting and admiring each other, as actors and as friends.

"David had the ability to be a great comedic leading man, although he never was able to display that ability on *The Fugitive* because of the nature of that show. David's skills as a comedic actor were excellent—on a par with a Cary Grant. In fact, I once said to David, 'You really ought to do a segment like *Arsenic and Old Lace*,'- -a light comedy where Dr. Kimble would find himself in jeopardy because of some oddball character's crime. David had the ability to do such a thing (which he displayed in other projects). But Quinn wouldn't allow him to do anything like that on *The Fugitive*, because the format of that show would not allow for a comic episode."

Pleshette added that Janssen had always set the tone for an extremely professional and exceptionally pleasant working environment on *The Fugitive*. "David was a gentleman, and he was always very concerned about the people he worked with," she said. "He treated everyone with respect—the staff, the crew, and the actors. That was his nature."

Assistant director Bob Rubin concurs. "Inside, David was shy; but he was real and he liked people," Rubin said. "When he talked to you, he looked you in the eye—no matter how little or how much clout you had. If David saw you on the street or on the studio lot, he'd stop you and say 'Hi.' He was open to chatting with you—whether you were a guest star of the caliber of Suzanne Pleshette or Melvyn Douglas; the newest crew member; or an actor with a one-day/one-line part. You were a person to him."

FUGE FACTS

Originally entitled "Wanted: Someone to Drive," this episode ties in several *Fugitive* themes: Kimble's affinity for animals (he's very much "a scared rabbit on the run"); his rapport with children (he cares for Nancy as if she were his own); his humanity (he buries the rabbit so as not to expose other animals or people to the meningitis); and the ideal of a legal system tempered with compassion (the marshal grants Kimble his freedom after the Fugitive saves Nancy's life).

Episode 68

AN APPLE A DAY

Original Airdate: November 2, 1965

Written by Dan Ullman. Directed by Ralph Senensky.

Guest Cast: Arthur O'Connell (Josephus Adams), Sheree North (Marianne Adams), Kim Darby (Sharon Wolfe), Walter Baldwin (Mr. Weaver), Amzie Strickland (Mrs. Crandall), Bill Quinn (Dr. Olner), Gene Darfler (Sheriff), Marlowe Jensen (Officer).

Prolog. *Briar County, Colorado, where a man runs in desperation before the guns and dogs of a sheriff's posse closing in for the kill. A move in the wrong direction, a broken stride, a waste of precious seconds in looking back—these are what can cost Richard Kimble his life.*

Synopsis. Dr. Kimble ("Ed Curtis") clashes with Josephus Adams, a country doctor who treats his patients with little more than a dose of honey and a reassuring word. The Fugitive intervenes after an elderly woman dies from a protracted bronchial infection. Meanwhile, Adams' wife stumbles onto Kimble's secret and tries to use that to her advantage.

Epilog. *Richard Kimble moves on again, searching for a day when there will be an end to running.*

As the creative (yet pragmatic) bridge between the producer, the director, the shooting crew, the production office, and the on-camera talent, the assistant director on a film or TV show has a unique perspective. The "A.D." is both a leader responsible for overseeing the various facets of day-to-day production, and a strategic insider whose knowledge of the entire operation leads to ideas that will make an already good production even better.

"I worked with a lot of seasoned pros on *The Fugitive*—people like Lou Place, Lloyd Allen, and Phil Cook," said A.D. Bob Rubin. "They were like big brothers to me (I was only 23 when I joined QM Productions)—they taught me a lot of that stuff you'd never learn in school. And our production head, Fred Ahern, was well-known and well-respected throughout the motion picture industry. Fred had worked closely and extensively with some of the legends of the film world—people like director Alfred Hitchcock and producer David O. Selznick."

Rubin worked very closely with David Janssen. "We developed a trust, a friendship—a personal friendship, in addition to a work relationship—throughout the last two seasons of the show, as well as beyond the show," he recalled. "As far as the show was concerned, David became very open to me; we spent endless hours rapping. I drove out with him to every location, so we could talk. We discussed certain concerns—things he liked or didn't; people he cared about and didn't; where he was and wanted to be. I was quite flattered that he had taken me into his confidence in the way he did. He knew that I would give him my best and an honest, non-judgmental response.

"David used me as a sounding board, maybe *before* he'd say some things publicly to people, or even to try to understand better why a certain director or actor had never been rehired. David and I discussed every script: what it was really about (to Richard Kimble at that stage in the series); where we were shooting and why; who the guest stars were; was Gerard or the one-armed man in the show; would he have any evenings off this week; how the other QM shows were doing, behind the scenes and ratings-wise; and on and on and on...

"David had allowed me access to him... to be able to interrupt him whether he was on the phone, had visitors from the network, or was meeting with his publicist (Frank Lieberman). I could 'get to him' and get an answer. Well before the end of the third season, David and I became good friends, and I was thus particularly able to help QM—the company—by becoming a kind of buffer for Quinn, the producers, and the production staff; whereby, if they wanted to get even more rewrites and changes to David, it would go through me."

FUGE FACTS

"An Apple a Day" was partially filmed at the White Oak Ranch, located in Malibu Canyon and owned by comedian Bob Hope.

Episodes 69 and 70

LANDSCAPE WITH RUNNING FIGURES (Two-parter)

Original Airdates: November 16 and 23, 1965

Written by Anthony Wilson. Directed by Walter Grauman.

Guest Cast: Barbara Rush (Marie Gerard), Herschel Bernardi (Capt. Ames), Jud Taylor (Sgt. Rainey), Arthur Franz (Bus Driver), Noam Pitlik (Salesman), Rodolfo Hoyos (Luis Bota), Bill Zuckert (Sergeant), Ronnie Dapo (Oldest Boy), Sy Prescott (Officer), Stuart Nisbet (Desk Clerk), John Clarke (Jarvis), Stephen Coit (Ticket Seller), Don Ross (Policeman), Adam Williams (Truck Driver), Robert Doyle (Tommy), Judith Norton (Joanie), Robert Biheller (Beavo), James Devine (Intern).

(Part One)

Prolog. *There is a point beyond which a man cannot push himself, a final defeat of the spirit that cannot be overcome. If it is to end for the running man, this is the way it will be. It is 2:00 a.m. in the city, and Richard Kimble, doctor of medicine, moves to the start of another working day. To those with no past and little future, the city only offers the most menial of labors, those designed to provide nothing more than day-to-day survival. But to Richard Kimble, kitchen helper in an all-night diner, survival for even a day has come to be enough.*

Synopsis. A physically and emotionally weary Kimble ("Steve Carver") commits a colossal mistake—he signs in for work under his real name. Although a co-worker helps Kimble slip away, the police alert Gerard, who cuts short his vacation so he can monitor the search—much to the dismay of his wife, Marie. The years of her husband's single-minded obsession with the Fugitive have finally taken their toll. Marie leaves Gerard, arranging for a bus ride home under her maiden name (Lindsay). Meanwhile, after hitching a ride from a trucker, Kimble ends up on the same bus. But the bus crashes, and Marie becomes a victim of hysterical blindness. Marie's cries for help snap Kimble out of his emotional doldrums. Kimble commandeers a truck and drives Marie to safety, neither party aware of who the other is.

Epilog. *In the city, the search for Richard Kimble goes on. But it is one more grim appointment that he will not keep. The relentless steel jaws will close on an empty trap. But for Richard Kimble, the Fates are preparing another appointment, at another time, at another place.*

The two-parter "Landscape with Running Figures" stands out for two reasons: (1) it offers a tremendous amount of insight into the Kimble and Gerard characters; and (2) it is, quite simply, the best episode of the series.

Lt. Gerard's obsession with capturing the Fugitive and his unyielding interpretation of his role as "instrument of the law" have been well established to this point in the series. The Kimble case represents a personal Humpty Dumpty which Gerard has determined to reassemble, regardless of the cost. The previous episodes which examine the effect of this obsession of Gerard's family ("Never Wave Goodbye," "Nemesis") leave the impression that Gerard's wife and son tolerate his behavior because they understand why the hunt for Richard Kimble is so important to him. They seem to accept the fact that, given the nature of Gerard's work, the family's personal life becomes secondary until he recaptures the Fugitive.

"Landscape with Running Figures" builds on this particular theme by focusing on the progressive strain Gerard's prolonged absences (and fruitless searches) have had on his family. While the lieutenant remains bent on capturing Dr. Kimble, Marie Gerard has reached her breaking point. She describes herself as "the losing end of a modern-day triangle," only she's lost her husband not to another woman but a man who's "never there." Gerard's obsession with Kimble has twisted her marriage, and Marie has clearly had enough. But she can't even leave the hotel without escaping the Fugitive. After checking out of her room, she sees Kimble's name emblazoned on an elaborate newspaper display—KIMBLE, KIMBLE, KIMBLE, KIMBLE, KIMBLE. Her breakdown and ensuing hysterical blindness were two accidents waiting to happen.

When Gerard last spoke about his obsession ("The End is But the Beginning"), he admitted it mostly as a point of concession during his duel with Aimee Rennick ("I'll find him, perhaps in spite of myself"). But in "Landscape with Running Figures," he's clearly torn, wavering between his concentration on the dragnet and his concern for Marie's safety. When he greets her in the hospital at the end of the story, Gerard discusses his fixation on Kimble explicitly (although he never uses the word "obsession"). The Kimble case is stuck so deeply in his throat that Gerard cannot swallow until the matter is cleared up. Equally clear is his love for Marie. Gerard sees his wife in a way very similar to Kimble's relationship with his sister Donna: a pillar of certainty in a life increasingly marked by uncertainty and near misses. Losing Marie would prove more devastating than never finding Kimble. "You're the only thing he hasn't touched, the only part of my life he can't ever get to," Gerard tells Marie. "If I lost that, there'd be nothing left but the thought of Kimble choking at me."

Barry Morse drew briefly on personal experience as he discussed the impact of the Kimble hunt on Gerard's family. "I think probably almost every job, to some degree, affects a man's family relationship, and the degree of his dedication to that job will affect the degree of the impact upon his family," he said. "Some jobs, of course, are more demanding than others. I know a bit about this because in our 54 years of marriage, Sydney [Morse's wife] and I have had to be separated a great deal, and there have been times when separations have put a great strain on our family relationship. It's not greatly different, in Gerard's case, that the impact of absences and the general stress that is generated by the nature of his job is bound to have an effect on his family."

The Fugitive reaches an important peak with "Landscape." While the series would continue to produce some excellent episodes the rest of the way ("Wife Killer," "Ill Wind," "The Judgment," to name a few), the overall quality of the writing declines noticeably over the course of the remaining 50 episodes. With the possible exception of Stanford Whitmore, no one knew *The Fugitive*, in terms of understanding the premise and the characters, better than Alan Armer and George Eckstein. Both men would leave the series at the end of the third season. It is no coincidence that the fourth season's writing suffered because of their absence, so much so that Quinn Martin convinced Eckstein to return to *The Fugitive* in the middle of the fourth year, specifically to help shape the scripts.

FUGE FACTS

Although Kimble has shown signs of despair in past episodes ("World's End," "The End is But the Beginning"), nothing compares to his emotional state in "Landscape with Running Figures." He has reached rock bottom. Even when he spoke wearily later in the series ("The Judgment"), Kimble seemed to have his wits about him. But in "Landscape," he is uncharacteristically careless (he logs in his real name), a sure indication that something is troubling him. In this respect, "Landscape" parallels another two-part episode, "Angels Travel on Lonely Roads." In both instances, "time stops" for Kimble after fate introduces him to a stranger on the road who helps him replenish his spirit.

(Part Two)

Prolog. *A police dragnet, a bus accident, and an ironic fate have brought together two people on a lonely country road. The woman, blinded in the accident, is unaware that the man beside her is Richard Kimble. And neither is aware that the other is fleeing from the obsession of Lt. Philip Gerard, hunter of the man, husband of the woman.*

Synopsis. After warding off three hoods, Kimble directs Marie to a nearby town that has been evacuated due to flood warnings. Finding shelter in an abandoned bar, they find comfort in each other's company—until Marie slowly discovers who her protector really is. Meanwhile, Gerard closes in on their location.

Epilog. *For a brief moment, time also stopped for Richard Kimble—and for a while it had been good to be able to stop and look back and find that there was something there. But now it is over. For the Fugitive, time has started again.*

Associate producer George Eckstein paid the late writer Anthony Wilson (*Lancer, Lost in Space*) one of the highest compliments possible. "Having worked on the show three out of the four years, and discounting my own episodes, only one first-draft script came in that we could have shot word for word, and that was Tony Wilson's show," he said. "That was a brilliant piece of work. In fact, in my whole experience in producing television, that was about the only first draft that could have been put in front of the camera and shot word for word. There were some very good episodes, but they didn't come in that ready to go. 'Landscape with Running Figures' was."

Unlike the previous two-part episodes, which lagged slightly in the second part, "Landscape" is a deft mixture of action, suspense and interpersonal drama that holds up for the entire two hours. Considering that the episode was originally written as a one-part show, this is all the more remarkable. "Tony Wilson came in with 84 pages, and they were beautiful," said Alan Armer. "It was a gorgeous script. George and I decided, rather than try to lop out 25 pages, to add another 30 pages and make it into a two-parter."

As a result, Wilson created several new scenes featuring a trio of teenaged degenerates—Beavo and company—who harass Kimble and Marie throughout Part Two. "When I said to Tony, 'Let's make it into a two-parter,' he was delighted because he'd be paid for two scripts instead of one," laughed Armer. "That whole set of characters appeared in the new, second part of 'Landscape with Running Figures.'" Wilson later wrote (and received an Emmy Award nomination for) "The Night That Panicked America" (1975), a TV-movie based on Orson Welles' famous 1938 radio broadcast, *War of the Worlds*.

FUGE FAMILIAR FACES

Barbara Rush turns in an outstanding performance as Marie Gerard. "Barbara was a real trooper in 'Landscape,'" recalled assistant director Bob Rubin. "She had an incredibly difficult, physical role to play, particularly in the second part of the show. She had to wear knee pads for those scenes where she had to crawl around. We filmed those scenes in the wee hours of the morning, and we shot take after take after take until it was perfect. But Barbara never complained. She just continued giving us that extra effort. She was fabulous on that show. I can't say enough about Barbara Rush as an actor and as a real pro."

Ironically, Rush was Martin's third choice for the role (behind Julie Harris and Hope Lange). When neither actress was available, David Janssen did some lobbying on behalf of his good friend Barbara Rush. "We let David cast that one, and he cast Barbara," according to Alan Armer.

Episode 71

SET FIRE TO A STRAW MAN

Original Airdate: November 30, 1965

Written by Jack Turley. Directed by Don Medford.

Guest Cast: Diana Hyland (Stella Savano), Edward Binns (George Savano), Joseph Campanella (Jesse Stangel), Clint Howard (Johnny), Kelly Thordsen (Sgt. Kelly), Shelley Morrison (Ginny), Lewis Charles (Max), Barbara Baldavin (Mickey), Wally Shannon (Waiter).

Prolog. *Tractor, New Jersey—a small industrial town where a passerby has summoned the police to a mugging in a dirty alley. But this senseless beating is about to take on far more significance to a man not even witness to it—a man named Richard Kimble.*

Synopsis. Kimble ("Chris Benson") reluctantly becomes involved with Stella Savano, the sister of George Savano, who runs the trucking company where Kimble now works. Stella is an emotionally disturbed woman with a dangerous attraction for Johnny, the adopted son of Jesse Stangel, Kimble's co-worker. The Fugitive learns that Stella is Johnny's mother—and that she believes that Kimble is the father.

Epilog. *For each of us, there is an occasional moment of fantasy, a search for a straw man of our own. But Richard Kimble can only hope that the memory of a face caught once in the glare of headlights is made of something other than straw.*

Joseph Campanella (Jesse) starred in *The Doctors and the Nurses*, the CBS medical drama that aired Tuesdays at 10:00 p.m. in 1964-65—until *The Fugitive* knocked it off the air. Campanella's lean, hard face has been a fixture on television in either guest star or regular series roles for nearly 40 years, in such programs as *Suspense*, *Mannix*, *The Lawyers*, *The Name of the Game*, *One Day at a Time* and *Dallas*.

Diana Hyland (Stella) also appeared in "When the Bough Breaks," "The Devil's Disciples," and "Dossier on a Diplomat." She later starred in *Peyton Place* and *Eight is Enough*, and won an Emmy Award for her role as John Travolta's mother in *The Boy in the Plastic Bubble* (1976). Hyland died in 1977.

Episode 72

STRANGER IN THE MIRROR

Original Airdate: December 7, 1965

Written by Don Brinkley. Directed by Joseph Sargent.

Guest Cast: William Shatner (Tony Burnell), Julie Sommars (Carole Burnell), Norman Fell (Lt. Green), Paul Bryar (Sgt. McKay), Jeff Burton (Berger), Tony Face (Benny), Kyle Johnson (Chuck).

Prolog. *For every acquaintance he makes, a man reveals a different face, a different identity. To the people of this midwestern city, this man is John Evans, itinerant laborer. To those who know him better, he is Dr. Richard Kimble, convicted murderer.*

Synopsis. Kimble is now the custodian for the Saturday Morning Club, a weekend camp run by Tony and Carole Burnell. Two police officers are found beaten to death. The police recruit Tony, a former cop (and one-time delinquent), to speak to the teenager whom the police suspect of the murders. But the real killer is Tony.

Epilog. *A man with a dozen names, a dozen identities, but none that he can claim as his own. Richard Kimble moves on, in search of justice, and the elusive privilege of answering to his rightful name.*

Writer Don Brinkley cites four reasons for *The Fugitive*'s success. "One, it was very well cast," he said. "I think the leading character was very, very sympathetic: he was the underdog who was fighting City Hall, and I think everybody could identify with that, certainly the ordinary TV viewer, sitting at home. Here's a man who's struggling for survival, against all kinds of odds, and somehow managing to make it from week to week. You could relate very easily to Janssen.

"Two, was the situation. I think that people related to the underdog aspect of the series. Three, it was very well produced." And the most important reason for *The Fugitive*'s success? "It happened to have a pretty good time slot!" chuckled Brinkley.

Episode 73

THE GOOD GUYS AND THE BAD GUYS

Original Airdate: December 14, 1965

Written by Don Brinkley. Directed by Alexander Singer.

Guest Cast: Earl Holliman (Charley Judd), Collin Wilcox (Laura McElvey), Bruce Dern (Hank), Michael Witney (Roy), Erik Holland (Wally).

Prolog. *In a civilized society, a network of laws protects man against his own brutality. But for Richard Kimble, living outside the law, the civilized world has become a jungle. His only protection is his animal instinct, his will to survive. But always there is the hunter, even here in Drover City, Montana.*

Synopsis. In Drover City, Montana, Kimble ("Bill Watkins") stumbles onto the annual "vigilante roundup," a carnival of sorts where the locals "hunt" down anybody who is not wearing "Western duds." After being "lassoed," Kimble is held "prisoner" in the cafeteria. Meanwhile, Gerard arrives and shows Kimble's picture to the town marshal, Charley Judd—who recognizes Kimble. But Charley thinks there's a reward out on the Fugitive (and wants to keep the money for himself), so he sends Gerard off on a false lead and has Kimble transported to a real jail.

Epilog. *Some men break the law, others are broken by it. But Richard Kimble continues his endless quest, pursued by the law he respects, a fugitive from the justice he seeks.*

Gerard's conversation with Charley Judd about the law (Act II) highlights "The Good Guys and the Bad Guys." Charley's humane interpretation of the law clashes with Gerard's code, which allows no room for doubt or emotion. Charley owes his career to the people of Drover, so he tends to give them the benefit of the doubt before he administers the law. "The way I look at it," Charley says, "most of the people who make the laws aren't exactly perfect. So I figure that the laws can't be too perfect, and maybe every once in a while they deserve to get broken."

Gerard naturally bristles at the sound of this, because in his view a police officer does not concern himself with making judgments: that is the responsibility of the judge and jury. But what Gerard finds most troubling about Charley's interpretation is its basic assumption that the law is fallible.

"I think that, if you really got into Gerard all the way, you'd find some deep, dark insecurities in the man," said Don Brinkley. "He's built his life according to the law. He's the kind of man who has to have the program laid out for him. He has to be told what's right and wrong; and having been told that, he'll accept it and he'll uphold it—to the death if necessary—because the law is that important.

"I think that Gerard is basically an insecure guy. What makes him secure is the gun on his hip and the fact that he feels he has the law on his side. This is what makes him strong: I represent the law, and the law represents me. Therefore, the law must be right, and anyone who challenges the law is challenging me."

Early in his conversation with Charley, Gerard reveals a perhaps unconscious respect and admiration for the Fugitive. He first describes Kimble as desperate, but then refers to him as clever, resourceful—and even courageous. "I think Gerard has great respect for Kimble," said Brinkley. "Over the years *The Fugitive* was on the air, it goes that way. It's almost like *The Old Man and the Sea*, or *Moby Dick*. They had respect." Kimble, in turn, explains Gerard's motivation to Charley ("He's dedicated") and in effect defends the lieutenant's integrity after Charley attacks it. "Maybe he thinks he's entitled [to a reward]—like you and your pension," he tells the marshal.

"The Good Guys and the Bad Guys" provides Barry Morse with a rare opportunity to inject humor into his role. Gerard absolutely loathes wearing the cowboy hat that Charley practically fastens onto his head. He tries to leave it behind on a couple of occasions, but Charley just won't let him. Morse is very funny in these scenes, as Gerard fights hard to maintain his dignity.

FUGE FACTS

Charley's comments about the law ("the people who make the laws aren't exactly perfect") brings to mind a key passage from Stanford Whitmore's pilot script: "Laws are made by men and carried out by men, and men are imperfect."

Episode 74

END OF THE LINE

Original Airdate: December 21, 1965

Written by James Menzies. Directed by William A. Graham.

Guest Cast: Andrew Prine (Neil Hollis), Barbara Dana (Betty Jo Unger), Crahan Denton (R.T. Unger), Richard Rout (Glenn), Len Wayland (Chief Kress), James McCallion (Sammy), Eddie Firestone (Taxi Driver), James Hong (Hee), Jon Lormer (1st Conductor), Ted Gehring (Truck Driver).

Prolog. *A man's image can be shaped by society's opinion of him. A fugitive must ask himself then, how long can a running man hold out against that opinion? How many miles, how many accusations before he becomes what society has labelled him?*

Synopsis. After losing his wallet, Kimble ("Bob Mossman") steals a wallet in order to pay his train fare. The wallet belongs to R.T. Unger, who owns the local dairy. Kimble finds work to repay his "debt," but Unger discovers the theft and reports Kimble to the police. After returning the money intact to Unger's daughter, Betty Jo, Kimble tries to earn train fare out of town. While at the dairy to deliver empty milk bottles, Kimble overhears a heated argument between Unger and Neil Hollis, the disreputable youth who fathered Betty Jo's child. Unger offers Neil $1,000 to leave town. When Neil demands the entire amount up front, the two men struggle. Kimble sees Neil kill Unger.

Epilog. *Some people run for exercise, some are professionals chasing a record, and still others run to live. Theirs is the longest race—if they can last until tomorrow, their reward is one more day of running.*

Originally entitled "Never Take the Milk Train," this episode answers the question "Whatever happened to Ray Kimble," the character played by Andrew Prine (Neil) in "Home is the Hunted." Ray not only missed the Fugitive's last family reunion ("Trial by Fire"), he never returned to the series. Kimble's father also appeared only once on-screen, but the series continued to refer to that character until "Running Scared," when Kimble learned that his father died. But Ray simply vanished from the scene. Perhaps once the Kimbles found out he was running amok in Florida (where this episode takes place), they disowned him.

Episode 75

WHEN THE WIND BLOWS

Original Airdate: December 28, 1965

Written by Betty Langdon. Directed by Ralph Senensky.

Guest Cast: Harry Townes (Russ Atkinson), Georgann Johnson (Lois Carter), Johnny Jensen (Kenny Carter), Larry Ward (Steve Jackson), Don Hanmer (Jake Wilkins), George Brenlin (Will), Gregory Mullavey (Carl Ritter), E.A. Nicholson (Truck Driver), Elmer Modlin (Postman), Don Saroyan (Officer).

Prolog. *For a fugitive, there is no rest from the past and no safety in the present. Even here, in the remote village of Small Groves, Wyoming, the most ordinary day may explode in his face. Rumors that Richard Kimble had been seen in the city of Casper have been relayed to every law enforcement agency in this corner of the state.*

Synopsis. In Wyoming, Kimble ("Jim McGuire") seeks refuge from the local constable at a hotel operated by a widow, who hires him as a handyman. He soon befriends the woman's son, a particularly sensitive young boy who protects him from the police.

Epilog. *For Richard Kimble, there is no sanctuary from the night wind. There is no cave in which to hide. But, occasionally, along the road, a fugitive will find a hand extended in trust, and the night wind will not seem so cold.*

Kimble recognizes that Kenny is a gifted child with a unique outlook on life. "Dead things" to Kenny are "things that don't do anything," such as clothes you can't wear anymore or toys you can no longer play with. He also possesses an acute sensitivity—he felt the fish screaming for air as it struggled on the ground. The boy senses his mother's apprehension about him ("Kenny's not like other kids"), so he retreats to his special place, the cave, where he finds protection from the way adults and other children mistake him. Not surprisingly, Kenny keeps other people away from the cave—until he meets Kimble, the first person who understood the boy's perspective. Kimble can also feel the screams of a fish struggling for air, because that plight is not far removed from his own. Kenny also senses their bond: "We're *both* different," he tells Kimble near the end of the episode.

"When the Wind Blows" harkens back to an observation Kimble made about himself in the pilot ("I used to think I was good with kids"). By urging Lois to stop worrying about Kenny's "differences" and start encouraging his gifts, Dr. Kimble shows a keen understanding of the child that comes from his years of experience as a pediatrician. "The things you worry about are the things that make him two feet taller than the rest," he tells Lois. "He's an original, and that's rare." If there were any doubts as to Kimble's ability with children, this episode clears them up. The Fugitive, indeed, is "good with kids."

David Janssen was as comfortable with children off the set as he was on-screen. "He had an affection for children, and an empathy for them," said George Eckstein, adding "He was very easy around them." Producer Alan Armer seconds the thought. "David seemed to get along with these youngsters," he said. "Of course, he got along with almost everybody who came in. There were never any problems, any fights, any personality clashes."

Episode 76

NOT WITH A WHIMPER

Original Airdate: January 4, 1966

Written by Norman Lessing. Directed by Alexander Singer.

Guest Cast: Laurence Naismith (Dr. Andrew McCallister), Audrey Christie (Nurse Murdock), Lee Meriwether (Willis Hampton), Joseph Perry (Counterman), Garrison True (Sergeant), Marcelle Hebert (Teacher), Jimmy Stiles (Joey), Jack Dodson (Lieutenant).

Prolog. *No matter how far a man may run, he cannot escape the emotional ties which bind him to his past. So Richard Kimble finds himself drawn to the factory town of Hempstead Mills. The reason: the chance of a small item in the local newspaper.*

Synopsis. Kimble ("Dr. Richard Spaulding") arrives in the factory town of Hempstead Mills, West Virginia to visit Andrew McCallister, his longtime mentor who is physically (and, unbeknownst to Kimble, mentally) ailing. McCallister's vigorous anti-smog campaign has earned him a reputation as the local crackpot. But the old man plans to go out with a bang—in the form of a bomb which Kimble unwittingly delivers to the factory. When McCallister discovers that a group of children will be inside the factory at the time of the explosion, he dispatches Kimble to evacuate the building and deactivate the bomb.

Epilog. *Richard Kimble, fugitive, on a brief visit to a dead past, is now once more in search of a future.*

Kimble uses the bomb threat to forge his way past the police. After submerging Dr. McCallister's bomb in a tank of test supply oil, he quickly constructs a makeshift "explosive," then completes the charade by taking Willis "hostage" and "ordering" her to drive him out of town.

Episode 77

WIFE KILLER

Original Airdate: January 11, 1966

Written by Dan Ullman. Directed by Richard Donner.

Guest Cast: Janice Rule (Barbara Webb), Kevin McCarthy (Herb Malone), Stephen Roberts (Chief Blaney), Bill Raisch (Fred Johnson), Lloyd Haynes (Ed Warren), Steve Wolfson (Reporter), John Luce (Reporter), Charles McDaniel (Male Nurse).

Prolog. *A fugitive is usually a man without a goal, aimlessly fleeing the Furies that pursue him. But for Richard Kimble, there is a goal, a phantom who has himself become a fugitive. And Richard Kimble, in turn, now becomes the hunter. But another hunter [Lieutenant Gerard] is also on the move.*

Synopsis. Reporter Barbara Webb spots Fred Johnson in a police round-up. Calling to mind the Kimble case, she prints the picture in the paper—which flushes out both Kimble and Gerard. But the one-armed man spots Kimble and takes off in a stolen car. Barbara and Kimble chase him down a winding mountain road, until the one-armed man crashes. Kimble tends to Johnson, while at the same time interrogating him about the night of the murder. Johnson admits to the murder, but he loses consciousness before he can sign the confession Barbara has prepared.

Epilog. *And Richard Kimble waits, not yet aware that his hope for salvation has again disappeared—waits to be reminded by Lt. Philip Gerard that he is still as much a fugitive as before.*

"Wife Killer" marks Bill Raisch's third appearance as the elusive one-armed man. Given Quinn Martin's desire to portray the character as a sort of spectre who looms over the Fugitive (very much like the figure of Lt. Gerard), it is no surprise that the one-armed man has appeared only in small spurts to this point in the series. This episode provides a little more flesh to the one-armed man's character. Fred Johnson is 47 years old, has Type B blood—and has an instinct for survival. Johnson's most marked trait is that he's a very mean-spirited man. Bill Raisch, the real-life man with one arm who played Johnson, felt that his physical disability would distract the audience, so he suggested that the writers make Johnson a brutal, vicious character—a strategy that worked. Johnson was never portrayed as a character with a physical disability. Rather, given Raisch's tremendous strength (he had been a motion picture stuntman prior to *The Fugitive*), the man with one arm was someone who could hold his own in a fight, and then some.

Like Kimble, Johnson will do whatever it takes to keep himself alive and away from the police. Unlike Kimble, however, Johnson has neither morals nor integrity to tie him down. In "Wife Killer" he "confessed" to Helen's murder simply because, as Gerard pointed out, he knew Kimble was a doctor and he still needed Kimble's help. If continuing to receive Kimble's medical expertise meant "confessing" to the murder of Kimble's wife, so be it. Johnson knew the risks were minimal—the confession was not recorded until after he lost consciousness. Once healthy, Johnson could always deny the confession and put the onus right back on Kimble.

Because of *The Fugitive*'s tremendous popularity during its network run, Raisch became closely identified with his role. Sometimes, a little too closely. Producer Alan Armer recalled an incident in which the police actually picked up Raisch for questioning. "Bill was in a restaurant or a bar, and he was picked up by the police, who remembered that he was wanted for 'something!'" said Armer. "They weren't sure what it was that he was wanted for, but they'd seen the face, and they knew he was wanted, and they put him in the police car and took him down to headquarters. Bill tried to tell them who he was, and they weren't having any of it! And it wasn't until he got downtown to police headquarters that he was able to straighten it out. The police just knew that this was a guy that had done 'something bad!'"

FUGE FINEST MOMENTS

"Wife Killer" contains one of the single best moments of the entire series—Dr. Kimble's reaction to the apparent admission of guilt. Literally taken aback as Johnson nods his confession, Kimble falls back into his chair: his mouth quivers, while his eyes beam a look of relief, confidence and hope. This scene is one of David Janssen's three best acting moments in the series. (The other two: the scene in "Fear in a Desert City" where Kimble reveals himself to Monica (Vera Miles); and the sequence in "Escape into Black" in which Kimble, amidst a barrage of oral recollections, struggles to regain his memory.)

FUGE FEATURE FILM MAKERS

Richard Donner, who also directed the episode "In a Plain Paper Wrapper," has directed such box-office smashes as *Superman*, *Radio Flyer* and all three *Lethal Weapon* pictures.

Episode 78

THIS'LL KILL YOU

Original Airdate: January 18, 1966

Written by George Eckstein. Directed by Alex March.

Guest Cast: Mickey Rooney (Charlie Paris), Nita Talbot (Paula Jellison), Phillip Pine (Pete Ragan), George Tyne (Sgt. Thorpe), Henry Scott (Harrison), Naomi Stevens (Gypsy), William Wintersole (Desk Clerk), Allen Joseph (Enforcer), Richard Gilden (Bracken), Don Ross (Driver), Carol Allen (Mrs. Belson), Dani Nolan (Woman).

Prolog. *The days of a fugitive run together as one, the fear and desperation unrelieved by the sounds of laughter. But Richard Kimble, now using the name Nick Phillips, will find that a man may laugh only to escape the terror of silence.*

Synopsis. Kimble finds work at a laundromat owned by Charlie Paris, a former comic and bookie who hopes to go straight. Kimble doesn't know that the underworld has put a contract on Charlie for testifying against them. Charlie hopes to make amends with his longtime girlfriend Paula, but she's more interested in Kimble—and the $8,000 she'll receive from the mob for turning in Charlie.

Epilog. *One man dies, and another survives for at least another day. For one, the sound of laughter has faded. For another, the echo of that sound remains. Richard Kimble's lonely flight continues. But now, perhaps, he will find an occasional moment to remember and smile.*

"When Elmer Ellsworth took over as costume supervisor, he decided that Kimble should only wear earth colors, monochromatic outfits that would help him to blend—and hopefully disappear—into any background, locale or situation that he might find himself in," said costumer Steve Lodge. "Because it was originally a black-and-white show, the first two years David had worn a black and grey herringbone tweed coat, grey windbreaker, and so on. After Elmer arrived, David wore a brown herringbone tweed sports coat, green Levi cords, blue chambray work shirt, etc. This change went into effect even before we went to color the following season."

Lodge added that the friendly atmosphere generated by the crew members made working on *The Fugitive* very easy. "We had a good crew of people who were allowed to be themselves," said Lodge. "I guess that was the end of the old days, and the beginning of the new days. Our crew was an independent crew that did every picture together. They weren't on a major studio lot, where they could get fired easily, and most of them had been together for years, from the very beginning of the show. And so, when we worked, we worked openly.

"Sometimes we got a little noisy while the actors were rehearsing. Although David was used to the 'noise,' it was a bit of a shock for some of our guest stars. One day while we were filming this episode, Mickey Rooney asked David 'How in the hell do you do it?' David said, 'Do what?' And Mickey said, 'Work with all this noise?' David said, 'What noise?' He couldn't hear it—he was so used to working on a high energy set.

"But whenever we'd shoot a scene, it was probably the quietest set you've ever heard. The assistant directors on our show saw to it that we reached the level of 'quiet' that we needed in order to get good sound—that was particularly important to Quinn Martin, because Quinn started off as a sound editor. It was the assistant director's responsibility to 'quiet us down,' to get us ready for shooting. Then our highly regarded sound mixer, John Kean, would record the dialogue while we were filming."

Episode 79

ECHO OF A NIGHTMARE

Original Airdate: January 25, 1966

Teleplay by John Kneubuhl. Story by Robert Lewin. Directed by James Sheldon.

Guest Cast: Shirley Knight (Jane Washburn), Arch Johnson (Mitch Jackson), Elizabeth Fraser (Millie Jackson), John Lasell (Mr. Kramer), Dennis Joel Oliveri (Wes Kramer), Kevin O'Neal (Perry Jackson), Harry Millard (Harry), Paul Lukather (Barney), Hugh Sanders (Al), Marc Winters (Little Boy), Ford Rainey (Lt. Wynn).

Prolog. *As a doctor, he had dedicated himself to the preservation of life. Now a fugitive, the life he must preserve is his own. Richard Kimble's safety depends on knowing where the enemy is—and who.*

Synopsis. Policewoman Jane Washburn witnesses three youths beat and rob Kimble ("Richard Taylor"), but she becomes suspicious after he declines to report the incident. Although she handcuffs herself to Kimble, he manages to flee the area with her. After Jane injures her ankle hopping a train, they break into an abandoned home so that Kimble can attend to her—and saw apart the handcuffs. But the family who lives there soon returns, and Kimble is held at gunpoint.

Epilog. *All men run the risk of being chained to their past. For Richard Kimble, that bondage is stronger than the steel which hangs from his wrist. And so, he moves on, searching, knowing that for him, now there can be no freedom.*

Although Kimble uses a hacksaw to cut through the handcuffs, the script originally called for the use of another tool. "David had to take a blowtorch and burn the handcuffs off," recalled director James Sheldon. "We were out on distant location, with no access to anybody, and David said, 'This is ridiculous! I can't do this—I mean, I'll burn [Shirley Knight's] hand!' I couldn't disagree with David—his instincts were good. So I let him change it to a hacksaw."

Sheldon caught some flak for the change by the time he returned to the studio. "I didn't know that David had already brought this up with the producers, and they had said no. But it was too late to change it," he said.

Episode 80

STROKE OF GENIUS

Original Airdate: February 1, 1966

Written by John Kneubuhl. Directed by Robert Butler.

Guest Cast: Telly Savalas (Steve Keller), Beau Bridges (Gary Keller), Malcolm Atterbury (Sheriff Bilson), Ellen Corby (Mrs. Barlow), Gene Iglesias (George), Argentina Brunetti (Mexican Woman), Olan Soule (Chet), Martin Priest (Guard), Don Eitner (Officer), George Savalas (Prisoner).

Prolog. *For many men, life is a ceaseless flight: each moment of each day must be escaped by fleeing somehow, somewhere, without rest, until one day, all hope dies, even the hope of further flight. Perhaps, for such men, death comes as a final and all-obliterating kindness: after a lifetime of nightmarish flight, an eternity of dreamless rest. But for Richard Kimble, there is no rest. Not free to live, he is also denied the freedom of death.*

Synopsis. Gary Keller, a promising art student, tests his new rifle by firing a random shot which instantly kills his mentor, the town minister, who happened to drive right into the line of fire. A devastated Gary wants to confess, but his father refuses.

Meanwhile, Kimble ("Frank Whistler"), who was riding with the minister, hides in the mountains in order to attend to his injuries. The police determine that Kimble was in the vicinity; believing him to be the killer, they notify Gerard. But Gary's father takes the matter into his own hands.

Epilog. *For Richard Kimble, the truth that will free him lies somewhere ahead, over the next horizon, beyond the next town, in another place, at another time.*

In "Stroke of Genius" Kimble becomes the top suspect in the shooting of the preacher simply because he is a stranger in town. But this time he has a character witness—Lt. Gerard, who tells the sheriff that Kimble has "never killed anybody while trying to escape, nor has he tried to." The lieutenant finds himself in a peculiar situation: he has to clear Kimble of suspicion so that the sheriff can release the Fugitive into his custody—where he can put him back on Indiana's Death Row.

On the surface, Gerard is motivated by his duties as an instrument of the law. But subconsciously, Gerard seems to demonstrate an outright concern for Kimble's welfare. He does not handcuff Kimble in the cabin, since Kimble is already injured; he opens a can of soup so that Kimble can eat; and he offers the Fugitive just a bit of compassion ("Everybody seems anxious to pin this on you"). Gerard, of course, would never admit this—his allegiance to the law does not allow room for emotion, doubt or anything that could put the infallibility of the law in question. But Gerard's actions certainly suggest that the lieutenant recognizes and (albeit begrudgingly) respects his adversary's numerous admirable qualities. Kimble, in turn, admires Gerard's powers—the lieutenant is not simply an enemy, but a human being whose life is just as important as anyone else's. This partially explains why Kimble continues to save Gerard's life throughout the series—he's a doctor and a humanitarian. (The other reason: Gerard is as much a part of the puzzle as Fred Johnson.).

FUGE FAMILIAR FACES

Harry O was David Janssen's best-known role following *The Fugitive.* But Janssen was not the first choice to play the weary private detective cum philosopher: the producers originally wanted Telly Savalas. The stocky Greek actor turned down that role because he was busy making films in Europe, but he later went on to achieve fame (and an Emmy Award) as *Kojak.*

Episode 81

SHADOW OF THE SWAN

Original Airdate: February 8, 1966

Written by Anthony Lawrence. Directed by James Sheldon.

Guest Cast: Joanna Pettet (Tina Andreson), Andrew Duggan (Harry Andreson), David Sheiner (Lou Jacobs), Don Quine (Carny), Ken Lynch (Concession Owner), Monroe Arnold (Dr. Moller), Carole Kane (Carny's Wife), Shirley O'Hara (Landlady), William Woodson (Carnival Barker), Robert Dornan (Doctor).

Prolog. *A carnival can be a place of fun and games, or the funhouse mirrors a reflection of man's uglier side. If you happen to be Richard Kimble, it can simply be another lonely street where the laughter belongs to someone else.*

Synopsis. An emotionally imbalanced young woman becomes attracted to Kimble ("Paul Keller"), as does her suspicious uncle—a retired detective.

Epilog. *The carnival has moved on, and so, too, has Richard Kimble. The carnival moves north, taking its rag bag of noise and excitement to another town, searching for the crowds that are its life. And Richard Kimble, a fugitive still, searches for the one man who can mean his life.*

"We filmed some of the exteriors of 'Shadow of the Swan' out at Malibu Lake," recalled assistant director Bob Rubin. "We were setting up to shoot the key dialogue scene between David and Joanna Pettet at the edge of the lake. Director Jimmy Sheldon wanted to include at least one swan swimming in the background of the scene behind David and Joanna. But none of the swans was interested in remaining in position for the shot. I asked Si Simonson, our veteran special effects expert, what we could do to ensure that the swan stayed in the shot when we were ready to film. Si paused a minute and said he had an idea. He walked down to the edge of the lake, rolled up his pants legs, and walked into the shallow lake. He carefully recruited one of the swans. He then tied a rock to the swan's legs with a piece of string. By the time the swan was in position, carefully anchored with the rock, we had one final dress rehearsal with Joanna, David and the swan in the background. It was perfect. However, because of various union regulations, it was time for the cast and crew to break for lunch. The plan was to shoot the scene as soon as we returned from the lunch break. The swan remained comfortably anchored in the three-foot-deep lake, while we ate lunch nearby. When I returned about twenty minutes later, I discovered that the poor swan had sunk! Si, with his pants legs still rolled up, rushed back into the lake and rescued the swan, which fortunately ended up being okay."

FUGE FUN

In this episode, Kimble tells the veterinarian that he'd never worked with animals before. Unless he was intentionally lying to protect himself, he seems to have forgotten his work with horses ("Fatso"), dogs ("Bloodline"), monkeys ("Last Second of a Big Dream"), rabbits ("All the Scared Rabbits") and bees ("An Apple a Day"). However, part of his story does check: Kimble also told the vet that he'd worked once as an hospital orderly (and he did, in "May God Have Mercy").

Episode 82

RUNNING SCARED

Original Airdate: February 22, 1966

Written by Don Brinkley. Directed by James Sheldon.

Guest Cast: Joanne Linville (Harriet Ballinger), Lin McCarthy (Len Taft), Jacqueline Scott (Donna Kimble Taft), James Daly (Michael Ballinger), Wright King (Joe Penny), Frank Maxwell (Sgt. Burns), Tommy Alexander (Bellhop), Ira Barmak (Airline Clerk), Arch Whiting (Reynolds).

Prolog. *A man on the run may manage to elude the law, but his yesterdays follow him like an everlengthening shadow. For some, the shadow of the past is an object of fear. But for Richard Kimble, it's a form of security. His memories are a bulwark against hopelessness and despair. When the memories falter, so does Kimble.*

Synopsis. Kimble contacts Donna after reading about their father's death. They arrange to meet at a hotel in Fort Wayne, Indiana, where Donna and Len register under an assumed name. But their rendezvous is threatened by Mike Ballinger, the prosecuting attorney at Kimble's trial. Ballinger hopes to clinch his gubernatorial campaign by capturing Kimble himself.

Epilog. *Without a past, a man has no future. For Richard Kimble, his memories are the source of his courage. They give him the strength to face another uncertain tomorrow.*

"I've always said that nobody can make me cry that can't make me laugh," said Jacqueline Scott. "David was very funny—you don't think of him like that: you think of him as kind of a glamorous movie star type. And to me there was never any ego about his looks. He was just a very natural, very nice and very funny man. He'd tell these kind of crazy Jimmy Durante jokes, and that'd be the last thing you'd ever expect to come out of him! And I just adored him. You'd be laughing and carrying on, and then I'd turn around and see him in trouble [as Dr. Kimble] and it would tear my heart out. I was very, very fond of David. He was really a nice man."

"Running Scared" marks a turning point in the series. With the passing of John Kimble, Donna becomes the sole surviving member of the Fugitive's immediate family (since brother Ray has apparently dropped out of view). Consequently, she becomes the only remaining anchor in Kimble's life, the one constant source of emotional support to whom he can turn. That's why Kimble asks Donna to pull herself together at the end of the picture: he needs her to remain strong during the balance of his ordeal. While Donna was by no means a weak character (she held her own against Gerard during "Home is the Hunted"), she does seem noticeably stronger when she returns for the fourth season ("The Judgment").

"In a show like *The Fugitive*, you have to accept the reality of the situation right off the bat," said Scott. "The man is a fugitive from justice, and any time you're around him he's not just your sweet loving brother: there is great danger. Not everybody who encountered Kimble in other episodes knew who he was, but I [as Donna] always knew the danger, and I had to accept the reality of those circumstances. I don't know whether she became 'better' or 'worse' at dealing with her brother's situation, but the covers became stronger. With time, she developed a harder and harder crust to prevent people from breaking in and trying to get to him."

FUGE FACTS

According to this episode, Mike Ballinger was the prosecuting attorney in *The People v. Kimble.* However, in "The Girl from Little Egypt," the prosecutor's name was Lester Rand.

Episode 83

THE CHINESE SUNSET

Original Airdate: March 1, 1966

Written by Leonard Kantor. Directed by James Sheldon.

Guest Cast: Laura Devon (Penelope Dufoir), Paul Richards (Eddie Slade), Ned Glass (Sam Vogle), Wayne Rogers (Fred Bragin), Sandra Warner (Frankie Topps), Sheldon Allman (Orin), Connie Sawyer (Mrs. Hull), Mary Gregory (Rita), Karl Held (Buddy), Val Avery (Gordie), Melville Buick (Woody), Robert Brubaker (Cooper), Jhean Burton (Waitress), James Oliver (Cab Driver), Robert Yuro (Saul).

Prolog. *The Chinese Sunset Motel, situated on a tarnished hyphen called the Sunset Strip that separates Los Angeles from Beverly Hills. For Richard Kimble, working as man of all jobs under the alias of Jack Fickett, it is a welcome bit of limbo.*

Synopsis. Undercover policeman Fred Bragin registers at a swank Beverly Hills hotel in order to survey notorious bookie Eddie Slade. When Slade leaves town for a short time, Bragin monitors the bookie's girlfriend, Penelope. The focus on the girl brings an unexpected bonus when the cop discovers she's being tutored by the hotel's "general factotum"—Kimble.

Epilog. *A fleeting moment, to laugh, to be warmed, to contemplate what could have been. An hour ago, he was Jack Fickett. Now he must find a new name, a new place. A man who must lose himself in order that, someday, he might someday find himself: Richard Kimble, fugitive.*

The tutorial relationship between Penelope and Kimble provides the spark to "The Chinese Sunset," a reworking of George Bernard Shaw's *Pygmalion* that could have been called "My Fair Fugitive." Penelope refers to Kimble as her "professor" several times during the show, and Kimble's alias ("Fickett") even sounds a little like "Higgins" (the Rex Harrison character in the play). The *Pygmalion* angle gives David Janssen ample opportunity to play off the humor generated by the unlikely pairing.

Episode 84

ILL WIND

Original Airdate: March 8, 1966
Written by Al C. Ward. Directed by Joseph Sargent.

Guest Cast: John McIntire (Lester Kelly), Jeanette Nolan (Naomi Kelly), Lonny Chapman (Jock Sims), Tim McIntire (Jonesie), Bonnie Beecher (Kate), Lew Brown (Sheriff), Renata Vanni (Mrs. Herrera), Mel Gallagher (Deputy #1), Silvia Marino (Josephine Herrera), Laurence Allen (Deputy #2).

Prolog. *The work is hard, to be endured from day to day. But here, just 20 miles north of the Gulf of Mexico, Richard Kimble has found reason to gain a new foothold on life, his first in a very long time.*

Synopsis. Gerard captures Kimble ("Mike Johnson") outside a migrant community near the Gulf of Mexico. But a violent hurricane quarantines them, along with the rest of the farm workers, inside a fragile barn. Gerard suffers severe blood loss after the roof collapses on him. To the astonishment of the workers, Kimble pleads for a blood donor who can help save the lieutenant's life.

Epilog. *The storm has come and gone. But few of those who sought shelter together that night will ever forget it. And Richard Kimble, the next hill now in his eye, will find occasion to look back and remember—a fugitive has time for that.*

A ballad is a song with the same melody for each stanza that passes on a legendary or traditional event from generation to generation. In "Ill Wind," the haunting lyrics of "The Running Man" (the acoustic ballad written by associate producer George Eckstein) recount the story of Richard Kimble and his flight from the law for the benefit of the migrant community who befriended him, protected him, and enabled him to escape "the sheriff's gun." The Kelly family may never understand why the Fugitive chose to save Gerard's life, but they will never forget the risk he took in doing so, and they will always cherish the time he spent among them. Nor will their daughter Kate ever forget Kimble's impact on her life. She now understands that a doctor considers *every* life worth saving—even his enemy's.

While many other episodes use music to create or punctuate a story's mood, this episode stands out for its use of "The Running Man." "Ill Wind" slowly weaves the ballad into the story one stanza at a time—this device heightens the importance of each stanza and the drama of the scene it accompanies. The judicious use of "The Running Man" transforms "Ill Wind" into an hour-long country-western song. (This should come as no surprise, considering the episode's original title: "Ballad for a Bitter Land.") Like the omniscient narrator, the balladeer Jonesie governs the drama in a way that a straightforward rendering of the story could not convey. For the migrant community, the events of that stormy night are the stuff of legends. As the Narrator observes, "Few who sought shelter together that night will ever forget it." For that matter, neither will the Fugitive.

The impact of the night's events are not entirely lost on Gerard, either. The Fugitive saves him twice in this episode, and "the girl who'll surely cry" figures prominently in both cases. First, Kate nearly stabs Gerard with a pitchfork, then she donates blood so that Kimble could perform the transfusion that keeps Gerard alive. "What you did, it didn't surprise me," says the lieutenant to Kimble after the pitchfork incident. The two men then sit uncomfortably for just a moment, neither knowing what to say next—aside from the final moments of "The Judgment," this sequence is the only moment in the series in which the two characters acknowledge their mutual respect for each other. Given the nature of their relationship, the moment is necessarily brief. Kimble then informs Gerard that he will escape if he can. "That doesn't surprise me, either," responds the lieutenant.

But Gerard remains fastened to his own understanding of the law. He cannot allow any personal feelings to interfere with his duty as a police officer. The law holds Kimble guilty of murder, and Gerard must uphold that ruling, as best he can. So although his body has been weakened by the loss of blood, the lieutenant makes one last desperate attempt to capture Kimble at the end of Act IV. Gerard may be perceived as pathetic, calling after Kimble while he himself lies fallen on the ground—but to him a police officer has to make the effort, no matter how hopeless.

"Gerard was presented to us as a character who was obsessive, certainly neurotic, and maybe paranoid as well," according to novelist Stephen King. King points to the conclusion of "Ill Wind" as one of those instances where the long trail of near misses occasionally takes its toll on the lieutenant. As King puts it, "Ill Wind" is one of those episodes "where you could see Gerard edging into 'freako land.' At one point at the end of that episode, you could see him getting ready to lose it. He's going 'You're obstructing justice! I'm in search of a fugitive! I'll arrest all of you!' I mean, there are these poor little migrants, and you knew from looking at him he would do it."

FUGE FEATURES

"Si Simonson, our special effects technician, did a fantastic job on creating the 'hurricane' we saw in 'Ill Wind,'" said assistant director Bob Rubin. "All of the walls on the set were on gimbols—that means that the walls were off the ground—and we had crew members stationed at each level who pulled the levers that rocked the walls. That's how we created the effect of the winds battering the walls of the barn."

FUGE FUN

Costumer Steve Lodge recalls a prank that the crew pulled on David Janssen at the time "Ill Wind" was produced. "David was a devoted fan of *Batman* [which had premiered in January 1966]," he explained. "When we found that out, one of the guys on the crew cut a stencil resembling the Bat Signal, then taped it to a baby spotlight while David was rehearsing a scene with John McIntire and Jeanette Nolan (Mrs. McIntire in real-life). Then somebody turned on the spotlight so that the Bat Signal was projected onto the cyc ("cyclorama," or canvas backing) behind David and the McIntires. 'What in hell is that thing supposed to mean?' demanded the director, Joe Sargent. David just grinned and said, 'I think that someone's trying to tell me that I'm a 'Bat' actor.'"

FUGE FINEST MOMENTS

This episode also features one of the most chilling moments in the entire series: Gerard's sudden emergence at the rear of the train depot just as Kimble tries to escape (Act I). Amidst the night sky and howling winds, Gerard has never looked more menacing.

Episode 85

WITH STRINGS ATTACHED

Original Airdate: March 15, 1966

Written by John Kneubuhl. Directed by Leonard Horn.

Guest Cast: Donald Pleasence (Max Pfeiffer), Carol Rossen (Ellen Harned), Rex Thompson (Geoffrey Martin), Bill Quinn (Lyman), Jason Johnson (Watchman), Paul Pepper (Stage Manager), Jim Raymond (Officer).

Prolog. *The life of an artist is a restless, lonely one, without peace—like a man pursued, finding peace and rest only when he has created something of beauty. But then, after that, he is forced into flight again, and he moves once more into the unknown, searching. For Richard Kimble, a fugitive, there is also only pursuit and a lonely searching. Moments of beauty, even moments of rest, are rare, because for him, as for the artist, to stand still is to die.*

Synopsis. Geoffrey Martin, an accomplished violinist at age 17, has grown weary of his career and would like to stop playing professionally for four years. But he is contractually obligated to continue performing until he is 21. In order to "free" himself, Geoffrey manipulates his assistant Ellen and chauffeur Kimble ("Frank Carter") into believing that his demanding guardian-instructor is trying to destroy him.

Epilog. *Some men can never be free. From birth, they are their own jailors, they are their own prisons, they are trapped by their own talents. For Richard Kimble, a fugitive, freedom is flight. For flight brings hope, and with hope, there is always tomorrow.*

Carol Rossen (Laurel in "Middle of the Heat Wave") was among the "repertory" of performers Quinn Martin loved to use because she had an acting style that was particularly suited to television. Rossen often projected a hidden dimension onto her characters, the very quality that Martin looked for in his actors. Consider how coolly she plays Ellen. The character remains so poised throughout the episode that it's possible to think (until Act III discloses otherwise) that she knows more about Geoffrey's machinations than she lets on. After Geoffrey discovers the dead bird in Act I, for example, the camera cuts to a close-up of Ellen, who looks concerned, if not a little too poker-faced.

Martin clearly appreciated Rossen's work, because he used her in many of his programs (*The Untouchables, The Streets of San Francisco*). The actress in turn enjoyed working for Martin. "I was very, very much a fan of his," she said. "Quinn was one of those wonderful people who respected the autonomy and integrity of the people he hired—respected in ways that may no longer be possible, given the 'givens' of today's network control. I mean, he had his likes and his dislikes, and you might talk to another actor who said, 'Well, he never hired me, and so, he was a jerk.' But that wasn't my experience.

"Quinn functioned in an era when there was a real respect for the versatility of talent, so that you didn't just work *The Fugitive* and never work it again. You did, in one season, a couple of shows, three shows, whatever, and play very different roles. And Quinn didn't care. If he had respect for what you could do, he brought you back to do it again a different way. And so it *was* repertory in the best sense because people got to do all kinds of different things. Quinn was great. I mean, he really was what a television producer no longer—rarely—is now, but certainly ought to be. I don't know that he could exist in the world of television today."

The prolog compares the Fugitive's search for the one-armed man with the creative process an artist undergoes while creating a thing of beauty: both require ongoing "movement" that if stopped could lead to a kind of death. But the analogy, although thought-provoking, is imperfect. While the artist has been blessed with natural ability, the Fugitive has been cursed as a result of human error. And though the artist may know the fear of a fading talent, that feeling cannot compare with the indelible sense of urgency of an innocent man who faces a death sentence.

Episode 86

THE WHITE KNIGHT

Original Airdate: March 22, 1966

Written by Dan Ullman. Directed by Robert Gist.

Guest Cast: Steven Hill (Glenn Madison), Jessica Walter (Pat Haynes), James Callahan (Russ Haynes), Nancy Wickwire (Claire Madison), Ted Knight (Lt. Mooney), Robert DoQui (Evers), Peter Marko (Dispatcher).

Prolog. *Quick reflexes are necessary to a doctor. They are indispensible to a fugitive. For Richard Kimble, who is both doctor and fugitive, they can mean survival.*

Synopsis. After witnessing the crash of a small aircraft, Kimble ("Dan Gordon") rescues the pilot, senatorial candidate Glenn Madison, and his passenger, Pat Haynes. Glenn's PR man, Russ Haynes (Pat's husband), arranges for a police sketch of Glenn's rescuer—who quietly left the scene. Russ locates the Fugitive and brings him to Glenn. After the sketch artist recognizes Kimble, the police head for the Madison estate, but Glenn and Russ hold them off. Claire (Glenn's wife) recognizes Kimble: long aware that Glenn cheats on her, she threatens to turn Kimble in unless he reveals the identity of Glenn's passenger. Kimble remains quiet; Pat tells him about the affair later. Claire overhears Pat's confession and decides to smear her husband's "All-American" image. Glenn kills Claire, then tries to frame Kimble.

Epilog. *In the storybooks, when you save a man's life, you are richly rewarded. For a fugitive, it doesn't always work that way. And sometimes, when you are chased by the Furies, the life you must save is your own.*

"David loved to make the 140-mile trip to the studio from Palm Springs (where he owned a home) in his Jaguar XKE," said costumer Steve Lodge. "He also loved to make that drive in as fast a time as the Jag was capable, and every once in a while a cop would pull him over for speeding. But David never got a ticket. It happened every time, he used to tell us: the cop would approach him with a huge Cheshire cat grin saying, 'Well, well, well... Wait 'til all the guys back at the station-house find out that *I just caught the Fugitive!*' David would then have to sign his autograph for the officer, or if there was a camera nearby, pose for a picture. This may have taken some extra time for David, but he never got a ticket making the trip from Palm Springs."

Episode 87

THE 2130

Original Airdate: March 29, 1966

Written by Dan Ullman. Directed by Leonard Horn.

Guest Cast: Melvyn Douglas (Dr. Mark Ryder), Susan Albert (Laurie Ryder), Hampton Fancher (Homer), William Bramley (Tim Oates), June Dayton (Millie Oates), Don Mitchell (Laborer), Harlan Warde (Detective), Jason Wingreen (Donald Bassett), Lilian Adams (Store Owner), Clay Tanner (2nd Deputy), Jon Kowal (Police Captain), Pat Riley (1st Deputy), Peter Canon (1st Policeman), Stuart Nisbet (Richardson), Paul Hahn (Officer), Bob Duggan (Driver), Kevin Burchett (Alan Oates), Mark Russell (2nd Policeman).

Prolog. *If you are Richard Kimble, you lead a complicated life. However, certain decisions are simple: when the police start getting involved, you don't wait around to see what happens.*

Synopsis. In Denver, Kimble reluctantly covers for Laurie Ryder after she dents her father's car, but he flees upon discovering that the girl was involved in a hit-and-run accident. After learning Kimble's identity, Dr. Ryder summons Gerard (along with the entire Kimble file) and introduces the lieutenant to the 2130, a computer that can help capture the Fugitive by determining a pattern to his travels. After initially finding no pattern, the 2130 determines several probable locations where Kimble might surface, based on such factors as Kimble's preference to remain in warm climate during the wintertime. However, upon studying the data, Ryder determines that with the exception of one incident, Kimble seems to be a good man. After confronting his daughter about the car accident, Ryder warns Kimble about the 2130 by leaking the story to the press.

Epilog. *If you are Richard Kimble, fugitive, your already complicated life has become more so. You can no longer rely upon your instinct, because for all you know, your pursuers may be machines, and you are merely a human being.*

"The 2130" is really three stories in one: the 2130; the hit-and-run accident and the relationship between Ryder and Laurie; and Kimble on the run from one locale to another. The excess of plots hurt the episode, particularly in its characterization of Gerard. Normally, the lieutenant lets no stone go unturned. It's a little surprising, therefore, that Gerard never suspects Ryder of leaking the story to the press. The lieutenant is usually quick to figure out when he's been had—and who's had him. The hit-and-run angle could have been eliminated, and the episode would have been a lot tighter.

But "The 2130" is still fun to watch. Gerard's skepticism of the computer's capabilities reflects the attitude of a bygone era. Today, of course, computers are less intimidating, and not only in appearance—modern versions of the 2130 come in laptop and pocket sizes. We have incorporated computers so much in modern life that we practically take them for granted. Given how much the police rely on computers today, it would be difficult for Kimble to remain a fugitive for four days, let alone four years.

The writers of the feature film version of *The Fugitive* doubtlessly took this into consideration. "I also think about that every now and then," said Stephen King. "Every now and then I'll run across an episode, and you'll see Kimble working as a bartender picking an ad out of the newspaper and going down and applying for the job and getting it with virtually no ID. Now, he might have a piece, or two or three pieces of ID, and the guy's not stupid, obviously (he was a doctor!), so you'd be able to con off a certain amount. But the way the world runs now, with credit cards and everything else...."

King envisioned another way of reprising *The Fugitive*. "Wouldn't it be great if somebody did *The Fugitive* as, let's say, a six-hour mini-series," he speculated. "You could have the basic developing situation, one or two towns, and then have Kimble pick up the one-armed man and follow his trail, a converging trail, back to Indiana where the whole thing would solve itself. That's essentially what happened in the TV series."

FUGE FACTS

"The 2130" is the most picaresque episode of the series. Kimble bounces around from one locale to another, and assumes at least five identities along the way:

As "Jack Davis," he works as the Ryders' valet (Denver, Colorado);

As "Bob Grant," he meets the Oates family and joins them on their way to California to find work;

He gives his name as "Jack" during the train scene with convict Marty Macklin (a.k.a. "Homer");

As "William Smith," he finds work with the Multnomah County flood control gang (near Portland, Oregon);

In the epilog, we see him in the New England area, looking for work in the cranberry bogs.

Gerard is not completely off character in this episode. After the 2130 determines that the probability of Kimble's committing another murder is "98% negative," the lieutenant responds, "The 2% is good enough for me."

Hampton Fancher (Homer) wrote the screenplay for *Blade Runner* (1982), starring Harrison Ford, who plays Dr. Kimble in the 1993 motion picture version of *The Fugitive*.

FUGE FUN

The crew gave Susan Albert (Laurie) an impromptu lesson in driving a stick shift car in order to film one of the early segments of this episode. "We used a Ford Cobra on that show," recalled assistant director Bob Rubin. "We were shooting past midnight (because it was a night scene), and we were all ready to shoot the scene where Susan's supposed to pull into the driveway, when we discovered there was one small problem. Susan didn't know how to operate a stick shift! So Whitey Ellison, our transportation captain, had to give her a crash course in driving a stick shift so that we could shoot that scene."

Episode 88

A TASTE OF TOMORROW

Original Airdate: April 12, 1966

Teleplay by John Kneubuhl. Story by Mann Rubin. Directed by Leonard Horn.

Guest Cast: Fritz Weaver (Joe Tucker), Michael Constantine (Ben Wyckoff), Brenda Scott (Sarah Tucker), Dabbs Greer (Charlie Fletcher), Mary Jackson (Carolyn), Paul Sorensen (Shep), Paul Sheriff (Officer).

Prolog. *To a fugitive, only the past is real. Each morning, it rises with the sun, each night it returns with the darkness. There is no present. And, for Richard Kimble, the future is filled with uncertainty, and fear.*

Synopsis. Kimble ("Al Mitchell") stumbles onto the company of Joe Tucker, a man wrongly convicted for embezzlement who has returned to his hometown to seek the bank officer who framed him. When Kimble is picked up for car theft, he meets Joe's daughter, who tells him that the real culprit, who is now dead, confessed to the crime before he died. Kimble tries to prevent Joe from killing an innocent man—but Joe is delirious, and bent on revenge. Meanwhile, the police have uncovered Kimble and are out to capture him.

Epilog. *For some, an end finally comes to the running. But for Richard Kimble, the end has come only to one more day, and the running must go on.*

Writer Mann Rubin (*Barnaby Jones*, *Future Cop*) later wrote the screenplay for *Warning Shot*, a 1967 feature film that featured David Janssen in familiar territory (he played a police officer on trial for murder). Leonard Maltin's annual *TV Movies and Video Guide* describes *Warning Shot* as an exciting movie that's "even better on TV." As a matter of fact, the film was originally made for television: it was the pilot for a possible David Janssen series. *Warning Shot* also features such *Fugitive* guest stars as Ed Begley ("Man in a Chariot") and Carroll O'Connor ("Flight from the Final Demon").

Episode 89

IN A PLAIN PAPER WRAPPER

Original Airdate: April 19, 1966

Teleplay by John Kneubuhl. Story by Jackson Gillis and Glen A. Larson. Directed by Richard Donner.

Guest Cast: Lois Nettleton (Susan Cartwright), Michael Strong (Shaw), Kurt Russell (Eddie), Pat Cardi (Gary Reed), Michael Shea (Rick), Mark Dymally (Joe), Arthur Malet (Sawnzie), Wolfe Barzell (Hoffman), Bing Russell (Officer), Kay Riehl (Landlady).

Prolog. *A target may be paper, an animal—or a man. To a gun it makes no difference, nor does it care who pulls the trigger, or why. To Richard Kimble, a fugitive, guns are a familiar enemy, for he is always a target, a target for which the law has issued a mandate—if necessary, shoot to kill.*

Synopsis. Kimble's relationship with waitress Susan Cartwright becomes doubly complicated by the arrival of her orphaned nephew Gary, who himself is trying to break in with a local group of boys. Upon recognizing Kimble ("Bob Stoddard") from growing up in Stafford, Gary tells the other boys, who decide to capture Kimble with the rifle they just purchased from a magazine ad. Meanwhile, the social worker assigned to investigate Susan interrogates Kimble instead.

Epilog. *Love needs time to grow. And a hunted man has no time. Yesterday, a need that found hope in a look, a word, a touching of hands, is today denied by flight, a flight from guns. Today's guns are already miles behind—but the need remains.*

Although "In a Plain Paper Wrapper" was not the final episode to air this season, it was the last to be filmed—and therefore the last episode produced by Alan Armer, who would leave the series at the end of the year. "I did 90 hours of *The Fugitive*," said Armer. "After a while, you kind of feel that you've been everywhere, and done everything, and that there are just no more new roads to explore."

Armer felt ready for a new challenge, and he immediately accepted Quinn Martin's offer to produce the pilot for *The Invaders*, a projected science-fiction series about a lone man's effort to protect a disbelieving public from an alien takeover. "Quinn had a pilot for *The Invaders*," Armer said. "Larry Cohen [who conceived the idea for the series], brought it to Quinn, and Quinn let me read it. He said, 'What do you think?' I said, 'I like it. I think it's exciting.' And Quinn said, 'Do you want to produce it?'

"And I thought, after doing 90 hours of *The Fugitive*, you really feel you're kind of burned out, and I said 'Yes, I'd like to,'" continued Armer. "And we did a pilot—'Beach-head,' which was written by Anthony Wilson ('Landscape with Running Figures'). Joe Sargent ('Ill Wind') directed it, and the first cut was gorgeous! But we had to cut it down to 49 minutes from an original running time of 65 minutes, and it suffered, I'm afraid. My agent said it (the long version) was the single best pilot he had ever seen."

The Invaders premiered in January 1967. Like *The Fugitive*, *The Invaders* was based on one man's efforts to resolve a disadvantageous situation (invasion of Earth from outer space) despite tremendous odds (no one believes him). The series starred Roy Thinnes and featured such Martin trademarks as the superimposed demarcations ("Act I," etc.), excellent writing (including several scripts by George Eckstein and Don Brinkley), familiar guest stars (Barry Morse appeared in the episode "The Life Seekers"), and an omniscient narrator. Unlike *The Fugitive*, however, *The Invaders* never caught on, and was canceled after just one-and-one-half seasons. "*The Invaders* was such a way-out concept that I guess it would be more successful today than it was then," Armer speculated.

Armer later produced *Cannon* (1971) for Quinn Martin, plus several made-for-TV movies, including *Birds of Prey* (1973) with David Janssen. He truly enjoyed working on *The Fugitive*. "It was enormously gratifying," he said.

FUGE FACTS

"In a Plain Paper Wrapper" is one of the few episodes in which Kimble is not chased out of town by the police. The landlady calls the police in Act IV not so much to report Kimble, but to report Gary's injury. However, Kimble remains imperiled in this episode because Shaw, the social worker, has been interrogating him relentlessly. The Fugitive must leave town before the truth comes out.

John Kneubuhl, who wrote four other episodes this season, left television to teach English at the University of Samoa.

FUGE FOL DE ROL

Apparently Iroquois, New York, where this episode takes place, has Sunday postal delivery. Gary picked up the rifle from the post office on the day after Kimble took him to the movies (which was a Saturday).

Episode 90

CORALEE

Original Airdate: April 26, 1966

Written by Joy Dexter. Directed by Jerry Hopper.

Guest Cast: Murray Hamilton (Joe Steelman), Antoinette Bower (Coralee Reynolds), Patricia Smith (Lucille Steelman), Joe Maross (Milt Carr), James Frawley (Pete), Dabney Coleman (George Graham), Rusty Lane (Frank Reynolds), Harry Ellerbe (Minister), Peter Madsen (Policeman).

Prolog. *A derrick barge used for underwater salvage work off the coast of California. Richard Kimble has taken the name Tony Carter, and unknowingly taken the hand of trouble.*

Synopsis. Joe Steelman nearly had his company shut down six years ago after the harbor police found him guilty of negligence. After a diver named Johnny (who is also Joe's brother-in-law) dies due to an improperly fastened helmet, Joe blames the death on reputed jinx Coralee Reynolds, a local girl whom the diver had been dating. (By coincidence, several other men had died shortly after seeing Coralee.) Kimble ("Tony Carter") alone consoles the girl after the entire town abandons her. Kimble also knows about the broken helmet. Although the Fugitive is reluctant to testify at the harbor police's hearing on the matter, Joe decides to eliminate him anyway. In order to protect Kimble from Joe, Coralee has the Fugitive "arrested."

Epilog. *The highway north carries a fugitive to freedom, a freedom shadowed by his own special "jinx." He cannot look back now. He can only look ahead to the day when that jinx will ultimately be broken.*

"Coralee" was not a pleasant episode to film. The cast and crew suffered through seven days of seasickness and unbearable weather conditions on location, from heat and humidity to hail and rain squalls, while filming the episode aboard an actual derrick barge in the Pacific Ocean, off San Pedro. Perhaps the lasting stench of the polluted waters factored in the decision to banish "Coralee" to the end of the season, even though the episode was filmed very early in the year.

EPILOG: THIRD SEASON

In April 1966, top level entertainment programming executives from ABC in New York announced that *The Fugitive* would have several changes when it returned for its fourth season in the fall. The most noticeable change would be the switch to color from black-and-white, as part of the network's commitment to color broadcasting (each episode of the fourth season would begin with a tag emphasizing that the program would appear "in color"). Another announcement discussed plans to shoot episodes in such exotic locales as Mexico, Puerto Rico, and Hawaii.

The most intriguing announcement of all would have changed the entire complexion of the series. Apparently concerned that *The Fugitive* was not drawing enough young viewers (a survey conducted from October 1965 to February 1966 indicated that the program averaged nearly 17.5 million adult viewers a week), ABC disclosed plans to broaden the program's base of appeal by giving Dr. Kimble a young son. However, in a news conference announced in May 1966, the network realized that given the spectre of Lt. Gerard, burdening Dr. Kimble with a son was an idea that just wouldn't work.

1965-66 was a rewarding season for *The Fugitive* on two levels. The series averaged a 40% share of its time slot—this means that all of the households with televisions whose sets are in use at 10:00 p.m. on Tuesdays (the program's time slot in the United States), 40% of those households were tuned into *The Fugitive*. The series won a Raven Award from the Mystery Writers of America as the Best Mystery Show of the season. Finally, on May 22, 1966, the National Academy of Television Arts and Sciences named *The Fugitive* as Best Dramatic Series of 1965-66—a definitive retort to everyone who had ever doubted that Roy Huggins' "repulsive" series concept would ever be accepted by the television public.

For producer Alan Armer, receiving the Emmy statue was the crowning achievement of an exciting career. He would subsequently leave the series to produce *The Invaders* for Quinn Martin. "*The Fugitive* was a very rewarding series," he said. "It's very gratifying when you do a successful series—people leave you alone, they figure you know the answer. When you do a series that is not successful, everybody has an answer, and everybody's prepared to tell you exactly what you're doing wrong. *The Fugitive* was a series that in the beginning ABC was watching very closely. After a while, they backed off and let us do pretty much anything we wanted to. And it was lovely...by the third year, Quinn figured we knew what we were doing, and left us alone."

Because the Awards telecast aired three hours later on the West Coast, Armer's children did not find out that their father had won the Emmy until much later in the evening. Armer could have called them with the news, but he wanted to surprise them. "All the time while my kids were watching the show, they never knew I had won," he recalled. "They were really knocked out."

David Janssen and director of photography Meredith Nicholson also received Emmy nominations this season.

David in *Ticket to Alaska.*

Barbara Rush.

Suzanne Pleshette.

Brenda Vaccaro.

Hope Lange.

Mickey Rooney.

Telly Savalas.

Clint Howard and strawman.

Elizabeth Macrae and Tuesday Weld.

Glenda Farrell, Jack Weston and David in *Fatso*.

David with Antoinette Bower in *Coralee*.

David with mother Berniece Janssen and sister Teri-Jean in 1943.

Berniece Janssen with Harrison Ford in Chicago on the set of the 1993 Warner Bros. feature film, *The Fugitive*.

PHOTOGRAPH © STEVE LODGE

The Fugitive on location. Left to right: Ray Rich (key grip; holding branch), Bob Hoffman, Ed Nugent (operating camera),Jim Crowell (Janssen's double), Unidentified camera assistant, Barry Morse (who also directed this episode, Vince Martelli (camera assistant), David Janssen, Phil Cook (assistant director).

David and Celeste Holm in *Concrete Evidence.*

FOURTH SEASON, 1966-1967

PRODUCTION CREDITS

Starring David Janssen as The Fugitive
Also Starring Barry Morse as Lt. Philip Gerard
and William Conrad as The Narrator

Executive Producer: Quinn Martin
Created by Roy Huggins
Producer: Wilton Schiller
Assistant to the Executive Producer: John Conwell
In Charge of Production: Arthur Fellows, Adrian Samish
Co-Producer: John Meredyth Lucas, George Eckstein

Director of Photography: Robert Hoffman
Production Manager: Fred Ahern
Art Directors: James D. Vance, James Hulsey
Music: Peter Rugolo
Post-Production Supervisor: John Elizalde
Location Manager: Bud Brill
Casting: Meryl Abeles O'Loughlin
Film Editors: Walter Hannemann, James D. Ballas, Richard H. Cahoon, Jodie Copelan
Assistant Directors: Lou Place, Phil Cook, Robert Rubin
Property Masters: Irving Sindler, Don Smith
Chief Electrician: Vaughn Ashen
2nd Cameraman: Edward Nugent
Special Photographic Effects: Howard Anderson
Special Effects: Si Simonson
Music Supervisor: Ken Wilhoit
Set Decorator: Sandy Grace
Assistant Film Editors: Anthony Friedman, Tom Neff Jr., Martin Fox, Orven Schanzer, Harry Kaye, O. Nicholas Brown
Makeup Artist: Jack Wilson
Costume Supervisor: Edward McDermott
Costumers: Stephen Lodge, Karlice Hinson
Hair Stylists: Carol Meikle, Jean Austin
Key Grip: Ray Rich
Script Supervisor: Kenneth Gilbert
Editorial Consultant/2nd Unit Director: Carl Barth
Sound: The Goldwyn Studio
Production Mixers: John Kean, Barry Thomas
Sound Editor: Chuck Overhulser
Re-Recording: Clem Portman

PROLOG (FOURTH SEASON)

To me, *The Fugitive* was essentially a mood piece, and the black-and-white shows really brought out that element," said Stanford Whitmore, who wrote the pilot episode. "The black-and-white shows gave the series an edge that was lost when the show switched to color. I felt that the show became a little too 'pretty' when it switched to color, and that it lost a lot of the moodiness that was created by the black-and-white."

"From an aesthetic point of view, the black-and-white did bring a dimension to the drama that was lost by the switch to color," added co-producer George Eckstein. "But from a practical point of view, we had to make the switch, because most of the network shows by that time were broadcast in color—that became the rule rather than the exception."

With the switch to shooting in color, an already expensive series began to cost even more to produce. "The film itself not only costs more, but the film processing, print, and editing costs are also higher," explained assistant director Bob Rubin. "Because we could no longer use our huge library of stock footage from the first three years (which was all shot in black-and-white), editor Carl Barth, who was also our second unit director, and I spent many a freezing night shooting drivebys, cutaways, establishing shots, and photographic process plates (used in the background of interior car scenes actually shot in the studio) for use on our rear projection dialogue scenes."

The fourth season brought several other changes to the series, including a new producing team of Wilton Schiller and John Meredyth Lucas (both formerly of *Ben Casey*) and a new director of photography, Robert Hoffman. As part of a gradual slant toward action-oriented stories, the new team added new wrinkles to the series, such as establishing a $10,000 reward for the Fugitive and incorporating Fred Johnson (the one-armed man) into more stories. The shift toward action played up the chase element, leading to some exciting moments in such episodes as "The Ivy Maze," in which Kimble narrowly misses capturing his elusive prey.

However, the change in approach also took away from the series' strength—"emotionally" strong stories that, in executive producer Quinn Martin's view, were the key to impacting the mass general audience across the country. The quality of the writing, which began to decline slightly during the second half of the third season, suffered noticeably during the first few weeks of year four. Martin became so concerned about the writing that he convinced Eckstein to come back to *The Fugitive* about eight shows into the season. Not coincidentally, upon Eckstein's return, not only did the writing improve, but the series gradually regained its emotional balance.

Two more series with *Fugitive*-like concepts debuted in Fall 1966. Interestingly enough, one was *Shane* (starring a pre-*Kung Fu* David Carradine), a TV rendition of the Jack Schaefer novel (and 1953 Alan Ladd film) on which *The Fugitive* was partially based. The other series was *Run, Buddy, Run*, a situation comedy that parodied *The Fugitive*—Jack Sheldon played an accountant forced into hiding after mobsters mistakenly believe that he knows vital information about their organization. Both *Shane*, which was broadcast on ABC, and *Run, Buddy, Run* (CBS) were canceled by mid-season.

Episode 91

THE LAST OASIS

Original Airdate: September 13, 1966

Written by Barry Oringer. Directed by Gerald Mayer.

Guest Cast: Hope Lange (Annie Johnson), Mark Richman (Deputy Steel), Jaime Sanchez (Sam), Arch Johnson (Sheriff Prycer), John McLiam (Deputy Kelton), Lew Brown (Deputy O'Hara), Vincent Arias (Roger), Don Ross (American Guard), Eugene Iglesias (Mexican Guard), Silvia Marino (Nellie).

Prolog. *A fugitive has many enemies. A desert is among them. But the desert can also bring friends.*

Synopsis. Injured after being shot by local police, Kimble ("David Morrow") seeks refuge at an orphanage near an Indian reservation in Puma County, Arizona. Annie Johnson, the head teacher (and herself an orphan), removes the bullet and offers Kimble work as a teacher. Although the sheriff believes that Kimble has successfully escaped, his ambitious deputy continues the investigation, and soon suspects Annie of sheltering Kimble.

Epilog. *For Richard Kimble, a border is a dark tunnel whose other end might lead to the final encounter with the many-faced enemy. But for the moment, it leads to safety.*

"The Last Oasis" was the first episode produced by the new team of Wilton Schiller and John Meredyth Lucas. "I had worked with Wilton," recalled Lucas. "I was producer and he was executive producer on *Ben Casey*. He had also been my agent, then later on he became a successful writer and ultimately went on to produce. Wilton had hired me to write some of the *Ben Casey* shows, and I then went on to direct a lot of *Ben Casey*s. When the producer of the show left, I took over as producer of *Ben Casey* and Wilton was the executive producer. So we had a long relationship."

Lucas discussed some of the advantages and disadvantages of taking over an established series. "The advantages are that you have an operation that is completely in place," he said. "You're not having to worry about creating new characters, to build a new 'bible' of what the show is to be. The disadvantages are that you're limited in any change that you can make because you have very rigid parameters."

FUGE FOL DE ROL

Considering the name and background of Hope Lange's character, this episode could have been called "The Fugitive Meets Little Orphan Annie."

Except for a brief macho grimace, Kimble is noticeably quiet and expressionless as Annie removes the bullet from his leg. Perhaps Kimble is suggesting that once you've been shot a few times (as Kimble has to this point in the series), the bullets hurt less and less. Annie, however, is not as experienced in such matters—she herself looks a little queasy after removing the bullet.

Episode 92

DEATH IS THE DOOR PRIZE

Original Airdate: September 20, 1966

Written by Oliver Crawford. Directed by Don Medford.

Guest Cast: Lois Nettleton (Marcia Stone), Ossie Davis (Johnny Gaines), Howard da Silva (Pete Dawes), John Lasell (Mr. Lee), Kevin O'Neal (Gary), June Vincent (Mrs. Lee), Len Wayland (Boles), Wolfe Barzell (Tailor), John Harmon (Texan), Harlan Warde (Anderson), Jess Kirkpatrick (Ben), Bill Erwin (Man), John Ward (Dan).

Prolog. *For a fugitive, there must be wariness in even the simplest chore: an extra sense, sharpened by the two-fold chase—the fugitive hunted and the fugitive hunting.*

Synopsis. In his rush to follow a one-armed man into an electronics exhibit, Kimble ("Ed Sanders") accidentally knocks over a sales representative, Marcia Stone, who loses her purse as a result. After discovering that the man's arm is broken, Kimble returns the purse, but a bystander who thinks Kimble has stolen it has already reported him to security. Kimble hides inside a storeroom, where he witnesses Pete Dawes, a security guard, shoot a young robber in an apparent act of self defense. Kimble runs off, unaware that without his testimony, Dawes faces possible manslaughter charges.

Epilog. *A fugitive moves on, through anguished tunnels of time, down dim streets, into dark corners. And each new day offers fear and frustration, tastes of honey—and hemlock. But if there is a hazard, there is also hope.*

"Death is the Door Prize" is a badly-paced episode that is excruciating to watch, despite good performances by Howard da Silva and Lois Nettleton. The jarring cuts from scene to scene, together with the choppy dialogue ("Hey, Pete/Hey, Johnny"), keep the viewers from getting into the story. The one attempt to draw the audience's emotions (Dawes' plea to Kimble) comes far too late; the viewers by this point are too distanced to care.

The pivotal scene of this episode occurs in Act I, when Dawes kills Stu, one of the young thieves. Even after several slow motion replays, it's difficult to determine what the boy was trying to do when he reached for his side. The description of that sequence in Oliver Crawford's teleplay is no more helpful: "He makes a gesture—it could be fright—or a threat—a definite move to his rear pocket—[before] Dawes fires." It looks like Stu was reaching for a weapon, although none was found on his person; however, since he was on a ladder, he may have been trying to keep his balance (assuming he was scared). The sequence takes place too quickly to tell for sure—and the rapid cut back to Dawes does not help.

Episode 93

A CLEAN AND QUIET TOWN

Original Airdate: September 27, 1966

Written by Howard Browne. Directed by Mark Rydell.

Guest Cast: Carol Rossen (Cora), Michael Strong (Oliver Enright), Bill Bramley (Lynch), Bill Raisch (Fred Johnson), George Brenlin (Cab Driver), Peter Brecco (Dry Cleaning Man), Susan Davis (Miss Moretti), Ted Gehring (Sergeant), Alan Emerson (Hamp), Lloyd Haynes (Officer), Robert Karnes (Chief Abbott), Orville Sherman (Hotel Clerk), Ed Deemer (Ralph), Eduardo Cianelli (Victor Luchek).

Prolog. *A man on the run comes to expect neither justice nor mercy. Every hand is against him; every face turns away from his pain. In such moments, the thread of hope, of life itself, stretches to the breaking point.*

Synopsis. Kimble ("Paul Miller") surfaces in the gambling town of Clark City, where he is badly beaten by two policemen dispatched by Johnson ("Steve Cramer"), who works as a numbers runner. After a street walker nurses Kimble (after first trying to steal his wallet), the Fugitive reports the incident to Oliver Enright, who manages the town on behalf of former mobster Victor Luchek. Suspicious that someone is undermining him, Enright uses Kimble to bait a trap. Meanwhile, Johnson puts out a contract on the Fugitive.

Epilog. *A man on the run must never stop. After every fall he must get up, push on toward the same elusive goal, a goal so close at times as to be only a heartbreak away.*

"The golden days of television" is a term usually associated with a specific time (circa 1950s and early 1960s) in the medium's seminal days that featured such excellent anthology programs as *Playhouse 90* and *The U.S. Steel Hour.* But to the people who worked during that period, the "golden days" reflected an attitude when the heads of the three major networks respected the abilities of the people they hired to perform their jobs without interference. "It was a time in which producers had power, and a passion for their material and developed it out of that passion, understood the show, and proceeded to do their show without having the endless input of network and studio executives, as is the case today," recalled Carol Rossen. "This [interference] simply wasn't done! So, therefore, producers who were really wonderful producers understood their material and understood how to surround themselves with really wonderful people to fulfill that material in all departments—acting, directing, etc.

"Quinn was one of those people, as you can see by his record as a producer. He had a real genuine respect for what everybody did. That's what made him a great producer. He hired whom he perceived to be the best people, and let them do it. So there was none of that feeling on *The Fugitive* that you were a 'less than,' or you were a hired hand. You were fully participatory in terms of what your contribution was."

Although Martin wielded a lot of control in his organization, he was not an obtrusive boss, but rather kept to himself and let his "people" do their jobs. "Quinn never 'big dealed' himself on the set," continued Rossen. "Some producers come on a working set to see how it's going, and actors get very nervous when 'strangers' suddenly appear like that. They feel they're being judged, that they are not free to experiment, to make mistakes, to find the scene or the character. Quinn never did that—never, ever intruded on the work process.

"I remember a wonderful story about that. One night after working very late, David and I were walking down a studio street to his dressing room to have a drink or something. And a man passed us in the dark on the street. And as he passed, he said simply, 'Hi, Carol... David. The dailies look wonderful!' So I asked David, 'Who was that?' And he said, 'Quinn!' I'd worked for him four or five times by then and had never met him. I didn't take that as indifference. I took that as smart."

Martin left television in the late 1970s, around the time when the networks began to usurp more control over their programs. The "golden days," where producers enjoyed creative autonomy, were over. Rossen believes that television has been adversely effected by the passage of this era, not only in terms of quality but in viewership. "People watched commercial television in those days. They don't now, not the way they did, if the polls are correct," she said. "I think they don't watch it because networks and other business executives, rather than the talent, are making the creative decisions, and therefore watering down concept and quality. But the networks still haven't put that little thought together!"

FUGE FIRSTS

Kimble willingly surrenders himself to the police—the only time he does so in the series. After overpowering Johnson in an alley, Kimble presents his longtime quarry to the police and turns himself in, so that he can later present Johnson to Lt. Gerard. The fight scene will remind viewers of the famous sequence in "The Judgment" in which Kimble beats the confession out of Johnson. The confrontation in "The Judgment" is far superior, however; the camera focuses clearly on Kimble's face (it cuts back and forth between Kimble and Johnson in this episode).

FUGE FOL DE ROL

Bill Raisch, who looks quite natty in this episode, is inexplicably billed as "Cramer." The one-armed man's name had already been established as Fred Johnson in "Escape into Black."

FUGE FEATURE FILM MAKERS

Since *The Fugitive*, Mark Rydell has directed box-office successes such as *The Fox*, *Cinderella Liberty*, *Harry and Walter Go to New York*, and *The Rose*. Rydell was once married to actress Joanne Linville, who previously guest starred in "Running Scared."

Episode 94

THE SHARP EDGE OF CHIVALRY

Original Airdate: October 4, 1966

Written by Sam Ross. Directed by Gerald Mayer.

Guest Cast: Robert Drivas (Roger Roland), Eduard Franz (Edward Roland), Madlyn Rhue (Liz Roland), Rosemary Murphy (Mrs. Turney), Richard Anderson (Lt. Sloan), Ellen Corby (Mrs. Murdock), Judee Morton (Millie), Henry Scott (Policeman), Paul Kent (Policeman), Walter Gregg (Boyfriend), Bobby Johnson (Man), Ralph Montgomery (Fingerprint Man), Sy Prescott (Plainclothesman), Bob Duggan (Policeman), Peter Madsen (Sergeant), Kay Riehl (Woman).

Prolog. *A big city: a jungle of anonymity, where nobody looks too close, and everybody is locked in with his own big problem. A hiding place for a man who, for the moment, calls himself Carl Baker.*

Synopsis. A descendant of royalty, Roger Roland is a troubled young man who rejects his family's heritage (he dyes his hair black). One night, Roger murders a young woman, then hides the weapon (a statue) inside Kimble's apartment. After a tenant reports seeing a figure dashing from the girl's room, the police suspect Kimble, despite his alibi (he was helping another tenant). After the police find evidence of black hair dye, Kimble hurries to his room, where he discovers the statue and hides it inside the air vent. Kimble thinks Roger is involved and notifies his family, but Roger's father suspects Kimble and phones the police. Meanwhile, Lt. Gerard arrives in town after hearing the story on the news.

Epilog. *One man is still the hunter, and the other is still the Fugitive.*

Gerard's first appearance of the season is a welcome sight after three disappointing episodes. Granted, "The Sharp Edge of Chivalry" is not much better, but the episode has its moments. The murder scene, staged from the victim Millie's P.O.V. (the camera is angled upward as Roger moves in on her), is quite chilling. Gerard's entrance and exit are nicely bridged—the camera zooms down on him in Act I, then pulls away at the final fade to black.

Episode 95

TEN THOUSAND PIECES OF SILVER

Original Airdate: October 11, 1966

Teleplay by E. Arthur Kean and Wilton Schiller. Story by E. Arthur Kean. Directed by James Nielson.

Guest Cast: Lin McCarthy (Jacob Lawrence), Joe Maross (Sheriff Mel Bailey), June Harding (Cathy Lawrence), Paul Mantee (Joe Burmas), Bonnie Beecher (Ella Lawrence), Ford Rainey (Ollie Corman), Simon Scott (Pierce), James Sikking (Deputy Marsh).

Prolog. *At dawn he rises to labor through the sunlight hours. His hands, skilled enough for a surgeon's knife, are forced to cruder tasks, tasks no longer of his own choosing. Not even his name is his own.*

Synopsis. Kimble ("Dave Livingston") finds work on Jake Lawrence's farm, where he develops a special friendship with Jake's autistic daughter Cathy. But he soon becomes nervous when the sheriff begins searching for Joe Burmas, another convicted murderer. Burmas nearly kills Kimble after trapping him inside a truck that crashes into a creek. Meanwhile, *The Stafford Chronicle* establishes a $10,000 reward for the Fugitive's capture. The local storekeeper recognizes Kimble's face on the newspaper and decides to collect the money himself. Kimble tries to evade the posse but again runs into Burmas. When Gerard and the sheriff investigate the Lawrences, Kimble's only hope lies with Cathy.

Epilog. *A fugitive gets his fill of goodbyes, of loyalties born and discarded, yet not discarded. For the fugitive game is a lonely one, with only two players to see it through, a game that would seem without end.*

"Ten Thousand Pieces of Silver" is a pivotal episode in two respects. It introduces the $10,000 reward for information leading to the Fugitive's capture, a plot device that will resurface several times over the remainder of the series. It also marks the final episode produced by Wilton Schiller and John Meredyth Lucas. The new team experienced many difficulties, particularly with the scripts, and the series was adversely affected as a result. "I know they had some problems," commented Alan Armer. "A couple of times, Adrian Samish came to me [on the set of *The Invaders*] and said, 'Can you give us some story ideas?' And I did—I don't know if they used them or if they didn't."

However, in discussing the fourth season, Armer refrained from criticizing the new producers because he knew exactly what they were experiencing at the time. "I was having problems of my own," he said. "Remember, in the first year of a series, you're kind of finding out what works and what doesn't, and *The Invaders* was a very tough series. I was having major struggles of my own, just to get the scripts and to get the shows filmed. I didn't really have a chance to see many of the fourth season *Fugitives*.

"I know Will was having some problems. Every series has its own character, its own personality, its own format, its own style of story telling. For someone to come into a series in the fourth year, it's hard to instantly grasp all of the subtleties in that. I'm sure it would have been difficult for anybody."

The biggest problem that plagued the Schiller/Lucas scripts was a matter of approach. The early fourth season episodes veered more toward the "melodramatic" (Quinn Martin's term for plot elements), and away from "emotion" (the pivotal element that enabled the program to reach the viewers). "I suppose Wilton's attitude was more that this was more of a melodrama than it was a drama," said George Eckstein. "That would have been reflected in that kind of change [from emotion to melodrama]."

Eckstein believes the change in approach was not so much a deliberate attempt to put a new stamp on the show, but rather a subconscious reflection of a new producer's style. "That sort of change happens unconsciously; there's no plan for that," he said. "You don't start the season with an overview. You don't start the season saying, 'Well, what are we gonna do different? How are we gonna approach the scripts differently?'

"Wilton as the producer, for the most part, brought in a whole different set of writers than Alan had," Eckstein continued. "Most producers in town have certain writers that they call upon again and again to write their scripts. Alan and Wilton were two different people that never crossed paths, so the individual writers that Wilton brought in were a whole different group than the writers who had been writing the show the first three years (except for me). And so, you get a different point of view, and different attitude, as communicated from the producer to the writer as to what the show is about. I don't know whether one is superior to the other. But the first three years probably were more personal dramas than were the last year, which was of a melodramatic line."

Quinn Martin, however, apparently believed that the first approach was better than the new approach. Without the emotional drive that fueled the first three seasons, the quality of the writing suffered considerably. Even though *The Fugitive* still enjoyed healthy ratings, Martin was concerned enough about the writing to ask Eckstein to return to the series as co-producer and help Schiller with the scripts. "George is a superb writer, and he knew the series," said Armer. "He was the perfect choice to go in and help Will."

The odd man out was Lucas. "I was not completely happy in the organization, and I felt I would rather work outside it," he said.

Ironically, Lucas left at the point where he and Schiller were beginning to grasp the particular subtleties of *The Fugitive*. Their final two episodes ("Nobody Loses All the Time" and "Ten Thousand Pieces of Silver") were "emotionally" strong stories whose dramatic pull came from Dr. Kimble's interaction with the characters. These episodes captured some of the flavor of the first three seasons. Lucas, who later went on to produce and direct several episodes of the original *Star Trek* television series, would return to *The Fugitive* as a writer and director later this season.

FUGE FUN

While Dr. Kimble rarely sees his sister Donna (only three times over the first three seasons), he certainly manages to bump into his brother-in-law Len Taft quite a bit. "Ten Thousand Pieces of Silver" features two of the three actors who played Len—Lin McCarthy ("Running Scared") and James Sikking ("Home is the Hunted"). The previous episode ("The Sharp Edge of Chivalry") featured the third—Richard Anderson, who played Len in "The Judgment."

Costumer Steve Lodge recalls some of the shenanigans that took place during the filming of "Ten Thousand Pieces of Silver," parts of which were filmed on the old Crash Corrigan movie ranch in Simi Valley, California. "We had put David into a lake, in a truck, while on location," Lodge recalled. "Then we were on the set, and we had to match him in a small tank, where later the sheriff rescues him, and they're driving back some place, and David's got to still be wet. We used warm water to make him feel comfortable. And somebody said, 'Why don't you put some ice cubes in it?' And I said, 'You can't do that!' And they said, 'Don't worry about it, he's got a great sense of humor!' After we had done it about 15 times, we'd put ice cubes in the water, and I went up to him before the shot and hit him with a couple sponges full of ice water—and he came out of that truck and chased me all over the place!"

Episode 96

JOSHUA'S KINGDOM

Original Airdate: October 18, 1966

Written by Lee Loeb. Directed by Gerd Oswald.

Guest Cast: Harry Townes (Joshua Simmons), Kim Darby (Ruth Simmons), Tom Skerritt (Pete), Walter Burke (Doc Martin), John Milford (Sheriff), Vaughn Taylor (Feeney), Mark Russell (Deputy).

Prolog. *A fugitive is like a long distance runner, with a difference: a fugitive's distance is infinity. Infinity is a long, impossibly long, way away, and there must be time for the hunted to rest, to gather strength to move once again.*

Synopsis. Kimble ("Jim Corman") assists a small town veterinarian. While he attending to Joshua Simmons' horses, Joshua's daughter Ruth asks the Fugitive to check her feverish baby. Joshua's strict religious beliefs prohibit the use of medicine. But when Ruth persists, Kimble prescribes antibiotics, although Joshua soon destroys the drugs. After determining that the baby is anemic, Kimble arranges for a transfusion (using his own Type O blood). Meanwhile, after stumbling onto Kimble's wanted poster, a would-be deputy searches for the Fugitive with the aid of two bloodhounds.

Epilog. *Richard Kimble, both the hunted and the hunter. The truth that will free him is somewhere ahead. He'll find it.*

Part of the fun of watching *The Fugitive* today lies in recognizing the many familiar (or soon to be familiar) actors that appear on-screen over the course of the series. In addition to showcasing such already prominent performers as Suzanne Pleshette, Melvyn Douglas, Angie Dickinson, and Ed Begley, *The Fugitive* helped paved the way for many stars in the making, such as Robert Duvall (*Lonesome Dove*), Kim Darby (*True Grit*), Tom Skerritt (*Alien*), and Dabney Coleman (*Nine to Five*).

But according to casting director John Conwell, no one person is responsible for "discovering" any performer. "A lot of people are involved," he said. "For instance, I had seen Robert Duvall on *Naked City*, and I just thought he was terrific. A script came up, and I mentioned it to Quinn, and he didn't know who Duvall was. I said, 'Do you want to look at the kinescope [which was what we had in those days]?' And he said, 'No, no, no. You just cast him.'"

Conwell also mentioned Tom Skerritt and Dabney Coleman as examples of how many people are involved in the making of a star. "Tom and Dabney were unknown people at that time," he said. "I'm not saying I 'discovered' them. You know, an agent would call me: 'Would you meet this actor? He's terrific,' and so I met, say, Tom and Dabney. And then when I had something I thought they were right for, I brought them in to read, and I cast them [Skerritt and Coleman worked on many QM series]. And later on, they both made names for themselves, in features and on television." Skerritt stars in *Picket Fences*; Coleman won an Emmy for Best Supporting Actor in *Sworn to Silence* (1987).

FUGE FAMILIAR FACES

"Kim Darby was excellent in both of the shows she worked on," said assistant director Bob Rubin. "She was only 18 when she did 'An Apple a Day,' and she could hardly believe she was acting opposite this very handsome, very famous, television star! She and David worked well together—they proved very strengthening to each other's performance. Because of Kim's fine work on the first show, David was very open to working with her again and again."

Darby later played Janssen's daughter in the motion picture *Generation* (1969), also starring Andrew Prine (Ray Kimble in "Home is the Hunted").

Episode 97

SECOND SIGHT

Original Airdate: October 25, 1966

Written by Dan Ullman. Directed by Robert Douglas.

Guest Cast: Tim Considine (Howie Keever), Ned Glass (Albert), Crahan Denton (George), William Sargent (Sgt. Denny), Ted Knight (Dr. Rains), James Noah (Detective), Janet MacLachlan (Nurse), Richard O'Brien (Macklin), Stuart Lancaster (Wingo), Sidney Clute (Bartender), Byron Keith (Foreman), Victor Millan (Garcia), Nancy Jeris (Policewoman), Angela Greene (Floor Nurse), Bill Raisch (Fred Johnson).

Prolog. *For a fugitive to survive, he must rely entirely on his senses. Richard Kimble has survived because his senses have become exceptional. The world is his jungle, and the tiger he stalks is a man with one arm. From Kimble's years in this jungle, he has learned to miss nothing, and to react quickly, as one must in a jungle.*

Synopsis. Working at a film supply store, Kimble ("Jack Anderson") discovers a photograph of Fred Johnson ("Walters"). After learning that Johnson works at a chemical warehouse, Kimble surprises Johnson. But the one-armed man ignites some chemicals, and the ensuing explosion blinds Kimble. Johnson then reports Kimble to the police while the Fugitive is in the hospital, but Kimble manages to escape. Kimble tries to locate Howie Keever, the boy who photographed Johnson. But the police question Howie and his uncle, who both learn about the $10,000 reward. Kimble arrives at Howie's apartment, but is soon arrested after Howie's uncle turns him in.

Epilog. *And so Richard Kimble, fugitive, is back in the jungle again, where, as always, he must be the prey of others, until the day where once more, he can become the hunter.*

This is the worst episode of the series, but not for the usual reasons (writing, acting, direction, editing, etc.). Although deficient in those areas, what makes "Second Sight" truly awful is David Janssen's wretched performance.

From the fan's point of view, it is embarrassing to watch Janssen in "Second Sight." Granted, he's following the script—a doctor instructs Kimble not to open his eyes—but

Janssen plays it so broad that his performance borders on camp. Kimble bumbles around with his arms flailing, and crashes into every garbage can he finds.

In a sense, Janssen was victimized by the premise of the story. Rendering Kimble blind meant robbing Janssen of one of his strongest acting features—his ability to convey emotion to the audience through his eyes. This problem could have been remedied by using more closeup shots. Although Janssen has some closeups—he displays genuine fear in the scene where Kimble seeks help from the two bums—the damage has already been done. Whatever tension the remainder of the story generates (a policewoman aids Kimble across the street) has been contaminated by the unintentionally hilarious setup.

What "Second Sight" needs is Gerard, who usually surfaces whenever Kimble closes in on the one-armed man. Gerard by his very presence would have added tension to the proceedings. Given Kimble's handicap, the lieutenant would finally have an advantage over Kimble—and would be hard pressed not to botch the arrest.

FUGE FACTS

The nurse notes the $10,000 reward after she is shown Kimble's wanted poster in Act II; this is noteworthy because "Second Sight" was actually filmed before the episode that introduced the reward ("Ten Thousand Pieces of Silver").

Episode 98

WINE IS A TRAITOR

Original Airdate: November 1, 1966

Written by Arthur Dales. Directed by Gerd Oswald.

Guest Cast: Roy Thinnes (Carl Crandall), Pilar Seurat (Elena Morales), James Gregory (Pete Crandall), Carlos Romero (Morales), Richard O'Brien (Sheriff), Dabbs Greer (Thomas), Robert Wilke (Johnny), Warren Kemmerling (Nick), Rodolfo Acosta (Mexican #1), Victor Millan (Mexican #2), Roy Jensen (Deputy), Chet Stratton (Guide), Grandon Rhodes (Physician), Jason Johnson (Mann), Martin Garralaga (Felipe), William Challe (Jim), Arch Whiting (Deputy).

Prolog. *For a fugitive, the offer of help—some simple, decent act of kindness—must be rejected. There are no relationships of any duration for him. Life consists of fleeting contacts.*

Synopsis. Carl Crandall thwarts a pending labor strike at his father Pete's winery by murdering the instigator and framing Morales, another worker. Kimble ("Taylor") knows that Carl is the gunman (he recognizes his shirt), but is unable to tell anyone. (He wrote the District Attorney, but the letter was confiscated.) When Pete suspects his son, he dispatches two men to watch him—unaware that the same men have a stronger loyalty to Carl. The two men set out to murder Kimble.

Epilog. *A hunted man can clutch at a single straw, that one day the hunters will lay down their guns. But for Richard Kimble, that day has not yet come.*

"Roy Thinnes was a fabulously talented, hard-working guy who was respected by probably everybody he ever worked with, but he was never fully appreciated by the front office," said assistant director Bob Rubin, who worked with Thinnes on *The Invaders.* "Like David Janssen, Roy was a dedicated, creative actor, but he never enjoyed the kind of clout within QM Productions that David had simply because *The Invaders* never became the smash—creatively and as a moneymaker—that *The Fugitive* was."

FUGE FIRSTS

This is the first episode co-produced by Wilton Schiller and George Eckstein.

Episode 99

APPROACH WITH CARE

Original Airdate: November 15, 1966

Written by Leo Loeb. Directed by William Hale.

Guest Cast: Denny Miller (Willie Turner), Collin Wilcox (Mary Turner), Malcolm Atterbury (Sheriff), Nick Colasanto (Matt), Dabney Coleman (Steve Edwards), Michael Conrad (Hogan), Paul Lukather (1st Deputy), E.J. Andre (Old Man), Don Ross (3rd Deputy), Marlowe Jensen (2nd Deputy), Art Lewis (Speiler), Marcelle Fortier (Woman), Phil Chambers (2nd Carney), Mark Allen (Wrecker), Jimmy Stiles (Joey), Roy Stevens (Boy #1), Marc Winters (Boy #2).

Prolog. *A traveling carny: here one day, there the next. A place for a man on the run. A place for Richard Kimble.*

Synopsis. Willie Turner, a mentally retarded young man wrongly accused of hurting a child, hides at the local carnival where Kimble ("Pete Allen") now works. Kimble tries to convince Willie to return to the hospital where his sister had him committed. An attendant from the hospital searches for Willie at the carnival, but instead recognizes Kimble. Trying to protect his new friend, Willie strikes the attendant, then warns Kimble. The two fugitives commandeer a truck and hide in an auto wrecking lot. But the sheriff is not far behind.

Epilog. *For some men the world has provided little room, no place for them to live as other men. But for Richard Kimble, there is such a place. And to find it he must now continue his lonely search.*

Kimble is remarkably callous and impatient with Willie at several points in "Approach with Care." While Kimble's plight does not always allow him the time to be patient with a person like Willie, this sort of behavior seems highly inappropriate, given Kimble's medical background. (In "Terror at Highpoint," we learned that Kimble was specifically trained to treat children who have learning disabilities.) Although larger and older than most, Willie is, after all, a child.

FUGE FACTS

The male nurse Hogan (played by Michael Conrad of *Hill Street Blues*) said that he worked with Kimble at Fairgreen Memorial Hospital, which (according to "The Survivors") is where Kimble interned—and met his future wife Helen.

Episode 100

NOBODY LOSES ALL THE TIME

Original Airdate: November 22, 1966

Written by E. Arthur Kean. Directed by Lawrence Dobkin.

Guest Cast: Joanna Moore (Ruth Bianchi), Phillip E. Pine (Lt. Rowan), Barbara Baxley (Maggie Tibbett), Don Dubbins (McCaffrey), Herb Ellis (Hallet), Ben Wright (Ferguson), Bill Raisch (Fred Johnson), Nora Marlowe (Woman in Hotel), Lawrence Atkin (Workman), Patrick Riley (Policeman), Pat O'Hara (Officer #1), Robert Munk (Officer #2), Guy Remsen (2nd Policeman).

Prolog. *Any public disaster will attract a crowd of spectators, people secretly pleased, perhaps, that they are not touched by the tragedy, that they may walk away from the dying and go on about their lives. But one man here today cannot remain so uninvolved, so insulated against another's pain. He is bound by an oath taken many* *years ago, an oath written by a man named Hippocrates: "I will follow that method of treatment which, according to my ability and judgment, I consider for the benefit of my patients. Into whatever houses I enter, I will enter them for the benefit of the sick." These words, remembered from better days, return to haunt Richard Kimble.*

Synopsis. While watching a TV report of a fire, Kimble spots Johnson, and heads downtown, but Johnson sees Kimble and flees. After a truck hits the woman accompanying Johnson, Kimble ("Dr. Harry Robertson") orders an ambulance and takes her to the hospital. After removing a key from the woman's purse, Kimble visits her hotel room and finds a picture of the woman (whose name is Maggie Tibbett) with Johnson. Maggie, hesitant to help Kimble, contacts Johnson—who then orders her to call the police.

Epilog. *"I will practice my profession with conscience and dignity. Even under threat, I will not use my medical knowledge contrary to the laws of humanity. I make these promises solemnly, freely, and upon my honor." And for Richard Kimble, fugitive, they still apply.*

"Nobody Loses All the Time" marks the third appearance this season of Bill Raisch as Fred Johnson, the one-armed man (Raisch had only appeared in a total of three episodes going into the fourth year). Apparently, as part of a gradual slant toward action-oriented scripts, new producer Wilton Schiller wanted to incorporate the one-armed man into more stories. As a result of the increased on-screen exposure, a few wrinkles are added to Johnson's character—in this episode, for example, he has a love interest (played by Barbara Baxley).

Although Raisch had plenty of experience as a performer (he was a professional dancer prior to becoming a movie stuntman), he had very little experience as an actor. "Bill had never spoken dialogue in his life," recalled Barry Morse. "He was quite terrified, I remember, when they started to use him more in the series, and actually require him to speak dialogue once in a while. I can remember him saying to me, 'What do I do with this, Barry? I've got lines, here!' And I'd say, 'It's all right, you know. You just talk like we're talking now.' And he turned out to be very good, didn't he?"

FUGE FACTS

Maggie's betrayal of Kimble puzzles Gerard. The Lieutenant has found that people usually want to help the Fugitive.

FUGE FAMILIARITY

Prime Time Proverbs: The Book of TV Quotes (Harmony Books, 1989) includes *The Fugitive* twice in its section "Life's a Bitch." The book borrows quotes from "The Breaking of the Habit" ("For a fugitive, there are no freeways: all roads are toll roads, to be paid in blood and pain") and this episode ("It's all one big roll of the dice, and nobody loses all the time").

Episode 101

RIGHT IN THE MIDDLE OF THE SEASON

Original Airdate: November 29, 1966

Written by Sam Ross. Directed by Christian Nyby.

Guest Cast: Dean Jagger (Tony Donovan), Nancy Malone (Nedda Donovan), James Callahan (Joe Donovan), Douglas Henderson (Lt. Irwin), James Seay (Morgan), Charles Wagerheim (Fisherman), Ron Stokes (Boatswain's Mate), Greg Benedict (Policeman), Robert Kline (Policeman), John Mayo (Fingerprint Man), James Johnson (Crewman).

Prolog. *The open sea is a perfect place for a fugitive: nothing but water and great horizons. But always the land pulls you back. And for Richard Kimble, the horizon is a small offcoast fishing island, now a strike-torn battleground. A dangerous place for a man on the run.*

Synopsis. Veteran fisherman Tony Donovan steers Kimble ("Eddie Carter") into a labor dispute organized by his son Joe. A fight breaks out, and Tony and Kimble are arrested. After being marked for fingerprints, Kimble tries to leave town, but the police refuse to let anyone leave until the trouble subsides. After the police question him, Tony offers to take Kimble to Mexico if the Fugitive helps him on the next fishing trip. But Joe sees Tony smuggle Kimble on board and notifies the authorities.

Epilog. *Another horizon, another haven to look for. The constant search of a fugitive.*

Director Christian Nyby spoke well of Quinn Martin, whom he had known professionally and personally for many years (Nyby used to play poker with Martin's father). "I directed *The Streets of San Francisco* and a few other series for him," Nyby said. "Quinn was very supportive. He knew ahead of time who he wanted, and how to get them, and they'd leave him not only as employees, but as friends. That was a good basis for a good relationship for making good pictures."

Martin not only knew how to get the people he wanted, he also knew how to leave them alone to do their jobs. "We did this episode down in the harbor of San Pedro, and we never even heard from Quinn," Nyby said. "I didn't hear from him for five days. Finally, when he called, he said, 'How do things look?' I said, 'Oh, great, great!' He would leave you pretty much alone. That isn't true of all producers, but Quinn was that way."

FUGE FAMILIAR FACES

Prize-winning actor Dean Jagger brings an element of frailty and despair to his role as Tony Donovan. The old salt clearly likes and trusts Kimble, and the loss he feels at the thought of Kimble leaving is evident. Jagger, who won a Best Supporting Actor Oscar for *Twelve O'Clock High* (1950) and an Emmy for *This is the Life* (1980), starred opposite James Franciscus on TV's *Mr. Novak* (1963-65). Jagger passed away in 1991.

Episode 102

THE DEVIL'S DISCIPLES

Original Airdate: November 29, 1966

**Teleplay by Jeri Emmett and Steven W. Carabatsos.
Story by Robert Dillon and Steven W. Carabatsos.
Directed by Jud Taylor.**

Guest Cast: Lou Antonio (Don), Bruce Dern (Hutch), Diana Hyland (Patty), Frank Marth (Sheriff Hendricks), Robert Viharo (Chino), Robert Sorrells (Curley), Crahan Denton (Benson), Hal Lynch (Andy), William Wintersole (Pilot), Harry Ellerbe (Dr. Crossland).

Prolog. *To Richard Kimble, the laws of society are threatening, for society has judged him guilty of breaking the law, and ruled that he be punished unto death. But there are other societies with laws no less threatening, no less extreme, and punishing those who violate its code.*

Synopsis. After saving Kimble from a sheriff's dragnet, a motorcycle gang known as the Devil's Disciples wants the Fugitive to avenge the death of a former member whose father sent him to Vietnam as punishment for robbing a filling station. When Kimble discovers that the gang is not completely unified, he seeks help from one of the members so that he can warn the police and prevent the killing.

Epilog. *For some, the future is a limitless vista, bright and shining, full of hope. For Richard Kimble, the future, like the past, is a recurring nightmare, in which hope is a cynic's smile.*

Assistant director Bob Rubin remembered that Bruce Dern was an avid, near Olympics-level, long-distance runner. "One morning Bruce called me at 7:15 and said he knew he was due at 7:30, but that he was running late getting to work at the Studio in Hollywood," he recalled. "He said, 'Don't worry, I'll be there. I'm about eight miles away, but I'm stuck in traffic: Coldwater Canyon is jammed with cars.' I very much appreciated the call; I had been concerned, since he was set to work in every scene that day. About half an hour later, Bruce showed up on the sound stage, wearing his running clothes. He hadn't driven his car at all. It was a nice day out, and so he actually ran to work. That's what he meant when he called to say he was *running* late!"

FUGE FIGURES

Executive producer Quinn Martin paid top dollar for his guest stars. "Actors of the caliber of Mickey Rooney, Diane Baker, Jack Lord, Melvyn Douglas or Suzanne Pleshette could command as much as $3,000 a show, which was the top figure for TV at the time," said Rubin. "*We* would pay them $5,000 a show. Quinn Martin was willing to do that—in front of the camera and behind it as well. He paid top dollar to assemble a great team, and then he let them work. In exchange, he had a Top 10 show, week after week. Advertisers loved *The Fugitive*."

FUGE FACTS

Director Jud Taylor, who previously appeared as an actor in "Glass Tightrope," "May God Have Mercy," and "Landscape with Running Figures," also directed David Janssen in the TV-movie *City in Fear* (1980)—Janssen's final screen appearance.

Episode 103

THE BLESSINGS OF LIBERTY

Original Airdate: December 20, 1966

Written by Dan Ullman. Directed by Joseph Pevney.

Guest Cast: Ludwig Donath (Josef Karac), Julie Sommars (Carla Karac), Arlene Martel (Magda Karac), Jan Merlin (Jan Karac), Tony Musante (Billy Karnes/Bowen), Noam Pitlik (Jim Macklin), George Tyne (Sgt. Charney), Edwin Max (Stark), Nolan Leary (Judge), Chuck Courtney (Detective), Bruce Manning (Attendant), Calvin Brown (Cop #1).

Prolog. *Richard Kimble, fugitive, like everyone else, has to stop long enough to work, and eat, and rest, even though every time he does any of these things, his own personal danger increases tenfold.*

Synopsis. The police, searching for an escaped murderer named Bowen, stake out the apartment of a Hungarian family and assign policeman Jim Macklin to work undercover at the upholstery shop where the killer was last seen. After Kimble ("Ben Russell") finds work at the shop, Macklin recognizes him and begins a second investigation. Meanwhile, Bowen returns and takes the family hostage.

Prolog. *He stands convicted of a crime he did not commit. His full-time occupation is a search for the guilty man. There is no one who has a greater appreciation of freedom, and of the blessings of liberty, than Richard Kimble—fugitive.*

"When Elmer Ellsworth was the Costume Supervisor, every police department depicted on *The Fugitive* was wardrobed 100% authentic," said costumer Steve Lodge. "Ellsworth would spend hours on the long distance line with the various police officials, getting every minute detail of that particular law enforcement (city, state, county) agency's uniform. Then Western Costume Company would prepare 'costume' uniforms to look exactly like the real thing. This is one reason, I feel, that those first three years looked so much better than the final year.

"After Elmer left [replaced by Ed McDermott in the fourth year], all the police wore nondescript blue uniforms and the sheriffs wore nondescript green and tan," Lodge continued. "The prop department was affected in the same way: in the first three years, *all* law enforcement vehicles were matched exactly to the real ones in the depicted locale. But in the fourth year: black and white for police, tan for sheriffs."

FUGE FAMILIAR FACES

Tony Musante (Bowen) later starred as *Toma* (1973-74), a Roy Huggins series based on real-life undercover cop Dave Toma. When Musante left the series after one year, ABC revamped *Toma*, which reappeared in early 1975 as *Baretta*. Musante later co-starred with David Janssen in the TV-movie *High Ice* (1980).

Best known as the obnoxious Mr. Gianelli on *The Bob Newhart Show,* Noam Pitlik (Macklin) later became a prolific TV director (he won an Emmy in 1979 for directing *Barney Miller*). Likewise, Jan Merlin (Jan) experienced success outside of acting—he won an Emmy in 1975 for outstanding writing on *Another World.*

FUGE FACTS

"The Blessings of Liberty" was co-produced by John Meredyth Lucas: although it aired 13th, it was the fifth episode produced.

Episode 104

THE EVIL MEN DO

Original Airdate: December 27, 1966

Written by Walter Brough. Directed by Jesse Hibbs.

Guest Cast: James Daly (Arthur Brame), Elizabeth Allen (Sharon), David Sheiner (Sheriff Robinson), James McCallion (Delaney), Bill Zuckert (Clark), Barry Russo (Sgt. Endicott), Tom Signorelli (Mechanic), Jhean Burton (Waitress).

Prolog. *A temporary job in the peaceful meadows of the Pocono Mountains in Pennsylvania. Calling himself Russell Jordan, Richard Kimble has had a rare chance to relax, to catch his breath, at least for a few days.*

Synopsis. Gerard receives word that Kimble has been spotted in the Pocono Mountains of Pennsylvania. After Kimble saves the life of his employer, Arthur Brame, the wealthy rancher (and former mobster) is determined to repay the debt. When he discovers that Gerard is after Kimble, Brame puts out a contract on the lieutenant.

Epilog. *"No real menace to anyone but himself"—that's the way it must be for Richard Kimble, still alone and hunted. Even the good he might do is unable to balance the scales of justice which has made him, and keep him, a fugitive.*

"The Evil Men Do" is the fifth episode in which Kimble saves Gerard's life (the others: "Never Wave Goodbye," "Corner of Hell," "Stroke of Genius," and "Ill Wind"). If anything could sway Gerard's thinking about his longtime adversary, that ought to be it. In fact, Gerard says as much to Kimble in Act IV: "I think I know you well enough to know you wouldn't [hire a hit man]." But while the lieutenant's personal opinion of the Fugitive has evolved, his duty as an instrument of the law remains the same—he must apprehend Kimble because the law has pronounced him guilty.

"He's highly scrupulous," said Barry Morse of his alter ego. "We always managed—I hope I was consistently vigilant, and I know the writers were—we always managed to be absolutely scrupulous and careful in making it clear to anyone who cared to observe that Gerard was functioning with utmost propriety—some people might say with excessive propriety. (*He* wouldn't, of course!) He was functioning with the utmost propriety within his duty as an instrument of the law."

Still, one would think that a conflict of interest would emerge after the very same man saves your life five times. But if you're Philip Gerard, you are bound by a duty to uphold the law, and you cannot allow emotion to sway you into doing otherwise. "I suppose Gerard would say that personal relationships, as between himself and Kimble, are not affected by the accidental happenings which befall them," Morse continued. "He would simply say, 'Whether or not this man saved my life doesn't affect my duty to deliver him to the legal system which employs me and which has convicted him. Whether he has been wrongly convicted or not is not my business.'

"I can't count the number of times I've said that to people in the streets, because people used to become enormously involved in this series, and would assume, in the rather touching way that audiences do, that I was personally responsible for all these attitudes! And I had, first of all, of course, to explain that this was purely a fictional confection, and that any views expressed by this character were not necessarily mine. But then, I also had to remind them that this man Gerard was, after all, an instrument of *their* legal system, the U.S. legal system. Did they want it upheld or didn't they? I had many interesting conversations with people based on that question. Although, of course, it simplified itself in some instances where elderly ladies would hit me with their handbags or their umbrellas in airport lounges, or tough-looking guys would loom over me and offer to take me apart in restaurants or bars....It was quite flattering in a way that they should vicariously involve themselves so much in the rights and wrongs of the whole series."

Episode 105

RUN THE MAN DOWN

Original Airdate: January 3, 1967

Teleplay by Barry Oringer. Story by Fred Freiberger. Directed by James Sheldon.

Guest Cast: James Broderick (Owen Tripp), Edward Asner (Joe Bantam), Georgann Johnson (Laura Craig), Robert Doyle (Larry), Val Avery (Jim Ross), John Davis Chandler (Kenny), Sam Melville (Lee Runnels), Roy Engle (Lt. Rodgers), Stuart Nisbet (Ossie).

Prolog. *For some, a highway is just a road to travel for business or pleasure. For Richard Kimble, it is sometimes the only means to freedom. But at the moment, just minutes ahead of the law, it can be a one-way street leading to sudden death.*

Synopsis. Three armored car robbers hold a widow, a mountain ranger and Kimble ("Tom Anderson") hostage in an isolated cabin in the woods.

Epilog. *For Richard Kimble, freedom is a precious gift, sometimes found in a trackless wilderness, sometimes granted by strangers. But he knows that, always, it is a gift that may be taken back from him, suddenly—and forever.*

In *Hunt the Man Down* (1950), Gig Young played a public defender who tries to clear his client—an innocent man named Richard Kinkaid—of a 12-year-old murder conviction. "That's definitely a coincidence," said series creator Roy Huggins. "I thought of the name 'Richard Kimble,' but I honestly don't remember how I came up with it. I wasn't aware of that movie, and I've never known anybody named Kimble."

Hunt the Man Down has two other coincidental parallels to *The Fugitive*: Young's character was assisted by a one-armed investigator; and the key witness resided in Tucson, Arizona, where the pilot episode took place. "That's amazing," said Stanford Whitmore, who wrote the pilot and created the character of the one-armed man. "I hadn't heard of that movie, although I did base the one-armed man on some of the horror movie villains that scared me when I was a kid. As far as Tucson is concerned, the only reason I set it there was that Quinn wanted the pilot set somewhere outside of California. I chose Tucson because I knew the area. I had some friends who went to the University of Arizona, which is in Tucson, and I used to visit them all the time."

Episode 106

THE OTHER SIDE OF THE COIN

Original air date, January 10, 1967

Written by Sam Ross. Directed by Lewis Allen

Guest Cast: John Larch (Ben Corby), Joseph Campanella (Harry Banner), Beau Bridges (Larry Corby), Melinda Plowman (Ellen), Parley Baer (Al Cooney), Claudia Bryer (Mrs. Blake), Pitt Herbert (Sears), Glenn Sipes (Associate Deputy), Buck Young (Officer), Don Eitner (Associate Deputy), Jim Raymond (2nd Deputy), George Simms (Deputy).

Prolog. *A stranger in a small town, a hunt for safety: the fate of a fugitive on the move. But for Richard Kimble, there can be no safety—only danger.*

Synopsis. Now a clerk in a small grocery store in Ocean Grove, California, Kimble ("Jim Parker") becomes embroiled in a conflict between Larry Corby and his father Ben (the sheriff). When Ben refuses to support Larry and his pregnant girlfriend, the boy robs the store where Kimble works. After being shot, Larry drives off, but he loses control of the car and spins off the road. Ben, who had been chasing, is shocked to discover his own son. He takes the boy and promises to find drugs after Larry refuses to go to the hospital. Meanwhile, Kimble becomes suspected of the robbery and tries to escape after the police take his fingerprints. Although Ben soon captures Kimble, he makes a bargain: if Kimble can save his son, Ben will set him free.

Epilog. *For some people like Larry, there is justice tempered with mercy: a sentence of five years, suspended. For Richard Kimble, there is no understanding judge. He must find his own justice.*

"David was probably one of the most charismatic personalities that I've ever met," said script supervisor Ken Gilbert. "He had come up through the major studio ranks (as far as his training was concerned), at Universal. He knew what he was doing on the set, and the professionalism was appreciated.

"When I worked with him on other shows after *The Fugitive*, I noticed that the other crews responded to him the same way. People were drawn to him, no matter what he was doing, and anxious to participate any way they could.

"He was an actor until the moment they said 'Cut!' Then he was David Janssen. He liked to kid and to have a few laughs, rather than keeping a somber, heavy mood on the set all the time."

Episode 107

THE ONE THAT GOT AWAY

Original Airdate: January 17, 1967

Written by Philip Saltzman and Harry Kronman. Directed by Leo Penn.

Guest Cast: Anne Francis (Felice Greer), Charles Drake (Oliver Greer), Charles Bronson (Ralph Schuyler), David Renard (Guillermo), Vince Howard (Brooks), Harlan Warde (Mitchell), Pepe Callahan (Calderon), David Fresco (Hodges), Thordis Brandt (Girlfriend), Rico Alaniz (Perez).

Prolog. *For men who go down to the sea in ships, time ashore is precious, measured in minutes. For this man, it is measured in apprehension, and danger. His name is Richard Kimble. He is a fugitive.*

Synopsis. Government agent Ralph Schuyler poses as a boat captain in order to spy on the wife of an international embezzler who is reportedly returning to the United States via Mexico. Kimble ("Bill March"), recently hired as a deck hand, is also under surveillance. When Ralph learns Kimble's identity is false, he takes Kimble's fingerprints. After an "emergency" landing, the agent leaves Kimble's fingerprints with a local shopkeeper and notifies the authorities of the woman's whereabouts. Kimble tries to escape after intercepting a cable with the incriminating report on his fingerprints. But Ralph hears the news over the radio and continues to pursue Kimble.

Prolog. *Somewhere back across the border is the one-armed man. Until he is found, there can be no reprieve from fear. Richard Kimble remains what he is today: a fugitive.*

Anne Francis, who co-starred with John Ericson ("Brass Ring") on *Honey West*, also played Charles Drake's wife on *The Invaders* ("The Saucer"). Francis was David Janssen's partner for the 1966 Emmy Awards network broadcast—they presented the awards for Best Actor and Actress in a Comedy Series. Francis later co-starred with Barbra Streisand in *Funny Girl* (1968).

FUGE FACTS

Between the two of them, Philip Saltzman and Harry Kronman had written 15 episodes of *The Fugitive* before collaborating on this story.

Episode 108

CONCRETE EVIDENCE

Original Airdate: January 24, 1967

**Teleplay by Jeri Emmett and Jack Turley. Story by Jack Turley.
Directed by Murray Golden.**

Guest Cast: Jack Warden (Alex Patton), Harold Gould (Tom Crailer), Celeste Holm (Pearl Saunders), Jason Wingreen (Nebbs), Larry Blake (Charlie), Ray Kellogg (Sheriff), Jim Crowell (Deputy), Billy Snyder (Pete), E.A. Nicholson (Roughneck), Jane Barclay (Townswoman), Ed Garrett (Townsman).

Prolog. *Along an isolated stretch of farmland in Nebraska a construction company builds the sleek asphalt ribbon of a new superhighway. Workers are needed. Richard Kimble takes his place in line with other nameless faces, seeking a job that will give him a new beginning, a new identity. But a superhighway, even one that is yet unfinished, can prove a dangerous road—for a fugitive.*

Synopsis. Alex "Pat" Patton, an unscrupulous building contractor, once built a theater in his hometown, but the theater soon collapsed, killing three children and crippling several others. Although exonerated from manslaughter charges, the townspeople have harassed him ever since. The company faces financial ruin, yet Pat pours money into a mysterious "motel." Pat has a heart problem, and has just one month to live. After recognizing Kimble ("Steve Dexter") from his wanted poster, Pat hires Kimble to keep him alive until the motel is completed.

Epilog. *A fugitive ropes his way into a small corner of darkness, hoping for sanctuary from the relentless force that eternally pursues him. Now thrust once again into the harsh inquisitive light, Richard Kimble must run, searching for the elusive place where a new life can commence.*

The cleverly titled "Concrete Evidence" veers slightly toward "disease of the week" territory (Pat dies at the end of the story), but director Murray Golden keeps the episode on a steady course. The performances of David Janssen and guest stars Jack Warden, Celeste Holm and Harold Gould also enhance the story.

FUGE FACTS

Kimble drinks his coffee black; his prison ID number is KB-7608163.

Episode 109

THE BREAKING OF THE HABIT

Original Airdate: January 31, 1967

Written and Directed by John Meredyth Lucas.

Guest Cast: Eileen Heckart (Sister Veronica), Linden Chiles (Father Taylor), Antoinette Bower (Sister Angelica), Heather North (Marie), Adrienne Hayes (Vicky), Kelly Thordsen (Tarleton Policeman), Dallas Mitchell (Highway Patrolman #1), Clay Tanner (Policeman Landers), Paul Hahn (Highway Patrolman #2), Peter Marko (Attendant), Pat Patterson (Intersection Policeman).

Prolog. *Between birth and death, a man travels many roads and learns to predict what lies around the next bend. But for a fugitive, there are no road maps—only blind instinct, sharpened by the knowledge that every step may be his last.*

Synopsis. Despite a bullet in the leg, Kimble ("Tom Marlowe") hops a truck headed for Sacramento, where he renews acquaintance with Sister Veronica, now the principal of St. Mary Magdalene School. Kimble asks Veronica to drive him to Tarleton, where Fred Johnson supposedly works as a runner for a numbers racketeer. A student notifies the police after recognizing Kimble from a newspaper photograph, but Kimble escapes by hiding on the roof. Meanwhile, Veronica learns that a delinquent student has run away, and is torn between driving after the girl and staying to help Kimble.

Epilog. *As one road is blocked, Richard Kimble takes another. For a fugitive, there are no freeways. All roads are toll roads, to be paid in blood and pain. There are many roads: there is only one goal.*

"Breaking of the Habit" is a sequel to "Angels Travel on Lonely Roads," the first season episode starring Eileen Heckart as Sister Veronica. It's the only instance in the series in which the Fugitive is reunited with a character (other than his sister or the one-armed man) whom he met in an earlier episode.

The reprise is welcome, and Heckart turns in another stellar performance as Veronica. "Heckart was wonderful," said director John Meredyth Lucas. "She is such a joy to work with."

Episode 110

THERE GOES THE BALL GAME

Original Airdate: February 7, 1967

Written by Oliver Crawford. Directed by Gerald Mayer.

Guest Cast: Gabriel Dell (Chester), Lynda Day (Nadine Newmark), Martin Balsam (Andy Newmark), Vincent Gardenia (Gibbs), Jonathan Lippe (Phil), Susan Seaforth (Vicki Walton), Joan Tompkins (Rose Newmark), Sidney Clute (Joe), John Ward (Jenny), Barbara Dodd (Aggie), Jon Kowal (Al), Michael Harris (Guard).

Prolog. *A man on the run has few moments to relax, to live as other men. But a fugitive cannot live by flight alone. Even he must pause for the rare moment to replenish.*

Synopsis. A former ballplayer dispatches a man to kidnap his ex-girlfriend, the daughter of newspaper publisher Andy Newmark, at a baseball stadium. After discovering that Kimble ("Gene Tyler") witnessed the proceedings, Newmark summons Kimble to identify the kidnapers, who demand $200,000 ransom. When the word leaks out, the police surround Newmark's home and Kimble unsuccessfully tries to slip away. After determining that Kimble is a witness, the kidnapers want the Fugitive to deliver the ransom money—so that they can kill him.

Epilog. *So darkness swallows The Fugitive. But it merely covers, not hides, him. He is still hounded, still hunting, but still free—until tomorrow.*

The Fugitive cost an average of $200,000 per episode, a very high figure for the mid-1960s (it would cost about one million dollars per show today). "Most hour shows, at that time, were shooting for six days to complete one episode," said assistant director Bob Rubin. "We shot a seventh day, which was unheard of. Also, when most shows were working, say, a 10-hour day, we budgeted 12 shooting hours (not including meal periods). So we shot not only an extra day, but we were focused on that work a couple hours a day longer than perhaps any other creative technical team in the history of television."

In addition to the sheer fatigue brought on by such a schedule, David Janssen also suffered from a chronic knee injury he sustained while in high school. But the producers and crew members of *The Fugitive*, fully aware that Janssen was *the* reason that tens of millions of Americans dropped what they were doing every Tuesday night to watch *The Fugitive*, took care of their star. They tried whenever possible to make his load easier—sometimes by rewriting certain scenes, sometimes by rearranging the shooting schedule, sometimes by using library footage from previous episodes.

"There Goes the Ball Game" brings to mind an incident from the first season that underscores just how exhausted Janssen had become from the grueling demands of the series. "David and his wife then, Ellie, had box seats right behind home plate at Dodger Stadium—that was a kind of 'Hollywood ghetto,' where everyone could see them," recalled Stanford Whitmore. "He would go to all the games because it was the 'in' thing at that time. There were a lot of celebrities right in the forefront.

"One day on the set he said to me, 'Stan, I am so tired from night shooting—last Friday night, Ellie and I went to the game, and we were sitting there, and Sandy Koufax was pitching to Willie Mays, and my wife elbowed me and said 'Wake up! 50,000 people are watching David Janssen fall asleep during one of the classic confrontations in all of major league baseball!' So David said, 'I am so tired from night shooting: would you write me a show where there's no night shooting?' So, we got him something ['Come Watch Me Die'] where we had very little night shooting."

FUGE FACTS

The 1945 Washington Senators baseball team included a shortstop named Dick Kimble.

Episode 111

THE IVY MAZE

Original Airdate: February 21, 1967

Written by Edward C. Hume. Directed by John Meredyth Lucas.

Guest Cast: William Windom (Fritz Simmons), Geraldine Brooks (Caroline Simmons), Lorri Scott (Sally), Bill Raisch (Fred Johnson), Bill Quinn (Chief Terry), Don Mitchell (Ken), Carl Reindel (Assistant), Victor Brandt (Volunteer), Dani Nolan (Landlady), Jill Janssen (Coed), Iris Ratner (Another Coed), James Farley (Al), Perry Cook (Bus Driver), Mark Russell (Bill).

Prolog. *A fugitive: a man driven by a dream. Two dreams: flight from an unjust punishment, where every town is an unjust town; and a dream of destiny, that one town somewhere where Richard Kimble will find his freedom.*

Synopsis. College professor Fritz Simmons (Kimble's former fraternity brother) uses his experiments in dream withdrawal to elicit a confession from Fred Johnson, now a janitor ("Carl Stoker") at Wellington College. By obtaining some new evidence that only the murderer would recognize, Fritz believes he can clear Kimble. While Johnson participates, Kimble ("Jerry Sinclair") observes from behind a hidden screen. When Fritz's wife Caroline discovers Kimble's involvement, she notifies Gerard, but Fritz hides Kimble. Later, Kimble confronts Caroline and convinces her of his innocence. Fritz sneaks Kimble onto campus when Johnson begins to disclose information about "the Kimble job"—just as Gerard arrives on campus.

Epilog. *For Richard Kimble, the mind's eye is always open, scanning the nightmare landscape for his pursuers. He waits for brief dreams of tomorrow's reprieve. But they are only dreams. And he runs on.*

Lorri Scott (Sally) was not aware that Bill Raisch was really a one-armed man, recalled assistant director Bob Rubin. "On her first day on this segment, I walked Lorri across the sound stage to have her makeup applied by Jack Wilson, our makeup artist," Rubin said. "We were standing in the makeup table area where Jack was finishing Bill Raisch's makeup. Lorri wanted to flatter Bill as to his acting talent and his overall work on the show. So she said to me (loud enough for Bill to hear), 'Bob, isn't it wonderful how Bill fakes this whole thing, and does all those stunts, plays the scenes, and runs, drives and shoots a gun so well! It's wonderful how he hides his real arm behind his back, and the camera can't tell. Only in Hollywood could you pull something like this!'

"At that point Bill looked up (he had been more in conversation with Jack) and took his right arm (which is a stump, of course) and then just moved the stump up in the air, while Jack and I just looked at each other, speechless. Lorri, I know, will never forget how she felt when she realized that Bill really was a one-armed man.

"It was no problem with Bill—by that time, he had heard everything you could possibly hear about having one arm. But Jack and I watched Lorri becoming real humble, real fast. As is often still today, many folks feel more awkward around people with disabilities than they themselves do."

FUGE FACTS

"The Ivy Maze" was filmed on location at the Claremont College in Pomona, California. "Most of the locations that we used were accustomed to the idea of motion picture companies coming in and filming," said director John Meredyth Lucas. "With this episode, we had to shoot with an agreement that we wouldn't disrupt university life totally, and that they would keep out of our way, and be quiet on a bell so we could record dialogue."

FUGE FAMILY

Jill Janssen (Coed) is David Janssen's sister; she is also seen briefly in the final scene of "The Judgment."

Episode 112

GOODBYE MY LOVE

Original Airdate: February 28, 1967

Written by Leo Loeb. Directed by Lewis Allen.

Guest Cast: Jack Lord (Alan Bartlett), Marlyn Mason (Gayle Marten), Patricia Smith (Norma Bartlett), James Lamphier (Paul), Jack Raine (Charles), Ivan Bonar (Detective), Hal Riddle (Policeman).

Prolog. *Parking attendant: a job for food and shelter, a place to rest. Another temporary haven for a man on the run. Richard Kimble, known in this place and to these people as Bill Garrison.*

Synopsis. Kimble becomes romantically involved with former recording star Gail Martin, unaware that she knows about his secret—and the $10,000 reward for his capture.

Gail implicates the Fugitive in a scheme to rid her weak-willed lover, Alan Bartlett, of his wife Norma, a former golf pro who now uses a wheelchair due to a physical disability created by a spinal injury. Gail and Alan plot to murder Norma and pin the crime on Kimble. But Alan soon realizes they will also have to kill Kimble.

Epilog. *Safe for one more night, Richard Kimble continues along the twin paths of the hunter and the hunted, continues along without the knowledge that either road will lead to freedom.*

"David was very quiet, in that he was very much to himself," recalled veteran makeup artist Jack Wilson. "But he did like to make people laugh, and he was pretty funny most of the time. David worked very, very hard: he really did. He told me that he did his lines in the mornings—you know, get up real early in the morning and run through his lines, because at the end of a hard day, it's terribly difficult to try and do it.

"I liked him so much that I can't even watch his shows now—I mean, it's just like he was my brother, even more so like my brother. Just a wonderful, warm guy."

Wilson recalled an incident that took place several years after *The Fugitive*, when he worked with Janssen on the TV-movie *The Golden Gate Murders* (1979). "I got sick, and I had to go to the hospital," he said. "There was another person in the room with me, and the guy's wife answered the phone one afternoon. She looked at me, and she said 'This is David Janssen!' And I said, 'Oh, okay,' and she looked at me like I didn't know who I was talking to. And David just said, 'I just want to tell you, you gotta get out of the hospital: don't listen to God, don't listen to anybody, just get out of there! Listen to *me*.'

"That was the last time I ever talked to him. He passed away after the following year."

Episode 113

PASSAGE TO HELENA

Original Airdate: March 7, 1967

Written by Barry Oringer. Directed by Richard Benedict.

Guest Cast: James Farentino (Rafe Carter), Percy Rodriguez (Emery Dalton), Phyllis Love (Laura Bensen), Russ Conway (Sheriff Thornton), J. Pat O'Malley (Joe McGinnis), Garry Walberg (Webster), Michael Mikler (Kline), Gene Kirkwood (Lockett), Orville Sherman (Prewit), Marc Winters (Tom).

Prolog. *Wyler City, a rugged frontier town in the mining country of northern Montana. To the ordinary man, a place where he can test himself against the harsh demands of nature. To the Fugitive, a corridor of danger.*

Synopsis. After arresting Kimble ("Tom Barrett") on a minor charge, a determined deputy attempts to transport the Fugitive and an accused murderer to the state capital for arraignment.

Epilog. *A fugitive's life is not measured in years: it is measured in moments won, a day gained. Richard Kimble has won another day. Tomorrow he must win it all over again.*

David Janssen liked to pull pranks on the crew members. "Every single day, it seemed, while he was in Jack Wilson's make-up chair, David would take advantage of poor Jack," recalled costumer Steve Lodge. "When Jack would turn his back, David would quickly flip Jack's powder container over on its top-side without spilling a particle. Then, when Jack would start putting away his equipment, he would reach to pick up his upside-down powder container and...well, I guess I don't have to spell out what happened!"

FUGE FACTS

Not all animals get along with the Fugitive: when Kimble reaches down to pet a sleeping dog at the start of the show, the dog becomes startled and runs away.

Episode 114

THE SAVAGE STREET

Original Airdate: March 14, 1967

Teleplay by Jeri Emmett and Mario Alcalde. Story by Mario Alcalde. Directed by Gerald Mayer.

Guest Cast: Gilbert Roland (Jose Anza), Michael Ansara (Miguel Anza), Miriam Colon (Mercedes Anza), Tom Nardini (Jimmy Anza), David Macklin (Banks), Ross Hagen (Harry Benton), Barney Phillips (Sgt. Harrigan), Kevin Coughlin (Cotton), Bobby Diamond (Ollie).

Prolog. *Big cities breed indifference to the problems of others. But some men cannot remain detached—men like Richard Kimble. And involvement can lead to danger.*

Synopsis. Kimble ("Tony Maxwell") now works for cigar-maker Jose Anza and becomes close friends with Jimmy, Jose's son. Jimmy is caught between the expectations of his demanding father, who wants him to learn the violin, and the harassment he endures from three street youths. When Kimble is shot in the leg after the police discover his identity, Jimmy hides the Fugitive from both his father and his uncle Miguel—a police officer.

Epilog. *A fugitive lives with many emotions: hope, gratitude, loneliness. But among the emotions, one stands out: fear. And every day it's embedded a little deeper, each step a little faster, as the contest continues to take its toll.*

Kimble shares a little of his background in order to encourage Jimmy to continue with the violin. "I'm a doctor because my father wanted me to be a doctor, at about the age I wanted to be a baseball player," he tells the boy. "So I became a doctor. I'm not better than my father. I just had it better. That was his gift to me. My gift to him was accepting it."

FUGE FIRSTS

"David was probably the very first TV star to get his own 'personal' motor home dressing room," according to costumer Steve Lodge. "The 'Silver Bullet' (that's what we called it) was probably a 'perk' from Quinn, in lieu of something else David may have asked for. David's motto was 'Always ask for everything you can think of and if you're lucky, maybe you'll get half!'"

FUGE FOL DE ROL

The youths who terrorize Jimmy are remarkably well-dressed and clean-cut: by contemporary standards, they look more like "nerds."

Episode 115

DEATH OF A VERY SMALL KILLER

Original Airdate: March 21, 1967

Written by Barry Oringer. Directed by John Meredyth Lucas.

Guest Cast: Arthur Hill (Dr. Howell), Carol Lawrence (Reina Morales), Carlos Romero (Sgt. Rodriguez), Valentin deVargas (Captain Gomez), Rodolfo Hoyos (Sancho), Stella Garcia (Nurse), Roberto Contreras (Diego), Sam Gilman (Ship's Captain), Robert Hernandez (Man), Bard Stevens (Sailor), Natividad Vacio (Delivery Man), Mike Abelar (Attendant), Raoul Perez (Officer Arenas), George Lymburn (Officer).

Prolog. *Richard Kimble, fugitive, for whom there are no neutrals, only enemies or friends. To such a man, a stranger's whim, a decision to lend a helping hand, means the difference between freedom or death.*

Synopsis. A pneumonia-stricken Kimble ("Thomas Barrett") seeks refuge at a hospital in Mexico, where he is recognized by an ambitious doctor conducting research on meningitis. After Kimble recovers, the doctor blackmails him into assisting with his research in exchange for protection from the police. Kimble soon discovers that several patients are being unwittingly sacrificed for research purposes, while a persistent police sergeant investigates his identity.

Epilog. *To Richard Kimble, fugitive, the respite of love is brief, the end of love a necessity of survival. In flight from the numberless enemy, darkness and loneliness are harsh, but sheltering, friends.*

Dr. Howell was supposed to be an arrogant, bellowing and unlikable character. But director John Meredyth Lucas thinks he allowed Arthur Hill to play the role a little too hard. "It went a little strident," Lucas admitted. "I must tell you that as a director today, I would not have let him come on as strong as he did. But Arthur himself was a joy to work with—he was nothing like the character he played on-screen."

FUGE FACTS

In this episode (which was originally entitled "I am the Lion"), Kimble uses the same alias ("Thomas Barrett") he went by in "Passage to Helena."

Episode 116

DOSSIER ON A DIPLOMAT

Original Airdate: March 28, 1967

Teleplay by J.T. Gallard and Jeri Emmett. Story by J.T. Gallard. Directed by Gerald Mayer.

Guest Cast: Ivan Dixon (Ambassador Unawa), Diana Sands (Davala Unawa), Diana Hyland (Alison Priestley), Lloyd Gough (Frank Hobart), Marlowe Jensen (2nd Detective), Vince Howard (Policeman), K.L. Smith (Cabbie), William Hudson (Detective), Don Kennedy (Mover), Jonathan Hawke (Police Lieutenant).

Prolog. *A fugitive, if he is innocent, is sustained by hope. It is more necessary to him than food or shelter. But, paradoxically, the greater the promise of that hope, the more agonizing it becomes.*

Synopsis. Kimble ("Charlie Farrell") travels to Washington, D.C. in order to meet with attorney Frank Hobart, whose book *Unjustly Convicted* states that Kimble was convicted without the benefit of a fair trial. Kimble soon attends to Unawa, an African ambassador, after the diplomat collapses on the street. The grateful ambassador shelters Kimble at the African ligation, despite the protests of the ambassador's wife Davala. Since the ligation is considered international soil, Kimble will enjoy the benefits of diplomatic immunity so long as he remains inside the building. Believing that Kimble's presence in the embassy will harm her country's diplomatic status, Davala notifies the police, but Unawa intervenes. But after Unawa collapses again due to a terminal brain tumor, Davala decides to relocate the embassy.

Epilog. *For Richard Kimble, a moment of safety ends. But the long search must continue, for he knows the only true sanctuary lies in the elusive proof of his innocence.*

"Dossier on a Diplomat" marks the second instance where Kimble seeks the help of a respected attorney who wrote about his case; he was also assisted by G. Stanley Lazer in "Man in a Chariot." Although Kimble tells Frank Hobart (played by Lloyd Gough, who previously appeared as the Fugitive's father-in-law in "The Survivors") that "there's no new evidence" to discuss, in truth much has come out over the course of the series. In "The Ivy Maze," Johnson indicated that he wiped the lamp base with Helen's dress, a fact that never came out in the trial. Although Johnson destroyed the tape of this confession, Fritz Simmons witnessed the confession, and could testify on Kimble's behalf. Kimble could also call on Barbara Webb (the reporter in "Wife Killer") who witnessed another Johnson confession. Plus there's always Captain Eckhardt ("Trial by Fire"), who stepped forward and testified that he saw Johnson running out of the Kimble home on the night of the murder.

FUGE FACTS

Gerard falls for one of the oldest tricks in the book when he chases after Alison and the trunk (he thinks Kimble is stuffed inside); after the police follow Gerard, Kimble quietly leaves the embassy building.

Kimble tells Ambassador Unawa (Ivan Dixon of *Hogan's Heroes*) that three things keep him going: avoiding capture; finding the man who killed his wife; and seeking a new trial.

Episode 117

THE WALLS OF NIGHT

Original Airdate: April 4, 1967

Written by Lawrence Lewis Goldman. Directed by John Meredyth Lucas.

Guest Cast: Janice Rule (Barbara Wells), Steve Ihnat (Art Meredith), Sheree North (Willy), Tige Andrews (Buck Leonard), Martin Brooks (Lt. Gould), Marcelle Fortier (Landlady), Jeane Wood (Margaret).

Prolog. *For Richard Kimble, a squawking radio phone has become a warm voice, a sympathetic human contact, a release—if only for a while—from the terrible ache of loneliness.*

Synopsis. Near Portland, Oregon, truck driver Kimble ("Stan Dyson") becomes romantically involved with telephone dispatcher Barbara Wells, unaware that she is a convicted embezzler on loan through a prison work-furlough program. Distraught after her parole is denied for another six months, Barbara flees to Seattle, where Kimble is staying at a lakeside inn. Barbara asks him to take her to Canada, but when Kimble learns the truth about her, he radios his boss that he'll bring Barbara in. Meanwhile, Barbara's parole officer Art Meredith soon learns Kimble's true identity. Art notifies Barbara and instructs her to stall Kimble while the police locate them.

Epilog. *Barbara's sentence will come finally to an end. But for Richard Kimble, there is no calendar on which to mark the days. Loneliness once again stretches ahead, as apparently endless as the city streets.*

"Quinn Martin set the pace for a quality show; he just wouldn't accept anything less," said assistant director Bob Rubin. "David thrived on that, and so did we. We could put our wares out there and be proud of the show we had made. It wasn't just another show this Tuesday night at 10 o'clock on ABC. Tens of millions of Americans stopped—literally stopped what they were doing—at 10 o'clock to see what was going to happen to Richard Kimble."

Episode 118

THE SHATTERED SILENCE

Original Airdate: April 11, 1967

**Teleplay by Barry Oringer. Story by Ralph Goodman.
Directed by Barry Morse.**

Guest Cast: Laurence Naismith (John Mallory), Antoinette Bower (Andrea), Paul Mantee (Robert Howe), Dabbs Greer (Jensen), James McCallion (Kugler), Jack De Maye (Second Deputy).

Prolog. *For some people, a railroad terminal is a weigh station on a journey. For Richard Kimble, the Fugitive, every escape route can be a trap, every move an unforeseen step toward capture.*

Synopsis. Somewhere in the Oregon hills, a sculptor named Andrea hides Kimble ("Ben Lewis") from the local deputy named Howe. When the lawman becomes suspicious, Kimble retreats to the mountains, where he finds refuge in the home of John Mallory, a former scholar who cut himself off from civilization 14 years earlier. The ailing Mallory takes a liking to Kimble; when the old man takes a turn for the worse, Kimble is compelled to help him—even as Howe closes in.

Epilog. *A fugitive is a man in exile. A woman's love can remain with him only long enough to remind him of his loss. For Richard Kimble, it is the price of freedom.*

"The Shattered Silence" was Barry Morse's American directorial debut, although the actor had already become an accomplished director by that time. "I had done a good deal of directing before [in the U.K. and Canada], both in the theater and in television, and so this was not new territory for me," he said.

Morse drew on his observance of other directors who worked on *The Fugitive*, but he also relied on the input of such key crew members as script supervisor Ken Gilbert. "When Barry directed his first show, he was quite solicitous of me to help him out, whenever I could," Gilbert said. "We worked very closely on that."

Morse agreed that the crew made his experience very pleasant. "Working as a director on *The Fugitive* was made wonderfully easy for me," he recalled. "By this time, we had gone through nearly four seasons' worth of episodes, and our crew had become so beautifully 'rubbed down,' so beautifully smooth operating, that the director's job—any director's job—was made wonderfully easy. The skill and efficiency of that crew contributed enormously to the polish of the finished product.

"When I came to direct, I'd only have to lift my head and look towards a particular direction and the crew would realize, even before I said it, that my thought was to have the camera there, then I would just indicate where we might have Laurence Naismith sitting, or David sitting, or whatever. It was a very easy ride to work as a director on that series."

ACT IV

The Day the Running Stopped

Finally, Kimble, the End Game; or, Who "Really" Killed Helen Kimble?

T*he Fugitive* will be a series which will be brought to a planned conclusion, that conclusion being of course Richard Kimble's release from his predicament and the ultimate salvation of justice.

—Series creator Roy Huggins, from his original 1960 series concept

While the idea to end *The Fugitive* with a definitive concluding episode clearly belongs to Roy Huggins, the decision to proceed with the finale was Quinn Martin's call all the way. Martin felt that, given the enormous emotional investment that viewers from over 70 countries poured into the program, he owed it to the audience to give them the conclusion they wanted. Richard Kimble *had* to find the man who killed his wife Helen. Richard Kimble's name *had* to be cleared.

But if Martin had to do it again, he would not have ended *The Fugitive* as he did. Martin felt that the resolution of the story ultimately hurt the series' syndication value. "I think Quinn was of two minds," said co-producer George Eckstein. "One of the problems was that his sister was dying of cancer at the time, and he was very close to her. He was going through a very painful experience, and so his focus was not that much on the preparation of the series—he knew what we were doing, and all of that, but he wasn't really on top of it.

"Afterwards, Quinn said that he wouldn't have ended the series the way we did. On the one hand, he felt that he should have—in order to satisfy the audience. But from a financial point of view, he felt it was a mistake, because it was difficult getting the series into syndication, at least the first few years after it ended, because everybody figured, 'Well, we know how it ended.'"

The revival of *The Fugitive* on the A&E cable television network has erased any lingering doubt as to the series' magnetism. The response to the reruns, which began airing in 1990, has been tremendously positive. Many viewers have either telephoned or written the network with their feedback, particularly in early 1992 when A&E's rights to the series were about to expire. But the bottom line, as usual in television, is the ratings. The key reason behind A&E's decision in 1992 to renew their rights to the program was that *The Fugitive* was one of the most highly-rated programs in the cable channel's daytime lineup at that time.

"I think the show has proved Quinn wrong," Eckstein said. "It's achieved a kind of a cult status over the years, and maybe because of that, it made as much money with the closed ending as it would have if it had been an open ending."

Although a Cleveland newspaper columnist reported in January 1967 that *The Fugitive* was "one of those shows said to be headed for cancellation," the show's ratings were still healthy enough to merit renewal for a fifth year. ABC wanted another season, but David Janssen pulled the plug.

"*The Fugitive* didn't go beyond four years because David was just exhausted," said Richard Anderson. "He was a shell of himself by the time it ended. I talked to post-production head Arthur Fellows about this on the set one day, and he said, 'We'll never do another show with one person again, because you put too much on one person.'

David was in nearly every shot, and I think it just wore him down. In addition, it was a night show, so he was working at night a lot of the time, and I think that broke his health. I think they wanted another year, but David just wasn't able to do it."

"David must have been the hardest-worked actor in any series that's ever been," added Barry Morse. "I know that he was always immensely relieved whenever I turned up in town, because it meant that he was going to get a few days off!"

When Martin's first choice to write the finale (Don Brinkley) was unavailable, the assignment went to Eckstein, who had already contributed nine scripts, and Michael Zagor, who had written for other series *(Ben Casey)* but not for *The Fugitive*. "I didn't know Michael at that time," said Eckstein. "Quinn had evidently seen a pilot of his that didn't sell, and liked his work, so he asked the two of us to work together on the final show."

"The Judgment" has been criticized by many as being illogical. Why would Gerard grant Kimble a reprieve, they ask, and why would the one-armed man climb *up* the tower in order to get away? Eckstein acknowledges that the script isn't perfect. However, he and Zagor had very little time to write it—a factor that the critics have apparently overlooked. Even under normal circumstances, writing for television requires a quick turnaround time. Because the decision to end *The Fugitive* did not come about until very late in the season, Eckstein and Zagor had to work faster than usual. That they still contributed an excellent script is a remarkable achievement.

"That script was not prepared at the beginning of the season, which is usually the case with TV series," said Eckstein. "Back then, the deadline for ordering a new season was around Washington's Birthday, and the series would go on in September. You would have the luxury of time (six to eight months) to prepare those scripts. But 'The Judgment' wasn't prepared until the end of the season, around late January or early February 1967. By the time the decision was made to end the series, we didn't have much time: we were being rushed to finish that script."

There are a few elements to the story that Eckstein would have fixed if time had permitted one last revision. "We had to find an amusement park in Indiana, where the show was supposed to take place," he explained. "We ended up shooting at Pacific Ocean Park on the Santa Monica pier, and we were trying desperately to hide the Pacific Ocean—which wasn't easy. There were other sequences and elements of that story that I wish I had been able to do a more graceful job with. But it sure got its audience!"

To the hardcore fans of *The Fugitive*, there was never any question as to who had killed Helen Kimble. The guilt of the one-armed man had been established, piece by piece, over the course of the series. But that didn't stop all sorts of rumors implicating other characters from surfacing. "Everyone wanted it to be Gerard," said Eckstein. "Quinn thought that was nonsense, because it would have made Kimble an idiot for chasing the wrong man for four years! If you think about it in those terms, all the speculation that it was Gerard who killed the wife didn't make any sense at all, and *The Fugitive* was a show that was deeply rooted in reality. So having the one-armed man do it was the only way we really could have gone."

But Martin wasn't adverse to making things a little interesting. When he learned that Len Taft, the Fugitive's brother-in-law, was going to be implicated in the plot, Martin knew exactly who he wanted for the part. "Early in my career, I had an ability to play heavies and good guys within the same part—I could bring out both sides of the same character," said Richard Anderson. "I believe Quinn wanted me to play Len because he felt that I would have that sort of 'ambiguous' effect upon the audience for that segment. I mean, Len was a nice guy, but I also played him in such a way that people would not quite know whether or not he was really involved in the murder."

Even Las Vegas bookmakers got drawn into the frenzy. Anderson's brooding interpretation of the character made Len the favorite of Vegas oddsmakers during the weeklong interim between Part One and Part Two. "I don't remember what the odds were, but there were a lot of bets going on in Las Vegas on who did it," Anderson said. "The smart person said, 'Len's a nice guy, it must be him,' and I played it that way, too. There was a lot of money lost there!"

The wildest speculation as to who murdered Helen did not come about until 10 years after "The Judgment" first aired. In his chronology of dramatic television programs (*Television Drama Series Programming: A Comprehensive Chronicle;* Scarecrow Press, first published in 1978), Larry Gianakos concluded his summary of *The Fugitive* with a rather startling observation: "We endured 118 hairbreadth escapes with Dr. Kimble only to discover...that our hero was guilty after all."

Gianakos based his conclusion on second-hand information he received from a man named Gerard Turner, who claimed to have worked with makeup artist Jack Wilson. According to Turner, David Janssen was so devastated by the assassination of John Kennedy in 1963 that he became a cynic in real life; from that point on, Janssen had decided that Dr. Kimble had indeed killed his wife, and that the actor wanted to show this by having Kimble remove a prosthetic arm in the final scene of the series.

Gianakos never met Janssen, so the key to this theory is determining whether Turner's claims are valid. "I don't remember any Gerard Turner," said Wilson. "He could be somebody I knew, but I can't really remember the name."

There is no way to contact Turner for verification (Gianakos said he died in 1990). But that really wouldn't be necessary because the crux of his claims are not true. "The person who made David out to be a dark person might have gotten his ire up at some time, because he wasn't," said Wilson. "David was very quiet in that he kept to himself, but he also liked to joke around. That story about wanting Kimble to remove his arm was completely a joke, and that's all there is to it."

"I can believe that David was much affected by John Kennedy's death," added Stanford Whitmore. "It was a tremendous shock. But to say that David thought it would be great if Kimble was really guilty, and this is how he thought the series should end—I think that's silly. I would really put that kind of talk in the category of the kind of 'bull sessions' that Quinn, David and I used to have when we were building the pilot—the kind of freefloating attempts to get something that David would respond to. I can imagine, if he seemed a little frivolous at the time, that David might have said 'Hey, I've got a great idea how to end this mess: I'm really guilty!' David did that all the time—he had a very dry sense of humor. If he made such a remark, he was only kidding around, and nothing further should be made of it."

Barry Morse agrees that any reference to Kimble removing a false arm was no more than an off-camera remark that was never meant to be taken seriously. "David and I were both somewhat mischievous by instinct, and we were always cooking up japes, schoolboy kinds of things that one does from time to time," he said. "If you were working as hard as we were at that time, you had to have a few laughs! We used to go on PR tours around the country to promote the series. David didn't like doing these (he wasn't the sort of fellow who is as instinctively 'gabby' as I am), so he relied on me to address all these people who assembled in some convention hall in Chicago, or wherever it was, to tell them to keep watching and keep showing *The Fugitive*, because it was going to get better next year, or whatever it was we were told to say. We used to cook up various kinds of stunts that we would have liked to do to liven up these things. We used to talk about coming onto the platform in one of these convention halls, and David would have a prosthetic piece built into his suit. After exchanging some polite chat with the local ABC boss of wherever we were, David and I would walk off in opposite directions, and I would be left holding the prosthetic arm!

"I suppose somewhere along the line, one of us must have talked to some journalist about pulling that—and of course, it would have sent ABC right through the roof! I mean, the idea of our sending up this sacred devout thing...but if you could have seen these hundreds of men in tight silk suits, all sitting there eating indigestible food and talking nonsense to each other, you would have itched to do something like that. But that probably was the genesis of the idea of the prosthetic arm. It never came into being."

In a 1968 interview with director Ralph Nelson, Janssen himself put to rest any speculation as what he meant by his remarks. "You say things in jest hoping that nobody will do much about it except maybe laugh with you a little," he said. "Then you find it's in print and then somebody else picks it up and all of a sudden you're quoted. Sometimes people don't understand the humor of the situation: they take it as reality.

"I said something to the effect that I was going to unscrew my arm and walk off into the sunset having killed my wife. It was really a sort of irresponsible statement that I made just to have a laugh, and I found it cropping up in a magazine here and a newspaper there."

Janssen also had told Nelson that neither himself, Quinn Martin, nor anyone else involved in the series had any preconceived notions how to end *The Fugitive* before "The Judgment" came about. Morse corroborates this. "We had far more important and pressing things to attend to than speculating about how the series was going to end," he said. "We were lucky to know what the next week's script was going to be about!"

Episodes: 119 and 120

THE JUDGMENT (Two-parter)

Original Airdate: August 22 and 29, 1967

**Written by George Eckstein and Michael Zagor.
Directed by Don Medford.**

Guest Cast: Richard Anderson (Len Taft), Jacqueline Scott (Donna Kimble Taft), Diane Baker (Jean Carlisle), Bill Raisch (Fred Johnson), Joseph Campanella (Captain Ralph Lee), Michael Constantine (Arthur Howe), J.D. Cannon (Lloyd Chandler), Diane Brewster (Helen Kimble), Louise Latham (Betsy Chandler), Skip Ward (Nat Harris), Dort Clark (First Policeman), Arch Whiting (Second Policeman), Michael Harris (Third Policeman), Paul Sorenson (Dispatcher), Lloyd Haynes (Detective Franks), James Nolan (Driver), Mark Allen (Trucker), Perry Cook (Attendant), Paul Comi (First Officer), Don Lamond (Newscaster), Walter Brooke (Devlin), Seymour Cassell (Cabbie), Paul Hahn (Plainclothesman), John Ward (Tom Palmer), Johnny Jensen (Billy Taft), Richie Adams (First Reporter), Al Dunlap (Second Reporter).

(Part One)

Prolog. *How long can a man search before the search destroys him? To Richard Kimble, working for a trucking firm in Tucson, Arizona, defeat has never seemed so mockingly near. Months have passed, and the trail stays cold. There is no trace of the elusive hope he seeks. But sometimes, hope lies no further than the next truck.*

Synopsis. Gerard flies out to Los Angeles after Fred Johnson, the one-armed man, is arrested for armed robbery. Gerard hopes that a newspaper item about the arrest will bring Kimble ("Frank Davis") out to investigate. While Gerard questions Johnson about the Kimble murder, the Fugitive notices the story in a Tucson newspaper and heads for California. Jean Carlisle, a court reporter and a longtime friend of the Kimble family, soon discovers that Kimble is headed for a trap. She intercepts the Fugitive at an L.A. produce market just as the police close in. Later, after Johnson is bailed out of jail, the one-armed man murders his bail bondsman and skips town. Upon snooping around the bondsman's office, Kimble and Jean uncover a shocking piece of evidence—a bail bond receipt apparently posted by Len Taft, the Fugitive's brother-in-law! Kimble and Jean return to Jean's apartment to plan their next move. Gerard arrives to interrogate Jean, but she holds her own against the lieutenant. But Gerard decides to investigate Jean's car and discovers a produce market box in the back seat. Moments later, Gerard arrests Kimble.

Epilog. *A free man, Fred Johnson, boarded a train that will take him east to Indiana, to Stafford. Hours later, two men boarded another train which will bring them to the same destination. For one of these, the moment of arrival will be one of grim and long-sought triumph. For the other, his homecoming will mark only one more stop on his way to a destiny decreed in a court of law four years before. Richard Kimble is on his way home, and to an overdue appointment—with death.*

Gerard momentarily loses his composure when he questions Johnson during Act I. After establishing that Johnson was in the vicinity of Stafford on the night of the murder, Gerard grabs the one-armed man by the shirt and asks him passionately, "Did you kill Helen Kimble?"

"What Gerard is saying, in his emotional state, is 'Tell me you didn't do it!'" said George Eckstein. "At least, that's what we intended in that scene. What Gerard wants to hear was that the one-armed man didn't do it, and that he's after the right guy in Kimble. He didn't want to believe that the one-armed man could have done it, because that's been Kimble's alibi through the whole four years. And now he's got a one-armed man, and he doesn't want to believe that Kimble could possibly have been telling the truth all this time."

Is Gerard beginning to believe that Kimble is innocent at this point in the story? "No, not yet," said Eckstein. "He didn't believe it until the second part of the show. Because just as Kimble has spent four years chasing the one-armed man, Gerard has spent four years chasing Kimble, and he would try to deny any possibility that Kimble was innocent. Otherwise, his whole quest would have been a mockery. The way Michael and I saw it, Gerard would have to deny the possibility of Kimble's innocence until the last possible moment."

Gerard looks genuinely deflated when he arrests Kimble outside of Jean's apartment building at the end of Part One. There is no triumph in his voice, but rather a sense of ambivalence. For the first time in the series, Gerard apologizes to Kimble for doing his job as an instrument of the law. "It wasn't that Gerard believed that Kimble was a heinous serial killer or anything like that," said Eckstein. "He was treating him at that moment as a human being rather than as an animal. Gerard may be obsessed, but he's not a savage hunter. He's gone through four years of tracing Kimble, so he knows that Kimble left a string of good deeds behind him, if nothing else."

There's also a sense of resignation in Kimble's reaction to the arrest: he does not attempt to resist, as he usually had done. "The attitude between these two was that this had been a gentlemanly quest between two opponents who respected each other," said Eckstein. "That attitude has been played out in other episodes. Each respected the other, regardless of the way they pursued or fled from one another. And at that moment Kimble knew that Gerard had nailed him, and that he couldn't do anything about it." Or perhaps, as he told Jean earlier in the show, he really is tired of running.

FUGE FAMILY

Jacqueline Scott had just given birth to her second child at the time of production. "My son Andrew was just three-and-a-half weeks old," she said. "There was some discussion whether they'd bring me in, because I was still pregnant at the time they were setting up the last show. Although I wanted to do the last show, because I always loved working on *The Fugitive*, I also didn't want to hold them up.

"After Andrew was born, there was another problem—I was nursing him. There was some talk about having a limo drive me to and from the set, because I live very near the Goldwyn Studios (where we shot the series). They finally decided it would be much easier if I brought Andrew with me, so they got me a suite of rooms on the lot. Andrew, the nurse and I would trot off to work at 6:00 a.m., while my son Devin, who was two years old at the time, stayed at home with the sitter. I was really perfectly amenable to what they did."

On a few occasions, the production stopped so that Scott could feed her baby. "Bob Rubin, our wonderful bachelor assistant director, thought it was great that I was taking care of my baby," she recalled. "Whenever it was time to feed Andrew, Bob would just yell 'Lunch break!' and everything would come to a screeching halt."

FUGE FACTS & FIGURES

Two elements of this episode serve as a kind of "book end" to the pilot episode, "Fear in a Desert City." First we find Kimble working in Tucson, Arizona, the setting for the pilot. Next, the epilog opens with footage of an oncoming train, a sequence very similar to the opening segment of the first season episodes. Gerard and Kimble sit in the same places as in that opening sequence (Kimble even glances at the window); also, both are silent (only the Narrator is heard).

According to *Daily Variety*, Part One registered a 37.2 rating and a 56.7 share in the United States.

(Part Two)

Prolog. *A man may travel many roads, and one day find his way home again. But for Richard Kimble, this road is not of his choosing, and this day has come too soon. Two men, traveling together, joined by links of steel and the memory of a senseless murder committed years before. Two hunters, one of whom has finally caught his elusive quarry.*

Synopsis. After convincing Gerard that Johnson has headed for Stafford, Kimble receives a 24-hour reprieve—one last chance to find the one-armed man and prove himself innocent. Meanwhile, Stafford city planning commissioner Lloyd Chandler learns about a phone call Donna received from a man who claimed that Len was with Helen on the night of the murder. Lloyd knows who made the call (Johnson) and why (Lloyd used Len's name to bail Johnson out of jail). In fact, Lloyd witnessed Johnson murder Helen, but he was too paralyzed with fear to stop the beating; he remained silent because he didn't want to damage his reputation as a war hero. Lloyd meets Johnson that night at the stable, where the one-armed man demands $50,000, to be delivered the following day at an abandoned amusement park. Just as Kimble's reprieve is about to run out, Kimble and Gerard learn the truth about Lloyd from Lloyd's wife Betsy. After Betsy tells them that Lloyd has decided to kill Johnson rather than pay him the money, Kimble and Gerard race to the amusement park to stop Lloyd—and arrest the one-armed man—before it's too late.

Epilog. *Tuesday, August 29. The Day the Running Stopped.*

The following memo appeared on the last page of the teleplay to "The Judgment":

To all QM staff, crew, actors, all guest actors, all ABC personnel, all advertising personnel:

This script marks the end of a very exciting and successful enterprise, and I would appreciate it if everyone would keep the contents a secret, and not discuss it with any members of the press or newscasters, except to acknowledge that it does prove Richard Kimble innocent.

To any members of the press or any newscasters:

If the above does not work, and by chance you find out the contents of the script, please honor the industry code of not giving the ending away, except to say Richard Kimble will be proved innocent. Thank you.

Warmest regards,

Quinn Martin

Daily Variety reported it as "a better kept secret than classified U.S. atomic information." Quinn Martin, as his memos to the media and to his own personnel indicate, was adamant about keeping the conclusion to "The Judgment" a secret until the night the episode was broadcast. But apparently even Martin couldn't resist total silence, because he tipped off a trade paper columnist that the one-armed man did it. Harriet Peters of *Showtime* reported the news in her column of August 18, 1967. "Well, when you think about it, there's no surprise ending," said George Eckstein. "I mean, it wasn't as if the sister did it! There simply couldn't be a surprise: Kimble was innocent, the one-armed man did it, and Gerard nailed him. It was exactly the way everyone should have expected."

Martin, therefore, knew exactly what he was doing when he "tipped off" the press. He may have mentioned that the one-armed man did it, but he never said a thing about the key element of the story (the surprise witness Lloyd Chandler). That *would have* given away the ending.

"I was with David when he reviewed the script and found out what was going to happen in the end," said assistant director Bob Rubin. "As part of my work, I used to give him each script, review the endless rewrites with him, and update him with an overview of that week's show, schedule and cast. It was funny, he really didn't know how to play the final scene—the showdown with Bill Raisch. He said, 'You know, I've waited four years for this moment, and now I don't know how to play it. I'm not sure really how to do this. I mean, is he happy? Is he sad? Is he up? Is he down?' It's like, I've finally caught up with this guy, and now I don't know what to do.' David really personalized that moment, and there was a lot of emotion as he read that scene. I think he saw it as the end to a lot of memories. He kept saying, 'I don't know how to play this. I hope what I do will be okay.'" It certainly was.

In the final scene of the series, after Kimble is exonerated, Gerard meets Kimble outside the courthouse, and the two men quietly shake hands. But the original plan was to have the two adversaries exchange a few parting words before going their separate ways. "In the first version of that final episode, our writers had gone a little overboard," recalled Barry Morse. "They wrote a scene of quite emetic mawkishness, in which David and I said sentimental things to each other. At one point, I remember I suggested to David that, in order to mock this overly sentimental dialogue, we should throw ourselves into each other's arms and kiss each other firmly on the mouth! Well, we threatened that, but we never had to carry it out. By that time, we were all on such good terms with each other that everybody realized the absurdity, and it was agreed that we would make some changes in the dialogue. And I think somebody said, 'Well, what would be the best thing to say?' And I said, 'I think it would be best if we say nothing!' As is often in the case on the screen, what you do and what you look is much more eloquent than what you say."

Gerard realizes that the Kimble matter is finally closed. "From that moment on, as far as Lt. Gerard is concerned, Richard Kimble ceases to be," said Morse. "It's as Othello says in the final act: 'Othello's occupation's gone.' The *raison d'etre* of what has been occupying him for the last four years no longer exists. The Kimble matter is now one for the files, and from the point of view of a professional police officer, Gerard would simply be feeling, 'All right now, turn the page, what's up next?'"

At the time "The Judgment" was telecast throughout the United States, David Janssen was on location in Columbus, Georgia, shooting the film *The Green Berets*, with John Wayne. Thirty minutes after the final episode aired, Janssen appeared via satellite on Joey Bishop's late night talk show on ABC-TV. "I killed her, Joey," Janssen cracked. "She talked too much."

Bishop then asked Janssen how he felt after the series was finished. "My feeling was not one of remorse and it was not one of melancholy," Janssen said. "For all of us involved in *The Fugitive*, we didn't feel as though we should sing sad songs, because of the acceptance of the show. [We all felt] that everyone had done a good job and we are all now going on to something better, hopefully. It's a positive rather than a negative."

Twenty-five years later, Bob Rubin answered the same question from the crew's point of view. "That last segment was an important show," he said. "Even though we had worked on that show, it wasn't just work—we really cared. Lots of us really were involved in the emotion of the final show. Our sadness at the day the running finally stopped, however, was replaced by a sense of pride in a job well done; a show well done; and a season and a four-year series well done. We 'did' good!"

FUGE FACTS

Because of practical reasons, a film or dramatic TV script is never filmed in the sequence that we see whenever we watch it on the screen. "You always get the exteriors out of the way first—in case of bad weather," said Rubin. "You shoot the exteriors first, then you go into the studio and do the interior scenes, where there is total control of the lighting... and not a drop of rain. The scene where Barry shoots Bill Raisch was one of the first things we shot, then a few days later we did the scene where David beats the confession out of Bill. The confession allegedly took place on top of the water tower at the amusement park, but we actually shot that scene on a set inside the studio. So the one-armed man was actually 'killed' several days before he 'confessed.'"

FUGE FOOLERY

Barry Morse recalled another "ending" to *The Fugitive* that he and Janssen concocted during one of their mischievious moods. "David and I cooked up this scenario where we would establish a shot on a handsome suburban house in Stafford, Indiana," he said. "It's moonlit, and you can hear a few crickets, and so forth. We're on a high crane and we push in, and we go through the upper window. Then, we go tighter onto, say, the left side of a double bed, where David/Richard Kimble is sitting up, alarmed, having obviously just awakened. Then he turns on the light, and shakes the shoulder of his companion in this double bed, whom we see, as she turns around and wakes up, is his wife—Mrs. Richard Kimble. And then David would cry out, 'Oh! Oh, honey! Oh, thank God! I've just had the most terrible nightmare!' That was our 'suggestion' for the proposed ending of *The Fugitive*."

J.D. Cannon once joked that, since he played the man who witnessed the one-armed man kill Helen Kimble, he "should have been paid" for all four years of the series.

FUGE FAUX PAS

There are two minor errors in the credits: Johnny Jensen, who also played Kenny in "When the Wind Blows," is listed as Bobby Taft, although throughout the episode he's known as "Billy;" and Diane Brewster, who returned to play Helen in the flashback sequence, is not listed at all.

FUGE FINAL FACTS & FIGURES

David Janssen received his third Emmy nomination for Best Dramatic Actor; the award went to Bill Cosby for *I Spy*. Janssen was also honored by the readers of *Photoplay Magazine*, who named him Actor of the Year in March 1967.

August 29, 1967 was "the day the running stopped" in the United States. However, because of problems encountered in dubbing the episode, other countries had to wait until sometime in September to see the finale (in West Germany, viewers had to wait until October).

According to *Daily Variety*, Part Two scored a 50.7 rating and a 73.2 share. ABC estimated that 26 million homes in America were tuned in to the finale.

EPILOG: FUGE FOLLOW-UP

DAVID JANSSEN starred in several feature films—*The Green Berets, Generation, Where It's At, Warning Shot, Marooned, Macho Callahan*—before returning to television as Special Agent James O'Hara in the Jack Webb-produced series *O'Hara: United States Treasury* (CBS, 1971-72). Although *O'Hara* disappeared after one season, Janssen remained a fixture on television throughout the 1970s. He headlined nearly 20 made-for-TV movies—including *Night Chase, Hijack, Birds of Prey, The Golden Gate Murders*, and *City in Fear*—as well as the mini-series *Centennial* and *The Word*. Janssen also starred as the sensitive, weary private detective Harry Orwell in two TV-movies and the outstanding series *Harry O* (ABC, 1974-76). Janssen died of a heart attack in 1980.

BARRY MORSE continued his diverse performing career on stage, screen and television. He starred in several other TV series and mini-series, including *The Golden Bowl, The Zoo Gang, Space: 1999, Master of the Game, The Winds of War, War and Remembrance*, and *Glory! Glory!* Morse also wrote, produced and starred in the Canadian stage production *Merely Players*, a one-man tour-de-force that successfully raised funds for the Performing Arts Lodges of Canada (based in Toronto) which aid elderly and needy actors and film industry workers throughout Canada. Morse provides the introductions to each volume of *The Fugitive* available through NuVentures; he donates his royalties to benefit the Performing Arts Lodges.

ROY HUGGINS has continued to shape the face of television in the thirty years since *The Fugitive*. He has produced such ground-breaking shows as *The Virginian*, *The Rockford Files*, *Alias Smith and Jones*, *Baretta*, and *Hunter*. Huggins is the executive producer of the 1993 feature film version of *The Fugitive* that stars Harrison Ford as Richard Kimble and Tommy Lee Jones as Lieutenant Gerard.

QUINN MARTIN parlayed the tremendous critical and financial success of *The Fugitive* into a string of popular dramatic series, including *Twelve O'Clock High*, *The F.B.I.*, *Dan August*, *Cannon*, *The Streets of San Francisco* and *Barnaby Jones*. In addition to featuring all the visual affectations of a QM Production ("Act I," "Act II," and so forth), these programs featured emotionally-strong characters that appealed to TV audiences on a human level. Martin also made one feature film—*The Mephisto Waltz* (1971), starring a pre-*M*A*S*H* Alan Alda—as well as several movies made-for-television. Martin died in 1987.

BILL RAISCH's international popularity as the "man with one arm" never ceased. In a interview with *TV Collector* given just before his death in 1984, Raisch recalled an incident that occurred while he was visiting the set of *Dallas*: "Five people from Europe came over to me and said, 'Will you sign this autograph?' I said, 'You don't want me, I'm not in this show.' They said, 'We know you're not—you're the one-armed man on *The Fugitive*!'"

JACQUELINE SCOTT has guest starred on many television series since *The Fugitive*, including multiple appearances on *Gunsmoke*, *L.A. Law*, *Equal Justice* and the daytime serial *The Bold and the Beautiful*. She also starred in such motion pictures as *Firecreek* (with James Stewart and Henry Fonda), and won the Drama-Log Award for her role in the stage production of *Embraceable You*.

Producer ALAN ARMER left television in 1978 to teach screenwriting full-time at CSUN (California State University/Northridge). Prior to that, his post-*Fugitive* credits included the series *The Invaders*, *Cannon*, *The Name of the Game*, and the TV-movie *Birds of Prey* (starring David Janssen).

Writer/producer GEORGE ECKSTEIN's many accomplishments after *The Fugitive* include *Banacek*, *Sara*, *The Rhinemann Exchange*, *79 Park Avenue*, and *Perry Mason: The Case of the Desperate Deception*.

APPENDIX 1

ROY HUGGINS' ORIGINAL SIGNATURE FOR *THE FUGITIVE* AND NETWORK PRESENTATION

Reprinted below is series creator Roy Huggins' original description of the train wreck that freed Richard Kimble, and his discussion of the philosophy of *The Fugitive*. These pages, which Huggins wrote in September 1960, are the basis of the presentation he made to Leonard Goldenson during the 1962 meeting that led to the series' premiere in 1963. Many of Huggins' suggestions ("he must change his appearance," "he must keep moving," "he must stay in this country," etc.) were followed to the letter.

The most intriguing aspect of Huggins' presentation is the idea stated in the final sentence: "This will be a series which will brought to a planned conclusion, that conclusion being of course Richard Kimble's release from his predicament and the ultimate salvation of justice." Although the idea for ending *The Fugitive* with a definitive final episode is generally attributed to executive producer Quinn Martin, it actually belonged to Huggins. Amazingly, Huggins didn't realize this until he retrieved the presentation from a box of old files shortly before this book went to press.

"I'd completely forgotten about that last sentence," he said. "I hadn't seen the signature in 30 years. As it turns out, I'd filed it in a box marked *Bus Stop* [one of the series Huggins produced for 20th Century-Fox]. Finding those pages after all these years was a very pleasant surprise."

We are extremely grateful to Roy for allowing us to share these pages with you.

THE FUGITIVE
A Series Format
September 19, 1960
Roy Huggins

FADE IN:

LONG SHOT - TRAIN   NIGHT

A passenger train, its enormous headlight glowing in the
distance, is racing TOWARD CAMERA through dark and lonely
country. The RHYTHMIC SOUND of the train RISES SWIFTLY as
it approaches and PASSES CAMERA, the HEAVY, CADENCED SOUND
reaching a climax which breaks off abruptly as we go into:

INT. PASSENGER CAR - (PROCESS)   NIGHT

The RHYTHMIC SOUND of the train continues in a lower key.

BIG CLOSE ON RICHARD KIMBLE

He is a prematurely grey-haired man in his mid thirties. His
eyes are turned toward the dark window where broad farmland,
with its occasional solitary glow of light, swiftly passes.
But we sense from his inward air that he is seeing little of
this, that whatever beauty there may be in the swift passage
of quiet, moonlit countryside has no meaning for him. From
the beginning of this CLOSE SHOT we have HEARD the off stage
voice of a NARRATOR, a voice suggesting an infinite detachment,
which gives it the authority of a disinterested, omniscient
observer.

                    NARRATOR
          This man is known by a number:
          565-9880. His name is Richard
          Kimble. Once a doctor: specialty,
          pediatrics.

The CAMERA has DRAWN BACK over this to reveal the MAN next to
Kimble and two MEN in the seat immediately behind him. These
men are all members of the State's Attorney's office, and in
their varying ways they suggest precisely what they are.
They look neither grim nor watchful. They are doing their
jobs, thinking their private thoughts.

                    NARRATOR
                    (continuing)
          He is returning from his fourth
          and final appeal from a conviction
          on a charge of murder in the first
          degree. The victim: Helen Kimble,
          his wife.

TWO SHOT - KIMBLE AND OFFICER

The police officer beside him, using his left hand, offers a
cigarette to Kimble and takes one himself. He lights both
cigarettes with a lighter, using the same left hand. During
this action we may notice a light topcoat covering Kimble's
left forearm and the officer's right forearm. The Camera
does not single this out because the action itself suggests
that the unseen wrists are joined by handcuffs.

                    NARRATOR
               (continuing)
          Richard Kimble had offered only this
          defense: He had caught one brief
          glimpse of the actual criminal, a
          gaunt and redhaired man.
               (brief pause)
          This was the simple but unprovable
          truth. The provable truth was that
          Helen and Richard Kimble were childless,
          and bitterly estranged by his determination
          to change that condition through adoption.

BIG CLOSE ON KIMBLE

                    NARRATOR
               (continuing)
          Crimes without plan, motive or
          evidence are not only insoluble,
          they often victimize the innocent.
          Richard Kimble is returning to
          Death Row, State Prison. Execution
          date: 10:00 A.M., July 18. No further
          appeals are possible.

EXT. THE TRAIN

It passes CAMERA, the SOUND almost deafening once again. As
the train roars AWAY FROM CAMERA the whistle SOUNDS, an eerie,
fading wail.

                    NARRATOR
               (continuing)
          But this train is the Capitol Limited,
          and this is the tragic night of
          July 2 ...

3.

CLOSE SHOT - A RAILROAD SWITCH

CLOSE SHOT

The engine of the Capitol Limited. The whistle SOUNDS again.

CLOSE SHOT

A division in the track, showing the rails set for a 15^0
turn onto a spur line.

INT. THE TRAIN - THE FOUR MEN

silent, utterly unaware of what awaits them.

EXT. THE TRAIN

It is still travelling at headlong speed.

ANOTHER ANGLE

as the train takes the unintended turn onto the spur.

THE WRECK

We HOLD only for the first, shocking impact and go into an
EFFECT DISSOLVE.

EXT. EMPTY COUNTRYSIDE   NIGHT

We DISSOLVE INTO A SHOT designed for the MAXIMUM EFFECT of
tranquility. The night sounds are distant, undisturbed.

INTO SHOT the figure of a man stumbles, and as the figure
comes into a

CLOSE SHOT

we recognize Richard Kimble. Breathless, he stops. We see
his face clearly in the moonlight. He is bewildered, emerging
from shock. He stands for a moment, listening. And as full
realization of what has happened rises in him, he turns as if
expecting to find the wreckage of the train behind him. We
see nothing. We hear nothing but the sounds of the crickets
and an occasional night bird.

4.

CLOSER ON KIMBLE

As we see him face the almost terrifying fact of freedom. He
glances quickly around him, then begins to run. The CAMERA
HOLDS and the MUSIC BEGINS. As his figure recedes we see an
odd configuration in the distance into which he is vanishing.
This jagged configuration begins to move toward us swiftly
as the MUSIC RISES. The configuration becomes two sharply,
violently formed words which finally fill the screen:

                    THE
                    FUGITIVE

We HOLD for the musical climax and

                                        FADE OUT.

The foregoing is the cinematic signature of a proposed new
hour-long series, THE FUGITIVE. Each week this 70 second
introduction will excitingly restate the premise and reset
the mood of the series.

Each episode will deal with a week, a month, a day, or an
hour in the life of Richard Kimble as a fugitive, a life which
involves flight, search, moral dilemma, friendship, love,
laughter, all underlain with unfulfillment, danger and
tragedy. In a heightened and imaginative sense Kimble's
life as a fugitive will relate to deep and responsive drives,
needs and fantasies in the American audience, not the least
of which is that Kimble lives with alienation and anxiety,
but in his case they are real and can be dealt with. At the
heart of the series is the preoccupation with guilt and
salvation which has been called the American Theme. Kimble
is pursued, and in the eyes of the law he is guilty. But no
American of any persuasion will find him so. The idea of
natural law is too deeply embedded in the American spirit
for anyone to question Kimble's right, after all recourse to
law has been exhausted, to preserve his own life. Even
Hobbes, the great philosopher of authoritarianism, acknowledged
one circumstance in which a man has a right to resist
Leviathan: when an attempt is made to take his life on
mistaken grounds.

In the summer of 1960 it became abundantly clear that the
Western on television was about to undergo an eclipse. I had
given much thought to the broad and durable appeal of the
Western, and I concluded that the essence of that appeal
lay solely in the character and mode of life of the Western
hero.

5.

That hero is a man without roots, without obligations, without fixed goals, without anxiety about his place in the order of things. He not only avoids commitment to one locale, one occupation, or one woman, he actually seems compelled to change his dwelling place, his occupation, his human attachments. This implicit factor of willed irresponsibility without a concomitant sense of guilt is the element of basic appeal in the Western. The good-vs-evil formula, the omnipotence of the hero, these elements are found in contemporary melodrama. But not the element of absolute freedom that the traditional Western contains. SHANE is the great example of the tradition in its most faithful and successful form, and strangely enough, SHANE also contained the element of pursuit. Early in SHANE we realize that he is in flight, but we are never told from what. At the end of the picture Shane moves on, still pursued, but by what we are not told.

THE FUGITIVE was a long time in gestation. My aim was to capture the essence of the Western in a contemporary setting. My confidence in the basic theory was boundless, but a truly workable solution did not come easily. In these regimented and conformist times, the protagonist had to be unregimented, apart from society, rootless, immune to permanent human commitment, and ever on the move. And we had to understand precisely why this was so and to accept it with no uneasy sense of guilt; otherwise there would be a rejection of the protagonist and the concept.

THE FUGITIVE met all these needs and more. Richard Kimble is guilty by act of law, but innocent in fact. As a fugitive he is compelled to live in a drifting, alienated way, and the specifics will be spelled out dramatically from episode to episode. Here they are:

1) He must change his appearance, and he does. This purposeful loss of identity is one of our most deep-seated fantasies. It is found in countless children's stories and in equally countless sophisticated novels (The Moon & Sixpence, The Art of Lewellyn Jones, The Count of Monte Cristo, ad infinitum).

2) He must keep moving. To stay in one place over long is to multiply geometrically the dangers of recognition and apprehension. He finally adopts an arbitrary rule against staying in any given locale for more than six weeks.

3) He must stay in this country. Here he is one American among nearly 200 million Americans. Outside our borders passports are required, questions are asked; he is the conspicuous stranger.

6.

4) He can take only unusual, no-questions-asked
   jobs. An ordinary job requires letters of
   recommendation, a social security number, often
   even a finger-print check. This necessity of
   course opens the door in a natural and credible
   way to a vast store of exciting and fresh story
   material.

5) He cannot make friendships that are not ended,
   or fall in love without heartbreak. In terms
   of the needs of a weekly series, the story-telling
   advantages in this are obvious and infinite.

Because the thematic base of the series is so explicit and yet
so much a part of the unconscious yearnings of the broadest
possible spectrum of the audience, the actual story content
of each episode can and should be on the most sophisticated
level possible in television. Implicit in each episode is
the ultimate in sympathy for the protagonist, and the never
ending presence of jeopardy; therefore the wpisodes can be
built around character and premise.

This brief presentation has left a multitude of questions
unanswered, but not because they are unanswerable. For
example: Is he being searched for? Yes. One man in the
State's Attorney's office has been assigned that task, and at
least one episode, and probably more than one, will deal with
the pursuit itself. The story of Jean Valjean and his Javert
has not remained a classic for insignificant reasons, and the
best will be distilled from those reasons. Does he ever meet
anyone who recognizes him? Yes, and at least one episode
will be built around it. Questions of this kind all lend
themselves to answers in terms of dramatic treatment.

An element that will be used in the series, but only in the
most limited way, is the faint, almost unacknowledged hope
in Richard Kimble that he might one day come face to face
with the gaunt, red-haired man he had so briefly seen on the
night of his wife's death. The reason for this is obvious.
This will be a series which will be brought to a planned
conclusion, that conclusion being of course Richard Kimble's
release from his predicament and the ultimate salvation of
justice.

.Lou Antonio and Paul Richards in *A. P. B.*

Jack Klugman in *Terror at Highpoint.*

Barry Morse as Lt. Philip Gerard.

Bill Raisch as the "one-armed" man.

APPENDIX 2

THE FUGITIVE'S ALIASES, JOBS AND LOCATIONS

NO.	ALIAS	OCCUPATION	LOCATION
1.	James Lincoln	Bartender	Tucson, AZ
2.	Jim Fowler	Handyman	Hainesville, MO
3.	"Mister"	None	West Virginia
4./5.	Jeff Cooper	Apprentice Sailmaker	Santa Barbara, CA
6.	Ray Miller	Boxing Cut Man	Los Angeles, CA
7.	Joseph Walker	Farm Worker	Hidalgo Grove (near San Diego), CA
8.	Al Fleming	Gas Station Worker	Sierra Point, NM/ Hollywood, CA
9.	Larry Talman	Construction Worker	Seattle, WA to Alaska
10.	Bill Carter	None	Pikesville/Ellsmore, KY
11.	George Porter	Lumber Man	New England area
12.	Harry Carson/ George Paxton	Stock Room Worker	Sioux City, Iowa
13.	Paul Beaumont	Timekeeper	Near Salt Lake City, UT
14.	George Browning/ George Norton	None Ruth's Brother	San Francisco, CA
15.	None	None	Stafford, IN
16.	Sanford	Caretaker	Westborne, CT
17.	Ben Rogers	Handyman	Black Mocassin, NE
18.	Jerry Shelton	Lifeguard	Reno/Wilkerson, NV
19.	George Blake	None	Chicago, IL
20.	Dick Lindsay	Kennel Man	Virginia
21.	Dan Crowley	Liquor Store Clerk	Ohio
22./23.	Nick Walker	Janitor	Lincoln City, NE/ Sacramento, CA
24.	Al Dexter/Paul Edson	Masseur	Michigan
25.	Bob Davies	Roller Rink Supervisor	Springfield, IL
26.	Johnny Sherman	Warehouse Worker	Unknown
27.	"Doc"	Former Field Hand	Southern California area
28.	David Benton	Research Technician	Tidewater, GA
29.	Larry Phelps	Dockside Worker	Webers Landing/ Key Blanca, FL
30.	None	Warehouse Worker	Chicago, IL
31.	Frank Borden	Dishwasher	Harrisburg, PA
32.	May	None	Stafford, IN/Kansas City, MO
33.	Joe Walker	None	Overton, WY
34.	Pete Broderick	None	Fargo/Grand Forks, ND
35.	None	Fish Hatchery Worker	Barden County, WI
36.	Frank Jordan	Gardener	Eugene, OR
37.	Paul Kelly	Farm Hand	Cornell, ID
38.	Jim Russell	Farm Handyman/ Sculptor's Model	Sioux Falls, SD
39.	Frank Barlow/ David Merrill	None	Decatur, IL
40.	Jeff Parker	Dockside Worker	Puerto Viejo, Mexico
41.	Pat Thomas	Sean's Uncle	Donnivale, IL
42.	Stu Manning	Hotel Clerk	Hazelton, WY
43.	Parker	Construction Worker/ First-Aid Man	Eronson, NV

44.	None	None	Corona, GA
45.	Pete Glenn	Spotlight Operator/ Handyman	Salisbury, OH
46.	Ben Horton	Personal Attendant	Santa Monica, CA
47.	Steve Younger	Truck Driver	Hurley, PA
48.	Richard Clark	None	Bixton, AZ
49.	Douglas Beckett	Chauffeur/Gateman	Los Angeles, CA
50.	Eddie Frey	Handyman	Black River, SD
	Bill Hayes	Construction Worker	Uncertain
51.	Paul Hunter	Truck Driver	Bleeker, LA
52.	Bill Martin	None	Michigan
53.	None	None	Fairgreen, IN
54.	Bill Douglas	Dispatcher	Colorado Springs, CO
55.	Harry Reynolds	Hospital Orderly	Selby, MI
56.	Leonard Hull	None	Clay City, OK
57.	Tom Burns	Apartment Janitor	Rutledge, OH
	Phil Mead	Representative from Good Neighbor Society	Cleveland, OH
58.	Ed Morris	None	Topeka, KA
59.	Jim Wallace	Ranch Foreman	Encinas County, CA
60.	Nick Peters	Animal Show Worker	Morgantown, NE
61.	George Eagen	Farm Hand	Oklahoma
62.	Jim Owen	Construction Worker	Lake City, NY
63.	Joe Warren	Gas Station Attendant	Midwest
64.	None	None	Chicago, IL
65.	Fred Tate	Hotel Attendant/ Doctor	Reeseburg, AZ
66.	Tom Nash	Chauffeur	Ardmore, OK
67.	Joe Taft	Driver	Iowa/Texas/New Mexico
68.	Ed Curtis	None	Briar County, CO
69./70.	Steve Carver	Kitchen Helper	Witchita, KA/Joplin, MO
71.	Chris Benson	Warehouse Worker	Tractor, NJ
72.	John Evans	Custodian	Sona Falls, WA
73.	Bill Watkins	None	Drover City, MN
74.	Bob Mossman	Dishwasher	Raiford/Fort Scott, FL
75.	Jim McGuire	Handyman	Small Groves, WY
76.	Richard Spaulding	Doctor of Medicine	Hempstead Mills, WV
77.	None	None	Baker City, MI
78.	Nick Phillips	Laundry Deliverman	Yonkers, NY
79.	Richard Taylor	None	Southern California
80.	Frank Whistler	Handyman	Santa Elena, NM
81.	Paul Keller	Veterinarian Assistant	Uncertain
82.	None	None	Stafford/Fort Wayne, IN
83.	Jack Fickett	General Factotum	Beverly Hills, CA
84.	Mike Johnson	Farm Laborer	Southern Texas
85.	Frank Carter	Chauffeur	Washington, D.C.
86.	Dan Gordon	Truck Driver	Phoenix, AZ
87.	Jack Davis	Chauffeur	Denver, CO
	Bob Grant	Walnut Grove Worker	California
	Jack	None	Portland, OR
	William Smith	Flood Control Laborer	Portland, OR
	None	Cranberry bog Laborer	New England area
88.	Al Mitchell	None	Boise County, ID
89.	Bob Stoddard	Bartender	Iroquois, NY
90.	Tony Carter	Radio Operator	San Pedro, CA
91.	David Morrow	Teacher/Classroom Aide	Puma County, AZ

92.	Ed Sanders	None	Uncertain
93.	Paul Miller	Bartender	Clark City
94.	Carl Baker	Apartment Janitor	"A big city"
95.	Dave Livingston	Farm Hand	Monroe County
96.	Jim Corman	Veterinarian Assistant	Utah
97.	Jack Anderson	Photo Lab Worker	Pennsylvania
98.	Taylor	Witness	California
99.	Pete Allen	Carnival Worker	Longdale, IN
100.	Harry Robertson	Doctor of Medicine	Burlington
101.	Eddie Carter	Commercial Fisherman	Southern California
102.	None	None	Uncertain
103.	Ben Russell	Upholstery Store Worker	Uncertain
104.	Russell Jordan	Ranch Hand	Pennsylvania
105.	Tom Anderson	None	Southern California
106.	Jim Parker	Grocery Store Clerk	Ocean Grove, CA
107.	Bill March	Deck Hand	Southern California/Mexico
108.	Steve Dexter	Catskiller/Office Aide	Coleman, NE
109.	Tom Marlowe	Janitor	Sacramento/Tarleton, CA
110.	Gene Tyler	Witness	Southern California
111.	Jerry Sinclair	Reporter/Researcher	Indiana
112.	Bill Garrison	Parking Attendant/Chauffeur	Uncertain
113.	Tom Barrett	None	Wyler City, MN
114.	Tony Maxwell	Cigar Store Worker	"A big city"
115.	Thomas Barrett	Doctor of Medicine	Puerta Bonales, Mexico
116.	Charlie Farrell	None	Washington, D.C.
117.	Stan Dyson	Truck Driver	Seattle, WA/Portland, OR
118.	Ben Lewis	Handyman	Oregon
119.	Frank Davis	Truck Company Worker	Tucson, AZ/Los Angeles, CA
/120	Richard Kimble	Doctor of Medicine	Stafford, IN

James Dunn   in *Decision in the Ring.*

APPENDIX 3

Continuing with its creative programming efforts, this past season ABC introduced a new addition to its "Doctor Show" and "Crime Show" TV trail-blazing . . . mainly a "Doctor-Crime Show" called:

THE PHEWGITIVE

ARTIST: MORT DRUCKER   WRITER: STAN HART

This is your stern-voiced narrator — Every week, we remind you of what the program is about, since you might not get the idea from the subtle title. We also kill 5 minutes of each show by using the same opening every week!

Dr. Richard Thimble is on his way to the Death House, convicted of murdering his wife. What thoughts are going through the head of the distinguished gray-haired physician at this moment?

As he stares into the night, contemplating the shafting he got from that Jury who wouldn't believe his story about the "one-armed man"—Fate steps into the life of Dr. Richard Thimble!

Instead of completing his journey, a curious event has made Dr. Richard Thimble a free man . . . free to run all over the country, searching for the "one-armed man", getting involved in people's lives, and narrowly escaping re-capture every week!

"The Phewgitive" used with permission from MAD Magazine,
©1964 by E.C. Publications, Inc.

APPENDIX 4

THAT WAS THE LIFE

It is widely assumed that Richard Kimble married Jean Carlisle, the woman who accompanied him as he exited the courthouse at the end of the series, and lived happily ever after. On that basis, syndicated columnist Mike Royko of *The Chicago Sun-Times* paid a "visit" to Dr. Kimble in an "interview" that appeared on August 30, 1967.

Many of Dr. Richard Kimble's fans wonder how he is doing, now that he is no longer *The Fugitive* and is back home in Indiana practicing medicine.

I took a drive down to Stafford, Indiana, where he lived before being wrongfully convicted of murdering his wife and going on the lam for four years.

He was mowing the lawn in front of his large, tree-shaded house when I arrived. He consented to an interview.

"You don't mind if I keep mowing the lawn while we talk, do you?" he asked.

Not at all, doctor.

"We've got a dinner date at the country club and she'll blow her stack if I don't finish the lawn."

She?

"My wife. You remember her—Jean Carlisle, the girl who helped me right at the end."

I remember. How is she?

"Getting a little plump."

Well, doctor, how do you like being free?

"Who's free?"

You are.

"Listen, I got this house to pay for, two cars, an expensive country club membership. I spend my days listening to hypochondriacs and my evenings attending civic meetings, medical association meetings, neighborhood improvement meetings. You call that being free?"

What I meant was, you are no longer a fugitive.

"That's right. Now I'm a prisoner. Just between you and me, I miss being a fugitive."

You can't be serious.

"Like heck I'm not. That was the life, moving from town to town, working as a bartender, truck driver, laborer, foot loose and fancy free, no income tax. I went everywhere and saw everything. Now I'm stuck in this hick town."

Doctor Kimble, I'm shocked . . . .

"And the women. Boy, there was always some good-looking woman falling for me when I was *The Fugitive*. It must have been the hunted look in my eyes. I guess women are attracted by that."

Possibly, but . . . .

"It might have been my dark hair, too. I had an excuse to dye it then, but now I don't. Be honest—doesn't the white hair make me look a lot older?"

Mmmmmmmm. A bit, yes . . . .

"And look at my waist. I'm getting fat."

Oh, a few pounds, maybe.

"When I was *The Fugitive*, I was really in shape. Hard as a rock, lean. Because I was always working hard, hiking on the road, getting in fights, jumping out of windows."

But now you are a doctor, a physician.

"I'd rather be a young, adventurous fugitive than a fat old doctor."

Nevertheless, you had the satisfaction of catching the one-armed man.

"That was my mistake. If I hadn't gotten such a complex about him and just forgot about him, I'd still be at large. Those bungling cops would never have caught me."

But the one-armed man killed your wife.

"So? Six more months with her and I'd have done it myself."

But he was an evil, crude man.

"Hah! You should see the crowd at the country club."

Isn't it a relief not to have Lieutenant Gerard constantly trying to catch you?

"Lieutenant Gerard couldn't catch the flu."

Do you ever see him?

"Sure. They busted him for wasting four years and all that money chasing me instead of the one-armed man. Now he's a traffic cop. He's always stopping me, but I slip him a fin and he lets me go. That's the only thing I enjoy."

But isn't it good to be reunited with your sister, your brother-in-law, your . . .

"My brother-in-law is a boob. They came over last night and he got drunk and spilled a drink all over the sofa. Frankly, I wish he'd been the killer, instead of the one-armed man."

Isn't peace of mind important to you?

"Who has it? Before, all I worried about was a few cops and brushing off some girl who fell for me. Now I read the papers and look at TV and I worry about Vietnam, air pollution, and college campus riots."

But you have a wife again.

"All she does is remind me of how she helped me. She'll never let me forget that, boy."

But isn't there some happiness in your life—something to look forward to?

"Oh, sure."

What?

"Another one-armed man."

Reprinted with permission from the Chicago Sun-Times (c) 1992

APPENDIX 5:

COLLECTIONS AND CONNECTIONS

Because Roy Huggins never released the merchandise rights to *The Fugitive*, only a few products based on the series were made available at the time the series was first on television. As previously discussed in our chapter on the pilot episode, the paperback novel *Fear in a Desert Town* was removed from the market after Huggins won a lawsuit for copyright infringement. Ideal issued a *Fugitive* board game, but Huggins did not learn about the product until long after it had left the market. Although no official soundtrack album was ever made, a few groups released instrumental pieces called *Fugitive*; however, the music on these records is completely different from that of the TV show.

RECORDINGS

Fugitive, The Fabulous Ventures, from the album *Needles and Pins* (Dolton Records, 1964)
Fugitive, The Fugitives (Collectable Records; reissued 1992)
The Hidden Island, David Janssen accompanied by the Tradewinds Orchestra and Chorus (Epic Records, 1965). Janssen does not sing on the album, but he recites the lyrics to each piece

MERCHANDISE

The Fugitive Game (Ideal, 1964)

PAPERBACK BOOKS/SCREEN PLAYS

Fear in a Desert Town, by Roger Fuller (Pocket Books, 1964). Unauthorized novelization of the pilot episode.
Some of the original teleplays are available through *Script City,* a mail order outlet specializing in TV and movie memorabilia. For information, write 8033 Sunset Blvd., Suite 1500, Los Angeles CA 90046.

PERIODICALS

Publications with articles on *The Fugitive* include *TV Guide, Television Quarterly, Emmy Magazine, TV Gold, TV Collector,* *Reruns Magazine, Model and Toy Collector, Epi-Log* and *The A&E Program Guide.*

FAN CLUBS

On the Run, P.O. Box 461402, Garland TX 75046-1492. Contact: Rusty Pollard.
The Fugitives, 6500 Brush Country Road, Austin TX 78749-1403. Contact: "Texas" Bob Reinhardt.
The David Janssen Appreciation Society, 83 Rue Pasteur, 54000 Nancy, France. Contact: Catherine Robert.
Morse Code, Box 8, RR2, Site 6, Sexsmith, Alberta T0H 3C0, Canada. Contact: Vivian Stanley.

APPENDIX 6:

THE FUGITIVE ON HOME VIDEO

The Fugitive is available on home video through NuVentures Video. Each tape contains two uncut episodes specially matched for content and duplicated on high-quality tape in the two-hour (SP) mode. Barry Morse provides a brief introduction for every episode. These tapes are available through mail order only: for more information, write NuVentures Video, 13101 Washington Blvd., Suite 131, Los Angeles CA 90066.

Volume 1	The Girl from Little Egypt The End is But the Beginning
Volume 2	Never Wave Goodbye (Part 1) Never Wave Goodbye (Part 2)
Volume 3	Search in a Windy City Wife Killer
Volume 4	Cry Uncle This'll Kill You
Volume 5	Nemesis Ill Wind
Volume 6	Nightmare at Northoak Escape into Black
Volume 7	Landscape with Running Figures (Part 1) Landscape with Running Figures (Part 2)
Volume 8	Home is the Hunted The Survivors
Volume 9	World's End Brass Ring
Volume 10	May God Have Mercy Trial by Fire
Volume 11	Ten Thousand Pieces of Silver The Evil Men Do
Volume 12	The Last Oasis The Walls of Night
Volume 13	Run the Man Down The Devil's Disciples
Volume 14	The Other Side of the Coin The One That Got Away
Volume 15	Nobody Loses All the Time The Ivy Maze
Volume 16	Stroke of Genius In a Plain Paper Wrapper
Volume 17	Fatso Stranger in the Mirror
Volume 18	Man in a Chariot The 2130
Volume 19	Passage to Helena Dossier on a Diplomat
Volume 20	Corner of Hell The End Game

"Fear in a Desert City" and "The Judgment" are also available on home video through Goodtimes Home Video; these tapes are available in many video stores. (Some copies of "The Judgment" have the Narrator announcing September 5 as "The day the running stopped," which is the date the final episode aired in Canada.) For more information, write Goodtimes Home Video, 401 5th Avenue, New York NY, 10016.

BIBLIOGRAPHY

Books

Brooks, Tim and Earle Marsh, *The Complete Directory to Prime Time Network TV Shows, 1946-Present.* New York: Ballantine Books, 1988. Fourth edition. First published in 1979.

Brooks, Tim, *The Complete Directory to Prime Time TV Stars, 1946-Present.* New York: Ballantine Books, 1987.

Castleman, Harry, and Walter J. Podriziak, *Harry and Wally's Favorite TV Shows.* New York: Prentice Hall Press, 1989.

o*Watching TV: Four Decades of American Television.* New York: McGraw-Hill Book Company, 1982.

Gianakos, Larry James, *Television Drama Series Programming: A Comprehensive Chronicle*, Volume I (1959-1975). Meutchen, New Jersey: The Scarecrow Press, Inc.

Goldenson, Leonard H., with Martin J. Wolf. *Beating the Odds.* New York: Charles Scribner's Sons, 1991.

Inman, David, *The TV Encyclopedia.* New York: Perigee Books, 1991.

Katz, Ephraim, *The Film Encyclopedia.* New York: Thomas Y. Crowell, Publishers, 1979.

McNeil, Alex, *Total Television.* New York: Penguin Books, 1991. Third edition. First published in 1980.

Meyers, Richard, *TV Detectives.* San Diego: A.S. Barnes & Company, Inc, 1981.

Murder on the Air. New York: The Mysterious Press, 1989.

Monaco, James, *How to Read a Film.* New York: Oxford University Press, 1977. Revised edition, 1981.

Newcomb, Horace and Robert S. Alley, *The Producer's Medium: Conversations with Creators of American TV.* New York: Oxford University Press, 1983.

Parish, James Robert and Vincent Terrace, *The Complete Actors' Television Credits, 1948-1988, Volume I: Actors.* Metuchen: The Scarecrow Press, Inc. 1989. Second edition.

Stallings, Penny, *Forbidden Channels: The Truth They Hide From TV Guide.* New York: Harper Perennial, 1991.

Terrace, Vincent, *Encyclopedia of Television: Series, Pilots and Specials. Volumes I and III.* New York: New York Zoetrope, 1986.

o*The Ultimate TV Trivia Book.* Boston: Faber and Faber, 1991.

Marc, David, and Robert Thompson. *Prime Time, Prime Movers.* Boston: Little, Brown. 1992.

Articles:

From *TV Guide*:

Amory, Cleveland. Review of *The Fugitive.* January 11, 1964.

Buchwald, Art. "If There's Anything I Can't Stand, It's Sloppy Police Work," January 5, 1965.

"Catching Up with the One-Armed Man," April 10, 1965.

Crist, Judith. Review of *The Fugitive*, July 16, 1966.

Dern, Marian. "Ever Want to Run Away From It All? The Fugitive does this every week, and herein lies the secret of the show's success," February 22, 1964.

Efron, Edith. "What Makes a Hit? Four Top Producers Reach Some Surprising Conclusions," April 27, 1974.

Hano, Arnold. "David's Drooping... Success has left Fugitive Janssen tired, tense and physically ailing," March 6, 1965.

Hobson, Dick. "Eyeball to Eyeball with David Janssen: If he knows who he is, he isn't saying," January 29, 1972.

Searle, Ronald. "Artist Ronald Searle Captures The Fugitive with His Trusty 3b," January 22, 1965.

"S.O.S.... which means, in the case of The Fugitive, Storm on Schedule," June 6, 1964.

Whitney, Dwight. "He's the Long Arm of the Law Who Always Ends Up a Little Short: the most frustrating role in television is played by a Canadian actor who is happy about it all," September 12, 1964.

Whitney, Dwight. "He Never Did Much Running: David Janssen of The Fugitive is now in full flight to catch up with his potential," November 2, 1963.

"Sometimes He Just Sits in the Bathtub: Quinn Martin is a Hot TV Producer, and Here's How He Works," October 23, 1965.

"The End of a Long Run: After four years, the climax of The Fugitive is at hand." August 19, 1967.

From other periodicals:

Albert, Stephen and Diane, "Do You Remember The Fugitive," *TV Collector*, Vol. 2: 12-15 (four issues), 1984.

Abramson, Dan, "Catching Up with The Fugitive," *TV Gold*, December 1986.

Coyle, Paul Robert, "Great Shows: The Fugitive," *Emmy Magazine*, November-December 1982.

"End of the Road," *Newsweek*, August 28, 1967.

Matheis, Paul, "The Fugitive," *Model and Toy Collector*, 1991.

Seltzer, Michael, "Chasing a Fugitive Dream," *TV Collector*, July/August 1991.

Strauss, Jon, "The Fugitive," *Epi-Log*, May/June/July 1992.

Thorburn, David, "Is TV Acting a Distinctive Art Form?", originally published in *The New York Times*, August 14, 1977.

Jacqueline Scott and David Janssen.

INDEX

45th Annual PHOTOPLAY MAGAZINE Gold Medal Awards, March 1967. David Janssen, Actor of the Year, Barbara Stanwyck, Actress of the Year and Fred Klein, publisher of PHOTOPLAY MAGAZINE.

Author, Ed Robertson.

PHOTOGRAPH © THOMAS ANDERSON

About the Author

Ed Robertson was born and raised in San Francisco, and earned his B.A. in English and Drama at Saint Mary's College of California. Ed's writing has reflected his fondness for popular culture since he was a kid, when he wrote stories for spelling class about his favorite TV characters. Ed's affection for David Janssen dates back to when, as a teenager, he often stayed up to watch *Harry O* reruns on *The CBS Late Movie*.

The Fugitive Recaptured is Ed's first book; he also writes plays and short fiction. He lives in San Francisco.